AWAKE!

'The best overall study of Blake I have encountered in a very long time. Rich and energetic, it brings together detailed readings of familiar (and not so familiar) poems with sharp contemporary application, and the deep insights of a therapist well-seasoned in finding a path through dreams. A joy to read, well worthy of its extraordinary hero.'

— Rowan Williams, former Archbishop of Canterbury

'I can't think of many writers today who make Christianity look like something worth getting involved with. Rowan Williams is one, Mark Vernon another. When I read them, I feel excited by the possibility of a mind and soul transformed. This book, an exploration of the art and thought of perhaps the most exciting Christian of his time, William Blake, is full of light and challenge. Deeply fascinating and spiritually invigorating, it left me unusually alert for the sound of angelic voices in the hum of the everyday.'

— The Reverend Richard Coles

'Vernon's biography is a glorious read. It tackles the misunderstandings surrounding Blake's life and presents a fascinating portrait of a deeply spiritual and politically radical man, who was one of the greatest visionaries of British history.'

— Alice Loxton, historian, broadcaster and author of
*Eighteen: A History of Britain in 18 Young Lives*

'Superb: a luminous book, wholly different from other accounts of Blake's life. Vernon understands better than anyone else why Blake matters urgently for today. The result is prescient, prophetic and compellingly readable.'

— Charles Foster, author of *Cry of the Wild*; *Being a Beast*;
and *The Screaming Sky*

'At this moment, we need the voice of Blake—however strange and wild it often seems—more than ever. He is one of those untimely prophets who have the power to make us see reality anew in every epoch. Vernon is a particularly sensitive reader of the great man, one who knows how to communicate Blake's vision with rare clarity.'

—— David Bentley Hart, philosopher, cultural commentator and author

'Vernon's undefended perception and intelligence meet Blake's, and re-enchanted wisdom issues forth on every page. I have rarely been so energised, goaded and inspired into wakefulness. This is a book that speaks to our age.'

—— Claire Gilbert, author of *I, Julian*

'Vernon brings Blake alive for our times, with an engaging guide to his life and work. In the face of pitiless politics, oppressive religion and soulless work, argues Vernon, Blake still points us to a way of innocence, joy and enhanced perception.'

—— Linda Woodhead, F. D. Maurice Professor in Moral and Social Theology, King's College London

'Mark Vernon writes of Blake that he "wanted to help his fellow man see more clearly". The same could be said of Vernon himself, who has written a fascinating, thought-provoking and highly quotable testament to one of our greatest—and most prescient—prophets.'

—— Elizabeth Oldfield, host of *The Sacred* podcast and author of *Fully Alive: Tending to the Soul in Turbulent Times*

'Not only a brilliantly entertaining and illuminating book about Blake, but also an uplifting, original and inspiring work of philosophy.'

——Tom Hodgkinson, editor of the *Idler*

MARK VERNON

# Awake!

## *William Blake and the Power of the Imagination*

HURST & COMPANY, LONDON

First published in the United Kingdom in 2025 by
C. Hurst & Co. (Publishers) Ltd.,
New Wing, Somerset House, Strand, London WC2R 1LA
Copyright © Mark Vernon, 2025
All rights reserved.

The right Mark Vernon to be identified as the author of
this publication is asserted by him in accordance with the
Copyright, Designs and Patents Act, 1988.

Distributed in the United States, Canada and Latin America
by Oxford University Press, 198 Madison Avenue, New York,
NY 10016, United States of America.

A Cataloguing-in-Publication data record for this book
is available from the British Library.

ISBN: 9781911723974

www.hurstpublishers.com

Printed and bound in Great Britain by Bell & Bain Ltd, Glasgow

*There is a Moment in each Day that Satan cannot find,*
*Nor can his Watch Fiends find it. But the Industrious find*
*This Moment & it multiply, & when it once is found*
*It renovates every Moment of the Day, if rightly placed.*

William Blake

# CONTENTS

| | |
|---|---|
| *A Note on Quotations* | ix |
| *Acknowledgements* | xi |
| Introduction | 1 |

## PART I
## FOUNDATIONS

| | | |
|---|---|---|
| 1. | Sing Your Infant Joy | 9 |
| 2. | By Came an Angel | 29 |
| 3. | All That We See is Vision | 45 |
| 4. | Create a System | 63 |

## PART II
## ENERGY

| | | |
|---|---|---|
| 5. | Money Is Useless | 79 |
| 6. | Love! Love! Love! | 95 |
| 7. | Why Does the Raven Cry? | 115 |
| 8. | A Mighty & Awful Change | 129 |

## PART III
## DIVINITY

| | | |
|---|---|---|
| 9. | Sympathy Came Forth | 151 |
| 10. | Nature, Mother of All | 167 |
| 11. | No Other Christianity | 187 |
| 12. | Fountains of Living Waters | 211 |

| | |
|---|---|
| *Notes* | 229 |
| *Select Bibliography* | 249 |
| *List of Illustrations* | 255 |
| *Index* | 261 |

# A NOTE ON QUOTATIONS

Quoting the occasional couple of lines by William Blake is straightforward enough. His references to cleansing the doors of perception, seeing the world in a grain of sand, or spying the fearful symmetry of the tiger are cited as frequently as any other great writer, including Shakespeare. But any sustained contemplation of his verse quickly runs up against the challenge of his irregular spelling and quirky grammar. Then again, the idiosyncrasies soon become intriguing and loveable, as if one were coming closer to the man himself. When quoting Blake here, I have therefore kept his spelling but adapted some of his punctuation so as to aid understanding. The citations in the footnotes refer to *Blake: Complete Writings*, edited by Geoffrey Keynes (Oxford: Oxford University Press, 1966), hence the "K" before a number which is the page number on which that quote can be found.

I have also put Blake's lines in italics, rather than quotation marks, so as to incorporate them more smoothly into my text. I have borrowed this idea from Joel Harrington's *Dangerous Mystic: Meister Eckhart's Path to the God Within* (London: Penguin Press, 2018). I found the approach immensely helpful when returning to read Eckhart himself and hope that will be the case with Blake; the spirit conveyed through their writing is no small part of what both writers offer, and developing a comfort with reading them is invaluable.

An unitalicised quote of Blake in inverted commas indicates that it was attributed to him, rather than having been written by him directly.

# ACKNOWLEDGEMENTS

The British poet and Blake scholar, Kathleen Raine, said that William Blake is someone to learn from, not just learn about. I first properly began to recognise this following a Blakean pilgrimage around London led by Henry Eliot, visiting sites associated with Blake accompanied by readings. Many thanks to Henry. Those steps in understanding were greatly aided through courses run by the Temenos Academy, which was founded by Kathleen Raine: in particular, reading groups led by Susanne Sklar and Valentin Gerlier. Huge thanks indeed to them both, as well as to my fellow participants in those groups. Finally, as I began to write about Blake myself, I was well advised by Marina Benjamin and Sibylle Erle, who edited essays I wrote for the magazines Aeon and Vala, respectively.

For the writing of this book, I am very much indebted to the thoughts and comments of Susanne Sklar, Rosemary Hill and Alistair McCulloch, who read the manuscript in draft, as did my loving partner, Nicholas George. My heartfelt thanks go to my agent, Jaime Marshall, for his clear guidance, energetic support and conviction that a book like this can find an audience. Sincere gratitude goes as well to my publisher, Michael Dwyer, editor, Alice Clarke, copyeditor, Alasdair Craig, and other members of the team at Hurst.

# INTRODUCTION

A Sunday afternoon in London. Hundreds of people assemble in a dappled cemetery called Bunhill Fields, just off Old Street. They have come to witness the unveiling of a new gravestone.

They are addressed by an eclectic group of individuals: the heavy metal rock star, Bruce Dickinson; the rector of St James's Piccadilly, Lucy Winkett; the poet who looks like Merlin, Malcolm Guite. The date is 12 August 2018. The crowd is there to celebrate the life of the man buried on that spot 191 years earlier, William Blake.

Bunhill Fields is a burial ground for Nonconformists. The author of *The Pilgrim's Progress*, John Bunyan, and the hymn writer, Isaac Watts, are laid to rest within its walls. Blake was interred in the unconsecrated soil when he died in 1827, aged sixty-nine. His views had been dismissed and he himself branded eccentric or mad by the art and religious establishments. And he could prompt offense: something is going very wrong in the modern world, he insisted.

Nowadays his fame has grown to the point of becoming endemic—renown for which he himself hoped. He knew he had a gift, a mission and a message, conveyed in flowing images and punchy verse. But of what exactly was he trying to speak? I suspect that his prominence today routinely discounts a crucial part of what he could show us.

At the gathering in Bunhill Fields, Bruce Dickinson proclaimed Blake as one of the 'greatest living English poets,' and the 'living' was not a slip: Blake never dies, he continued. That's partly because of his prophetic voice, which chastises overbearing politics, oppressive religion, soulless employment, and harsh social mores. It's partly due to his love of liberty and the longing to expose and dissolve the assumptions that lead to exploitation and crimes. He also had a keen eye for hypocrisy: *A truth that's told with bad intent, | Beats all the lies you can invent.*[1] But Blake stood for, stands for, more than that. He was a seer and was driven by what he called his *visionary studies*.[2] He knew agony and ecstasy as palpable presences, dwelt in a cosmos that is alert not mindless, and understood that he had a vocation *To open the Eternal Worlds*.[3] He sought to rewild our humanity so as to restore the living vitalities that are being erased by a collapse of the cultural imagination. He strove to re-enchant our experience of life. The question for us, two centuries on, is how to grapple with this promise of dramatically enhanced perception?

This bubbling abundance is surely detected by many who encounter his work. His popularity is propelled by the potent mix of fiery warning and kindly humanity that animates his verse. People want to learn more because they know that their soul longs for the spirit he transmits. This book not only explores Blake's creativity and polemic but takes him at his word. Using his verse, his images, moments from his life, and the sharp philosophical critique he had of his times that have become ours, the aim is to follow him along the path that he reckoned leads to an utterly transformed awareness of things. Blake understood that a way of life shaped from top to bottom by science and technology is inclined to reduce the transcendent yearnings of human beings to the production of a virtuosic but circumscribed portrayal of nature and the cosmos. And that redaction has a shadow, our era's love-hate relationship with consumption and life among *dark Satanic Mills*.[4] He found a way to accept uneasy times without being depleted by them and sought to share his regenerative discoveries with others.

The basics of his argument can be put succinctly. A new mindset has emerged—often now called the modern perspective. Its origins reach back at least to the sixteenth century. The viewpoint treats our existence as immensely intriguing, but essentially meaningless. Artists, thinkers and scientists under its sway explore the world as if it had no inherent purpose, with a further assumption that the creatures who inhabit it are, at heart, driven mostly by the struggle to stay alive. The upshot of this mix of wonder and pointlessness is that people feel as if they live in what Blake called a *cavern*; a universe that sparkles but also intimidates as it feels vast and impersonal.[5]

A welter of reactions is provoked by this conviction, from curiosity and possessiveness, to despair and zealotry, as human beings—both individually and at the level of societies—try to secure a sense of purpose. Blake parodies the increasingly frantic attitude when he writes, *By demonstration man alone can live, and not by faith*; we must tease apart and investigate, better exploit the environment that envelops us, and—as is increasingly felt today—work out how to survive.[6] The temperament

# INTRODUCTION

assumes that what is not empirically or logically graspable probably does not exist; it distances people from the wellsprings of existence that lie beyond sense and reason and so renders individuals and entire cultures forgetful of how *To see a World in a Grain of Sand | And a Heaven in a Wild Flower, | Hold Infinity in the palm of your hand | And Eternity in an hour*.[7]

Blake sought recovery. He strove to awaken and embolden a re-expanded imagination through the use of poetry, imagery, and piercing insights. Further, unlike many of the Romantic figures with whom he is often grouped, he did not proceed by rejecting the political and technological revolutions that so dramatically marked his era (and have continued in our own), or by appealing to lost times and distant moods, as if he were a lone, tragic visionary. Rather, he realised that the spirit of his age (and, I would argue, ours) is an expression of a true hope, though one that has become deeply, dangerously confused. As he summarises the alternative in possibly his most famous lines: *If the doors of perception were cleansed every thing would appear to man as it is, infinite*.[8] In other words, Blake's remedy is not to fear what is unfolding, nor, if we are of a more optimistic bent, to flatter ourselves with tales of how, after a long history of error and superstition, this is the moment in which we are truly making progress. Instead, he aimed to awaken the awareness lost to closed doors of perception by better discerning the boundless longings that drive all this activity. Working out exactly what he means by this thoroughly engaged approach, and how to direct the energies that buffet and inspire us, is a core part of the thrill and challenge of reading him.

The way to untangle the knots of optimism and anguish became clear to Blake in his early-adult life and he toiled throughout his almost threescore years and ten repeatedly to describe the path afresh. Reformulations were necessary partly because he was far from immune to despondency and terror himself, a susceptibility he called his *Nervous Fear*; being sensitive to the zeitgeist is to be vulnerable to it and, on occasion, he needed to regroup to recover.[9] His work also developed because his understanding deepened, as did the means of addressing concerns. The upshot is that to read Blake, and listen to what he is saying, is not just to be challenged but is to be changed and, in the changing, to detect in oneself the emergence of fresh vistas previously occluded.

A first phase of this thought can be said to have settled in the years during which he entered society, as a young artist, apprentice and thinker. He identified key principles as primary and much of his early verse and designs show him becoming clearer and bolder about what these truths mean. I've called this stage the establishment of his foundations. It forms the basis of a Blakean education in how to live well, as explored in the first four chapters of the book and linked to episodes in his early life: first, savvy innocence, second, perceptual openness, third, confident imagination and, fourth, fearless critique.

These virtues equipped him well, not least as he faced the practicalities of earning a living, getting married, and wrestling with the social and political strife that massively impacted Georgian England, as well as Europe, the Americas and the Indian subcontinent. The tumult is probed across the next four chapters—a second phase in which Blake has wonderful and alarming things to say about money and sex, poetry and death, work and warfare. In particular, he developed a skill when engaging with what he called *Contraries*.[10] These are the tensions we inevitably find ourselves caught by: *Attraction and Repulsion, Reason and Energy, Love and Hate*.[11] They are conflicting feelings and values that tug us first one way and then the other. However, from within this churning milieu, Blake realised something crucial: the conflicts point to an unexpected possibility that is revelatory. The tension itself is key, he concluded, for *Energy is Eternal Delight*, awakening liberating perceptions hitherto unimagined.[12]

With this realisation in place, the mature apprehensions of his later life emerged, pursued in the last section of my book: a third phase. Here can be found his richest responses to the business of being human. He offers ways of remaking our relationship with nature and lays the groundwork for a new kind of politics. He draws on the power of myth to capture what otherwise escapes our comprehension and turns to a largely lost form of Christianity. This mystical tradition was, in part, illuminated by his encounter with the sacred texts of India which, via the colonial activities of the British Empire, were inspiring what has come to be called the Oriental Renaissance.[13] Blake interacted with all these currents and discovered a way of embracing the contradictions of the human condition: that we are finite creatures with an irrepressible and potentially disastrous taste for the infinite. He is a guide who fully grasps the significance of our lot. He mostly doesn't offer advice but something far more valuable: the means to wrestle with that most powerful entity, the human psyche, which is not an odd bit of the world tagged onto the rest of it, but a sharing of the inside of the whole world.[14]

So what if Blake were not merely a genius artist who suffered from a disorder of the mind? What if he were one of the sanest souls who can speak to us now, his work not an impenetrable puzzle but a catalyst for

## INTRODUCTION

conversion? I think he was a strikingly clear thinker, as well as innovative communicator, able to skewer an opponent in a couplet; able to step over a horizon of awareness in a quatrain. We can not only learn about him, but from him.

He is brilliant and enticing and whilst regularly delightful, also often not easy. But then transformation isn't. To follow him is to trust his promise that powers of imagination can lead us to a side of life otherwise impossible to know. There is a boundless source, which we are equipped to converse and collaborate with. As I joined the throng around the new gravestone in Bunhill Fields, I was delighted to read, in elegant script, these words inscribed on the marble slab: *I give you the end of a golden string, | Only wind it into a ball. | It will lead you in at Heaven's gate | Built in Jerusalem's wall.*[15] Dare we take him at his word? Can we stay close and track the way?

# PART I

# FOUNDATIONS

# 1

## SING YOUR INFANT JOY

William Blake arrived in the world at 28 Broad Street, London—a hosier's shop in the Soho neighbourhood of Britain's capital city; the date was 28 November 1757. George II was on the throne, more loved by his yet-to-revolt American colonies than his troublesome Parliament at home. The Seven Years War had erupted, dubbed 'the first world war' by Winston Churchill—just one of the conflicts in the battle for global hegemony between the states of Europe that darkened decades of Blake's life.[1] Not that his era was only one of strife: not at all. London was the centre of a trading empire and was booming. The mercantile city was home to three quarters of a million people when Blake was born, a figure that was to grow to over three million by the time he died, transforming the conurbation from a bustling riverside centre to a 'madding crowd' metropolis. The deeds and misdeeds of the period, as the historian Penelope J. Corfield calls them, established the motley way of life that is still largely ours.[2] Blake's was the era in which modernity matured, which is why his diagnosis of what was going right, and what was coming undone, is so germane to our ambitions and nightmares.

He was born in the heart of the hubbub, as his tradesman father, James, sold knitted and woven stockings and goods; William was the third child of a prosperous family that would extend to six, over the half-dozen years following his first screams and cries. The Blakes were of dissenting stock. As Nonconformists, they were in a minority and, as minorities do, they simultaneously enriched and disquieted the body politic. In fact, attempting to tame the godly enthusiasm of Baptists, Muggletonians and Moravians had become a popular sport, with freethinking agnostics, like the French philosopher Voltaire and the Scottish historian David Hume, penning the sceptical works that atheists today take as gospel. Other literary innovations included the championing of human sympathy, articulated by writers like Adam Smith and Jane Austen, and the first feminist philosophy, ground broken in Blake's time by Mary Wollstonecraft. His contemporaries produced great novels, tremendous music and humane architecture; they thrived on burning coal and, in the first half of his life at least, trading in enslaved Africans. The world was a place of thrilling change and bloody ferment, and Blake observed what was unfolding and analysed it. In depth.

The specific time at which he was born was 7.45 pm, according to a later horoscope.[3] Apparently, the planets indicated 'in the highest degree' an instinct within him for the occult, though without any tendency towards madness, that dismissive judgement which dogged him in life and still does—never quite managing to tame him, thank God. For whilst his insights and imagery can be deemed amusing on the one hand and crazy on the other, they continue to conjure the feeling that he was on to something crucial and prescient. Blake was a prophet. An exhibition of hundreds of his works in 2019 at Tate Britain in London was a sell-out: something approaching a quarter of a million people wanted a piece of him, perhaps to be changed by him.

His mother, Catherine, had married James having been already widowed—a common fate at the time. Both parents are described as gentle and reliable by Frederick Tatham, Blake's first biographer, and they were sympathetic to the peculiarities of their child, who immediately struck them as different; they knew how to foster his gifts. Catherine encouraged the young William to make sketches illustrated with verse, which she blessed by having them pinned to the wall of her bedroom.[4] The habit of a lifetime was thereby established early on and, later, he made a note about an angel who *presided at my birth*. It addressed him as *Little creature, form'd of Joy and Mirth*, before adding with more weight, *Go love without the help of any Thing on Earth*.[5] Which Blake did: he was devoted to this art regardless of how his paintings and writings were received by others, which is just as well because, nowadays, he is credited with inspiring the Pre-Raphaelites and high modernist poets; influencing American transcendentalism and the counterculture; and informing everything from national pride to comic books. In him was born a potency that has spun in myriad directions.

Birth itself always carried positive connotations for Blake and so gives us a first clue as to his worldview and philosophy. Consider the sentiment expressed in one of the poems from his first significant collection, *Songs of Innocence*, which is entitled 'Infant Joy.'

# SING YOUR INFANT JOY

*'I have no name:*
*I am but two days old.'*
*What shall I call thee?*
*'I happy am,*
*Joy is my name.'*
*Sweet joy befall thee!*[6]

These are tender lines, brief but conveying an unrestrained love of life before, even, anything has been named. Blake imagines a conversation, as he regularly does in his poetry; a baby is too young to form thoughts or speak, of course, but in between the doting adult and adorable child emerges a marvellous affirmation. A mood is made manifest and honed, as is also shown in the design that Blake drew around the verse—another

Fig. 1: *Songs of Innocence*, plate 14, "Infant Joy."

technique that he consistently deploys to stir awareness in us. In this case, a luscious vine wraps around the written words. The leaves rise above the script to support a blowsy, supersized anemone. The commodious bloom is coloured a deep burgundy in some versions of the image, which Blake highlights by setting the velvety red against a purple-blue sky and washing the lower half of the design in sunrise yellows and oranges. Nursed within the massive waving petals are peaceful human figures; a mother is holding her child and both of them are attended by an angel.

The scene is contented and domestic, at once touching and a little strange; we are being invited to look again at the commonplace. Blake must have spent time with newborns, though he didn't himself become a father, and the experience convinced him that we could learn from a baby's guileless openness to the present moment. He says as much, as the poem continues in its second stanza:

> *Pretty joy!*
> *Sweet joy but two days old,*
> *Sweet joy I call thee:*
> *Thou does smile,*
> *I sing the while,*
> *Sweet joy befall thee!*

OK, babies a day or two old don't smile in response to cooing parents—that takes a month or more to develop. Blake must have been seduced by a burp-smile. And who wouldn't be? He is delighted by the moment, contemplates it, and focuses on what is basic and valuable in it: in a word, innocence—an attitude that might be defined as the habit of saying 'yes' to life in a way that is hopeful and much more than simply naive. Here is the first quality to highlight in a Blakean way of life: a generous, unaffected virtue that can underpin his philosophy. Innocence.

Consider the lines of 'Infant Joy' again. They are short and made up of simple words: *sweet*, *joy*, *pretty*. They sing unashamedly of gladness but simultaneously carry notes of fragility. The brevity implies that the delight is heartfelt and palpable, though inevitably soon to pass, if also likely to return. These shifting elements are also conveyed in the way that the word 'innocence' would have carried strong Biblical overtones for Blake—scriptural notes always being audible to him. Innocence is what Adam and Eve were said to have lost when they ate from the tree in the garden of Eden. The mythical first humans were originally free of shame and restriction, according to the book of Genesis, but lost that when they became burdened by a sickening diffidence, after eating the fateful fruit. The act is referred to in the Christian tradition as the Fall, with the assumption that sin was introduced into the world as a result of disobeying God. Blake did believe we live in a fallen world; evil and suffering are irrefutable evidence. However, for him, the Fall was not about transgression or blame, but was rather about the diminution of spirit people suffer following a narrowing of vision. Innocence offers potential recovery, a glimpse of a tragically lost state. It is a capacity to perceive expansively, with clarity, receptivity and unhindered imagination—not simplistically but with a searching hope because, as Blake puts it, *Innocence dwells with wisdom*.[7] The insight born of innocence resists sneering scepticism, possessiveness and fear.

However, the virtue is fragile, at least at first. Innocence brings vulnerability, which is one reason people so easily lose it—or, indeed, actively dismiss or want rid of it. Cruelty and heartache can lead some to conclude that they don't want to be innocent. The state of mind is too open to feeling exposed, being manipulated, or straightforwardly getting hurt.

*Saving Innocence*

Blake was well aware of this pain—he is not advocating shallow naivety—and so alerts us to it in his poems. The edginess is fully present in other *Songs of Innocence*, a good example being 'The Chimney Sweeper.'[8] This verse reflects on the short life of a youngster, Tom Dacre, whose story is wretched and heartbreaking. Maybe Blake knew a boy by that name and immortalises him to honour him, as well as forewarn and forearm us; be aware of the abuse of innocence, he implies, and don't let that mean you lose it.

Tom is a sweep and Blake's childhood home on Broad Street was typical of the middle-class abodes that exploited the 'climbing boys.' Their cheap labour was needed to deliver comfort to the bourgeois—a word that was first deployed during Blake's childhood to capture the new socioeconomic group of which his family were a part. A warm fireplace in every room had become de rigueur for such folk, much as central heating is the default today, though because of a hearth tax, which was calculated on the basis of the number of chimneys, many townhouses were built with fewer stacks attached to a maze of dark, tight flues that drew smoke and soot from multiple inglenooks and grates. The networks of ducts and

# AWAKE!

shafts were kept unblocked by troops of child sweeps who, according to Blake, roamed London's streets in their thousands. Unkempt kids with grimy red eyes were a common sight.

The nation of shopkeepers, to recall Napoleon's quip, was developing a taste for convenience, and what is convenient for one is drudgery for another, which Blake personifies in the figure of Tom Dacre. The poem tells us of Tom losing his mother when still a baby, leading his father to sell the child as soon as he could, as an indentured apprentice. And 'child' is the right description since the age at which climbing boys began practising their trade could be as early as four; being small was the main requirement for squeezing up the narrow, twisting vents. Thus the poem beings:

> *When my mother died I was very young,*
> *And my father sold me while yet my tongue,*
> *Could scarcely cry weep weep weep.*
> *So your chimney I sweep & in soot I sleep.*

Child labour provokes horror today as it did amongst social reformers in Blake's time. But what is striking about the poem is that it holds back from outrage and instead focuses on the underlying cause of the indignation. Blake exposes, without flinching, Tom Dacre's innocence. As the poem continues, the boy has a dream. He sees sweeps who have died. They are released from miniature coffins by an angel. Then, leaping and laughing, they *wash in a river and shine in the Sun*. The angel next turns to Tom and promises that if he is a good boy, which is to say if he works diligently, he will never lack joy because God will be his father. The bitter irony, which Tom is too young to grasp, is that he will know this love only after his little body has been broken by the work and also laid in a coffin. The last verse of the poem presents us with the painful consolation that Tom innocently takes from the angel's promise.

> *And so Tom awoke; and we rose in the dark,*
> *And got with our bags & our brushes to work.*
> *Tho' the morning was cold, Tom was happy and warm;*
> *So if all do their duty they need not fear harm.*

The ambivalence is rending. *So if all do their duty they need not fear harm* means coerced duty and an exploitation that will certainly bring harm. And yet Tom's mood is described as *happy and warm* because he trusts the angel. His innocence humanises his dire state, even as readers of the

Fig. 2: *Songs of Innocence and Experience*, plate 45, "The Chimney Sweeper."

poem feel offence. Blake was in no doubt that the existence of climbing boys was a crime; he was no apologist. In a later poem that revisits the theme, also titled 'The Chimney Sweeper,' he condemns the inhabitants of comfortable homes with their warming fires, *Who make up a heaven of our [the sweepers'] misery.*[9] But in the first poem, he does not want the natural ire to eclipse and ruin the innocence. Innocence's purity is worth seeing and honouring for its own sake. Conversely, when it's forgotten, outrage loses its point and, no matter how justified, risks turning destructive.

Blake is saying that innocence is crucial to sustain, doubly so when injustices and tragedies surround us. With it, the infinite dignity of ourselves and others can be appreciated. Without it, not only does the viciousness of life rapidly become unbearable, but the desire to redress wrongs itself goes wrong. You must know what you love more clearly than what you hate; delight must be stronger than disgust. Wise innocence secures this. Writing around 150 years after Blake, Aldous

# AWAKE!

Huxley expressed the perennially important insight in his book, *The Devils of Loudun*:

> No man can concentrate his attention upon evil, or even upon the idea of evil, and remain unaffected. To be more *against* the devil than *for* God is exceedingly dangerous. Every crusader is apt to go mad. He is haunted by the wickedness which he attributes to his enemies; it becomes in some sort a part of him.[10]

*They become like what they behold*, was the way Blake captured the truth.[11] What do you see? Towards what are you most fundamentally orientated? These are questions he puts to us and the answers we give reveal much about what forms us.

The complexity of the issue is captured in another uneasy verse from *Songs of Innocence*, called 'The Little Black Boy.'[12] A significant proportion of the wealth of Georgian England flowed into cities like London as a result of the sugar trade, which in turn rested on the export of human chattel—people taken from Nigeria and Congo, Ghana and Senegal to toil on estates in the southern American colonies. Blake was fully aware of the savagery of enslaving fellow humans; some of his later work makes that appallingly explicit. One of his engravings, which is almost too brutal to look at, depicts a black man hanging from a gallows by a rope strapped around his ribs. But in 'The Little Black Boy' he wants, again, to focus on the innocence.

The verse is about a child born *in the southern wild* of Africa, whose mother taught him about God and nature and how *to bear the beams of love*. That's a telling phrase and a disquieting summary of innocence as Blake understands it; the *beams of love* refer both to bright sunbeams and to the wooden beams of the cross on which Jesus died, having accepted the hate that killed him. Blake the Christian evokes the coexistence of good and ill, challenging us to hold in mind more than one view of things at the same time.

The little black boy absorbs what his mother teaches him, so that when he meets a little English boy, born to parents who might well own enslaved Africans, he is able to tell the white child about their shared place on Earth, where *round the tent of God like lambs we joy*. The implication is that the African boy can perceive their shared humanity more clearly than the London child, whose vision is likely distorted by his materially more favourable upbringing. You might say that when it comes to knowing these deeper truths, privilege and guilt can be impediments.

## SING YOUR INFANT JOY

*Growing Pains*

A related risk to complex but clear-sighted innocence is depicted in a longer poem that is not in the *Songs of Innocence*, though Blake wrote it at about the same early stage in his career. This composition is in the form of a fairy tale, the type of story that can deal very well with such subtle matters. *The Book of Thel* tells the story of another youngster—a girl called Thel who lives in the mythical vales of Har by the fictitious river Adona, an enchanting place of simple pleasures. Blake describes the children of Har: *Playing with flowers & running after birds they spent the day, | And in the night like infants slept, delighted with infant dreams.*[13] However, even in Har, Thel is confronted by a problem. She realises she is beginning to grow up; she has become aware that her young happiness cannot last forever and she is shocked. As it dawns on her that springtime passes,

Fig. 3: *The Book of Thel*, plate 2, title page.

she cries out in distress, thinking that she would prefer not to age but to die. However, the beings around hear her lament and start to converse with her. The tale is Blake's way of introducing another manner in which innocence profits us: we are not alone when we are innocent because innocence can open us to the love and presence of unexpected others. Horizons can surprisingly expand.

First a lily of the valley speaks to Thel, the flower testifying that growing up is a boon. Even for a *wat'ry weed*, the plant says, being *clothed in light* turns out to be wonderful. The ecstasy the flower has known isn't at all compromised by what awaits it next: fading, shrivelling and dying. It explains: *'I am visited from heaven, and he that smiles on all | Walks in the valley and each morn over me spreads his hand.'*[14] Life is a blessing, the bloom insists, even though living is followed by dying. But Thel is not convinced. She has noticed that the flowers are food for a lamb which mindlessly munches on them when grazing. *'He crops thy flowers while thou sittest smiling in his face,'* she says, horrified.[15] Many parents will recognise such jolts that strike a developing child: in the midst of life, there is death; that's an affront. But the lily of the valley is not perturbed. The flower suggests speaking to a cloud, to whom Thel has likened herself because clouds first appear as if on a *pearly throne*, only to vanish, too.[16]

A cloud dutifully descends and Thel asks why it doesn't complain at the swiftly passing existence it has been allotted. The cloud explains that it gives up its life happily because it becomes rain that nourishes the creatures of Earth. *'When I pass away | It is to tenfold life, to love, to peace and raptures holy,'* the cloud affirms.[17] But again, Thel is not convinced. She notes, with disgust, that when she passes away, she'll feed worms. Then speak to a worm, the cloud suggests, calling one up from the ground. Like the gardener who finds comfort in the soil, the lowliest, least appealing of creatures might be the best source of succour when in a state of distress. Can Thel become more grounded?

The omens look good: a worm climbs onto the lily's leaf and Thel sees it looking every bit like an infant in a green cradle. She is surprised and moved, which next prompts a clod of clay to speak words of crystalline wisdom: *'O beauty of the vales of Har! we live not for ourselves. | Thou seest me the meanest thing, and so I am indeed. | My bosom of itself is cold, and of itself is dark.'*[18] And yet, the clod continues, it knows that it has a place in the great cycle of life in spite of its meagre lot. To ponder that is enough, for that is to *live and love*, the dirt avers.[19]

## SING YOUR INFANT JOY

Thel is intrigued: being in the real world might prove her salvation. It seems as if her panicky resistance to the transience of things will steady and make way for a more accepting, less resistant stance: a matured innocence. The humble clod senses the moment and invites Thel to take a step further and undergo an initiation. She can enter into the very darkness of the soil, which is the land of the dead, and so learn of the great cycles that steer her path, and she does. In the final section of the poem, Thel hears lamentations, sees *the fibrous roots | Of every heart on earth* and, in a moment of premonition, stands by her own grave.[20]

But it is too much. The experience is a bad trip. Thel is overwhelmed by the vision of the trials that she must undergo if she is to change and blossom. She comes to with a shriek, and flees back in terror to the vales of Har. Maybe the clod acted rashly; maybe the realisation was too total, too sudden. That can happen, and compounding the tragedy, the Eden that Thel returns to can now only be a place of arrested development for her. She struggles to hold onto her childhood like a sad Peter Pan, which really means that she refuses life and becomes increasingly self-centred. Her decision condemns her to fear rather than joy, to retreat not increase.

The story tells us something further about innocence. There is an angular form of innocence that can easily tip into a petulant narcissism and so must be carefully educated to discover a wider, more robust kind. I saw the impact that this transition can make on people's lives when I was curate in the Church of England. The work was mostly pastoral and involved frequent visits to people in their homes. One regular call was to a person who, I can now see, had gained a second innocence. She was a retired teacher and frail, though managing to live alone, having outlived her husband. And she glowed. I felt energised after my visits, though her junior by decades. I came to see that whilst she had aged and endured personal losses, she had become transparent to a wider pulse of life. She channelled more than herself without being any less herself. She knew how to let go and, paradoxically, that let more in.

In Blake's poem, Thel backs off at the outset of this journey. But for us readers, Blake points to an innocence that is stronger than suffering. Growing up need not mean losing innocence and wonder, which can be deepened by struggle. *Innocence dwells with Wisdom* he had written, and there is a further clause: *Innocence dwells with Wisdom but never with Ignorance*.[21] When ignorance is present there is not real innocence but credulity.

# AWAKE!

*Suffering and Lamentation*

To burn bright and not splutter. The open soul must learn to tolerate the assault on its quiet joy. Fostering an attentive realism became a core part of Blake's task and, at times, like Thel, he feared the path was too demanding, too exacting. But he had a conviction that the relationship between surges of gladness and waves of despair is asymmetrical. Affirmation is the more enlarging, encompassing apprehension—it sees more—whereas despair blinds and encloses. Happiness can be eclipsed for a while but need not be lost to the anguished events of life.

A few years after he published *Songs of Innocence,* Blake made the challenges of this nuanced hope clear when he published the first poems alongside a second set, in a combined collection entitled *Songs of Innocence and Experience.* One of the new poems is called 'Infant Sorrow.' It complements 'Infant Joy' in the sense that 'Infant Sorrow' makes overt what is nascent in the earlier poem. The tempestuous side of a new arrival is explicit.

> *My mother groan'd! my father wept,*
> *Into the dangerous world I leapt:*
> *Helpless, naked, piping loud:*
> *Like a fiend hid in a cloud.*
>
> *Struggling in my fathers hands:*
> *Striving against my swaddling bands:*
> *Bound and weary I thought best*
> *To sulk upon my mothers breast.*[22]

Every parent has been there, and the image accompanying 'Infant Sorrow' reflects the turbulent side of parenthood. No longer is the scene tranquil and blessed by an angel. Blake depicts a moment that is stormy, with a young child upon a bed refusing to be comforted by its mother, who vainly reaches out to her offspring. The snapshot of childish meltdown is shown indoors, which must be Blake's way of indicating that weeping and yelling confine and darken the mind; the sunbeams have disappeared behind clouds.

He might be suggesting a parenting tip—when at a loss, take the brat outside—and, in fact, the expanded collection gave Blake the chance to explore other ways in which innocence and experience can grow together. 'Infant Sorrow' depicts one possibility: the trials of raising kids can be aided by remembering that, for the most part, fiendish piping and tears

# SING YOUR INFANT JOY

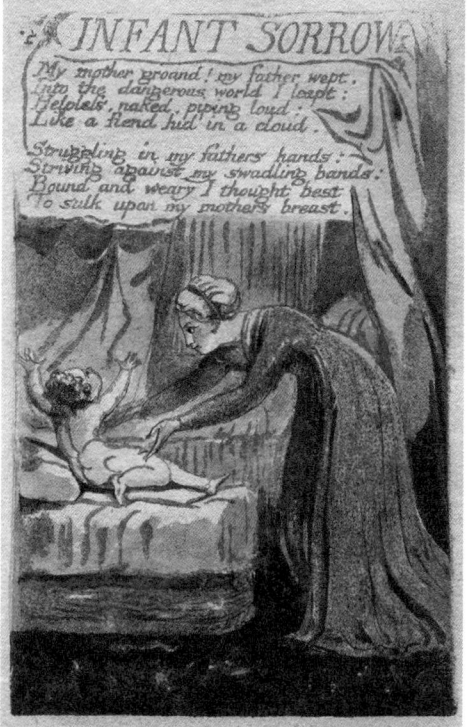

Fig. 4: *Songs of Innocence and Experience*, "Infant Sorrow."

sooner or later yield to a loving embrace, even if grudgingly. The good wins out, given time; that's a handy creed. But still, such outcomes are not automatic. Brutality can take on a life of its own and one of the best known poems in the new collection, entitled 'London,' recognises these harsher realities. The whole verse is given over to describing a bleakness that unleashes spiralling cruelty and seemingly inconsolable despair.

> *I wander thro' each charter'd street,*
> *Near where the charter'd Thames does flow,*
> *And mark in every face I meet*
> *Marks of weakness, marks of woe.*
>
> *In every cry of every Man,*
> *In every Infants cry of fear,*
> *In every voice, in every ban,*
> *The mind-forg'd manacles I hear.*

# AWAKE!

> *How the Chimney-sweepers cry*
> *Every black'ning Church appalls;*
> *And the hapless Soldiers sigh*
> *Runs in blood down Palace walls.*
>
> *But most thro' midnight streets I hear*
> *How the youthful Harlot's curse*
> *Blasts the new-born Infants tear,*
> *And blights with plagues the Marriage hearse.*[23]

The spirit is grim. Suffering floods unfriendly streets. Misery twists faces. Love is deadly. Things can fall so far that people become their own torturers, Blake descries with notable psychological astuteness; the vivid phrase, *mind-forg'd manacles*, captures the fretful stress that can overwhelm an individual if they become trapped by obsessive, reactive feelings. Was he so locked in himself on occasion and, knowing this hellish state of mind, could spot the dark brilliance that makes the 'manacles' phrase in the poem work? If so, he must also have reached a further point, realising that release depends, ultimately, on committing to overcoming darkness oneself. Social ills can spoil lives, experience can undoubtedly traumatise, but darkness need not be allowed the last word. Refusal is another facet of the power of innocence: the remarkable quality of resistance, a kind of holding out for what's good until it delivers its blessing.

That fruit is depicted in Blake's accompanying imagery. Around the bleak lines of 'London,' he etched more auspicious scenes. In the upper section of the plate, above the poem, an old man, blind and walking on crutches, is guided through the murky streets by a kindly lad. Then, alongside the chilling stanzas, a blazing fire is depicted, at which another figure warms herself. The *Songs of Innocence and Experience* are full of the hopeful possibilities that can co-exist with distressing actualities.

Nevertheless, things can be bad. Sometimes, straightforwardly lamenting a state of affairs is all that can be done. The pain known is unadorned. A poem of experience that portrays such woe is 'The Sick Rose.'[24]

> *O Rose, though art sick!*
> *The invisible worm*
> *That flies in the night,*
> *In the howling storm,*

## SING YOUR INFANT JOY

*Has found out thy bed*
*Of crimson joy;*
*And his dark secret love*
*Does thy life destroy.*

Fig. 5: *Songs of Innocence and Experience*, plate 39, "London."

The worm's devouring is not reconcilable with the rose's joy, period. The *howling storm* that heralds the bug's arrival portends that innocence must sometimes be ready to go so far as to sacrifice itself in the face of experience. That might be the only way to avoid bitterness taking root which, paradoxically and with real cost, might keep hope alive, for another unknown day. Better to have loved and lost than never to have loved at all. The poem expresses this tragedy, an undeniable aspect of the fallen condition of humanity. But the stance is still a refusal of a kind. It can be thought of as a resistance to 'solutionism'—the impulse that has become widespread in our technological era, which is to seek a fix for every problem; indeed, to treat life as a set of problems to which solutions can regularly be found. As a result, fewer think to say a prayer or sing a lament, light a candle or narrate a woe—the activities that can feed the soul and wait on a different energy: renewal or grace. Life hacks and system reboots are preferable to wilderness, as well as what Blake's near-contemporary poet, John Keats, called 'negative capability'—the virtue that can tolerate not 'reaching after fact and reason' and, in that patience, come to see all things in a different light, given time.[25]

Incidentally, Keats's references to 'fact' and 'reason' must arise from an awareness that the two words had been changing meaning across the course of the eighteenth century. 'Reason' had meant purpose, as is remembered in the phrase 'rhyme or reason,' though was coming to connote a robust argument that commends itself to the rational individual: 'a sort of light in which every mind must perceive.'[26] 'Fact' had meant a deed, coming from the Latin *facere* 'to do,' though was coming to connote an irrefutable truth, as in the phrase, 'facts and figures,' first deployed in the eighteenth century. Blake questioned the shifts because, for him, they signalled a loss of discovery to crisp reasoning, of experiencing to hard evidence. *Tell me the What* he insisted, because from the trials of life come not solutions but disclosures and, ultimately, they are more valuable.[27]

## Musically Minded

There is another aid to those undergoing suffering that Blake must have known as a child and pursued in his adult life. It is implicit in the title for the poems, not incidentally called 'songs': *Songs of Innocence and Experience*. These lines are designed to be sung and the musical dimension adds something crucial, as the introduction to *Songs of Innocence* reveals. It tells a story of how, one day, a piper is invited by a child to put down his pipe and sing. And then, when he had stopped singing, to write down his ballads *In a book that all may read*.[28] We are that 'all' and are invited to catch, in our imaginations, the echoes of Blake's original singing. The words can be joined not only by imagery but also by melody, because the poems can serve as lyrics. Blake was a believer in music which has its own power, restoring forgotten instincts and unknown energies; it *exists and exalts in immortal thoughts*, he wrote, which is to say, it enables insights that may be otherwise beyond us.[29] Blake held throughout his life a conviction that the three arts of painting, poetry and music can cut through our fallenness and reconnect us to the source of life; he strove to integrate all three in his work and so make that wellspring felt.

## SING YOUR INFANT JOY

He positively loved to sing, as we learn from several surviving anecdotes; he would, on occasion, introduce himself as 'Poet, Painter, & Musician as the Inspiration Comes.'[30] I imagine him first gurgling in the cradle, then humming as he toddled about the shop, and finally hymning much of the day. A gossipy observer of the artistic scene in Blake's time, John Smith, met Blake as a young adult at the soirée of a hostess, Harriet Mathew, one of the intellectual women known as the bluestockings. Smith recalled that the poet-painter would often sing as well as read his poems to the gathered assembly. Blake composed airs for his lines, or probably it's more accurate to say that the music and the words came to him simultaneously, although he had no formal training in music. But he had a talent. Harriet Mathew, for her part, had a musical ear and so would invite professionals along to hear. Smith says that sometimes Blake's tunes were 'most singularly beautiful' and 'were noted down by musical professors.' Smith continues: 'He was listened to by the company with profound silence, and allowed by most of the visitors to possess original and extraordinary merit.'[31] Indeed, the musicality can be heard in the verses alone, if you say them out loud, which is presumably why many of them have subsequently inspired composers to put the words to music.

Music was a huge part of eighteenth-century life and, before the invention of recording equipment, had to be performed live to be heard. Most people must have been practiced at singing and many in writing songs, from the great operas and oratorios composed for refined audiences, to the ballads heard on street corners and the drinking songs that rippled through taverns and inns. And there was singing in church: Blake belongs to the revival of lyrical spontaneity and sincerity that produced a surge of hymn-writing amongst his near contemporaries, not least Charles Wesley, who lived in the generation before Blake and composed more than 6,000 spiritual songs. Piety mixed with the profane, too. A book from 1783, *A Select Collection of English Songs*, includes eight plates engraved by Blake, featuring carousers at wooden tables raising goblets. One lyric reads: 'Busy, curious, thirsty fly, Drink with me, and drink as I; Freely welcome to my cup… Make the most of life you may, Life is short, and wears away.'[32]

The first critics of Blake's *Songs* were divided over whether, as poems, they helped or hindered the appreciation of our rocky lives. The stormy essayist, William Hazlitt, whose Soho burial plot is a stone's throw from Blake's birthplace, acknowledged beautiful moments in Blake's lines but couldn't hear the note of sophisticated innocence that chimes throughout the collection and concluded the poems were too much of a jumble. 'He [Blake] is ruined by vain struggles to get rid of what presses on his brain,' he said in a remark that could have been aimed at Hazlitt himself, given the way he loads his writing.[33] Another contemporary man of letters, Charles Lamb, declared Blake a 'mad Wordsworth'—a kind of damning with faint praise. That said, the literary circles of Georgian England were often tense and so the comment may say as much about Lamb as Blake; he had a touchy relationship with Wordsworth and the phrase could be more aimed at Wordsworth's poetry than Blake's.[34]

Wordsworth himself was entranced. He copied out the poems and read them repeatedly. It is likely that the combination of apparent simplicity and subtler depths helped him with his landmark 'experiments in Poetry,' the *Lyrical Ballads*, which were published in 1798—although where Wordsworth sought a first innocence via a return to youthfulness, Blake turned towards a state that could become a constant across the life-course, for those with the eyes to see. There is no nostalgia in Blake, which is but one way in which he is different from the Romantics who were to follow. Wordsworth's collaborator, Samuel Taylor Coleridge, greatly appreciated the *Songs*, too, understanding more clearly than Wordsworth what Blake aimed to reveal: how love outshines evil, though evils have a powerful reality. Coleridge was convinced of the value of the poems. He heralded Blake's 'Genius' in a letter to one friend, seeing at work in Blake the gift of a prophet.[35] In another letter, to the person who lent him a copy of the poems, he scored each one from 'gave me great pleasure,' through 'still greater' and 'greater still,' up to 'in the highest degree.'[36] 'The Little Black Boy' received the highest accolade of all, suggesting to me that Coleridge perceived precisely what Blake sought to surface: innocence is valuable because it is stronger than experience and can embrace the worst.

The virtue is doubly valuable in a harsh world, and Blake had re-expressed what is acknowledged within wisdom traditions. For example, Zen Buddhism has the concept of *shoshin*, or 'beginner's mind,' which is the art of dropping preconceptions in a readiness to see afresh. Christianity records Jesus telling his disciples to suffer the little children because an adult equipped with the unselfconscious attitude they more naturally embody can detect the kingdom of God, obscured by personal preoccupations.[37]

Living by innocence and experience, and avoiding succumbing to negative states of mind, proved to be a daily challenge. How could it be otherwise for a man who wanted, from his earliest days, to affirm the whole of life without reserve? His experiences as an infant readied his soul. And that was not the only sustenance he received. Soon after his birth, he began to become aware of celestial visitors and ethereal helpers he could turn to as well. I am referring, of course, to the encounters that fed accusations of madness and that interpreters still try to explain away: Blake saw angels. That type of report might be judged not so much innocent as straightforwardly gullible. But if not dismissed as purely fantastical, what can be made of his communing with spirits and, sometimes, their dastardly cousins, the demons? This question takes us to the second virtue that was foundational in his life: perceptual openness.

2

BY CAME AN ANGEL

When the infant William was two weeks old, he was baptised in the church of St James's Piccadilly, a few minutes' walk from the family house on Broad Street. The occasion was one of the few certain times that Blake attended a church service, which he and his parents seem to have done only on the occasions when, by law, they had no other option; at that time, baptisms and marriages had to be performed by Church of England clergy. Blake loathed such clericalism, though it did not make him irreligious. Quite the opposite: you could say that he was too religious to go to church.

Ecclesiastical Christianity clashed with his own vivid formulation of faith and he was far from alone in finding mainstream Georgian religiosity mind-numbing. The root concern was that going to church in the eighteenth century was an often banal activity, a sign of conformity not commitment, which meant that the sight of chocker box pews raised inquisitor-like questions. What were the people jostling in the nave really there for? Were they contemplating their salvation or passing the time of day with less important, more diverting matters? Busy churches caused moral panic, as empty pews can do now. Acknowledging the value of Christianity in a tokenistic manner was deemed corrosive, at least by some, including Blake. *A pretence of Religion to destroy Religion* was one of his pithy analyses.[1] I imagine he would say the same of cultural Christianity now.

Not that services were inevitably boring. Rousing hymns were on offer. The mellifluous King James Bible could be heard, the eighteenth century's most frequently reprinted book. Learned sermons lasting half an hour or more were preached. But educated figures like Jonathan Swift, author of *Gulliver's Travels*, asked themselves whether all this activity was elevating people's souls, and suspected it was not.

## AWAKE!

Dean Swift, as he was known because of his appointment as Dean of St Patrick's Cathedral, Dublin, is remembered for his wit, but in life he was a perturbed orthodox clergyman: prick a satirist and a puritan bleeds. He considered it an obligation to inform the people of their duty and so to counter 'the great decay of religion among us.'[2] In one of his surviving sermons, given the title 'On Sleeping in Church,' he relates what it is like to look down from the pulpit and see a congregation bothered neither with contradicting nor agreeing with him. Indifference reigns, as he spots people gossiping with friends, gawping desirously at their neighbours, gazing dreamily into the middle distance, or exchanging smirks and sniggers at the expense of the preacher, a beadle or warden. Most displeasingly of all, Swift eyes parishioners sleeping as if anesthetised by the preaching. 'Opium is not so stupefying to man-Persons as an Afternoon Sermon,' he despairs.[3]

The historian, Edward Gibbon, whose multivolume book on the decline and fall of the Roman Empire began appearing when Blake was in his late teens, referred to the 'fat slumbers' of the English clergy and feared that he was living in an age of civilisational decline, with religious laxity spreading the rot; he was another cultural 'pessimist,' to reference a neologism of the time, arguing that irreligiousness was linked to society becoming more liberal. The Act of Toleration, passed in the previous century, was a target for the concern. It brought Nonconformists in from the cold, though not Roman Catholics, who in Blake's youth were persistently associated with disloyalty and possibly treason.

Fear of decline always produces a passionate reaction—sometimes by identifying an enemy; sometimes in rhetoric like 'yes we can' or 'make America great again'; occasionally by championing a remedy. In Blake's time, lackadaisical church-going sparked a backlash in the form of a lively counterculture of idiosyncratic religiosity, of which he approved. No one was spiritual but not religious, as many are today, because the drift from institutions and the uncoupling of personal practices from creeds and doctrines had not yet occurred. Neither had self-help been invented. But the antecedents of these trends were appearing as people started buying volumes of popular moralising.

Improving tomes went by titles that included *The Daily Self-examinant: Or an Earnest Persuasive to the Duty of Daily Self-examination; with Devout Prayers, Meditations, Directions and Ejaculations for a Holy Life and Happy Death*. That barnstormer was penned by Robert Warren, a sincere clergyman from Kent, whose advice boiled down to having a good night's sleep. Plus ça change. Spiritual autobiography was another high-minded genre, as was the printing of sermons in the hope that, if ignored on a Sunday, they might be studied in the week. Evangelical revivals and apocalyptic prophets like Joanna Southcott and Richard Brothers became famous, awaking private piety and fierce devotion in some. Blake identified with this fiery scene and was to make something wonderfully distinctive of it. I find him refreshing to read partly because he was resolutely not agnostic about his worldview and the infant Blake might even have spotted a sign of the supernatural beings that were a mark of his experience on the day he was baptised.

The ceremony was conducted in the marble font that still occupies the northwest corner of the nave of St James's. As it happens, hanging over the font were images that might have pleased the child. Above was a cover suspended from a rafter and, as the gurgling William was presented to the minister, he might just about have managed to focus on a large, exuberant angel clinging to the garlanded hood. The celestial being was descending from a higher cluster of singing cherubim, also suspended aloft. Was the babe comforted by an already familiar scene?

*Tales of the Unexpected*

The thought highlights a stumbling block. Blake regarded angels as living beings and no small part of his impatience with the lukewarm religious attitudes of his contemporaries derived from the spectacle and, at times, shock of his frequent encounters with seraphs and otherworldly souls. He routinely reported throughout his life that he saw these visitors from ethereal spheres as regularly as the sunrise, and told of participating in other unusual activities, such as conversing with the dead. He immensely valued this contact with the beyond and avoided anything that he felt compromised it. He was also notably unaffected when talking about it, never becoming starry-eyed or manic, as can happen with those for whom peak experiences are the exception not the rule.

He was often witty about it, too. *I have always found that Angels have the vanity to speak of themselves as the only wise*, he observed.[4] *This they do with a confident insolence sprouting from systematic reasoning.* Prissy beings, those angels. I suppose that being on heavenly business means not being troubled by trivialities like doubt, and there are other literary seers who have concluded similarly. Dante, for example, depicts angels as conscientious to the point of obsession. In *The Divine Comedy*, they appear in a burst of light or on the wind, perform a task or deliver a message, and disappear as abruptly as they had come—rapt and wrapped-up, leaving surprised humans either astounded or terrified. Wrestling with their weird and wonderful presence is central to Blake: dodging that, out of distaste or embarrassment, is really dodging him. They are central to what is intriguing and, to be frank, fun about him.

The colourful stories of Blake's second sight, remembered by so many who knew him that they can't be discounted, reach back into his early childhood. Catherine Blake, his wife, one day dropped this causal remark into a conversation: 'You know, dear, the first time you saw God was when you were four years old, and He put His head to the window, and set you screaming.'[5] I love that 'first.' What happened when God appeared the second time, the third?

Alexander Gilchrist, an early biographer who was seminal in securing the reputation that Blake has come to enjoy, records perhaps the most famous vision. One day, as a young lad, William was walking on Peckham Rye, a grassy rise that is a mile or two east of the *lovely hills of Camberwell* south of the River Thames.[6] 'Sauntering along, the boy looks up and sees a tree filled with angels, bright angelic wings bespangling every bough like stars.'[7] He sped home and told his parents, who chastised him: don't lie, they said. Luckily, he obeyed them and told many such stories. On another occasion, whilst still young, he saw hay-makers in the evening, who were a frequent sight in his youth because London's outskirts quickly gave way to arable fields. The late summer light not only gilded the grasses and workers but 'amid them angelic figures walking,' Blake reported.[8]

Further tales of the unexpected abound and clearly such sightings were not infrequent. Thrashings were threatened when he ran in and announced that he had just seen the Old Testament prophet Ezekiel under the trees, as happened on another day.[9] His lucidity reached beyond perceiving the holy as well. There is a further story from his early years in which he interrupted a traveller who was describing the wonders of a foreign city. 'Do you call that splendid?' the precocious William interjected. 'I should call a city splendid in which the houses were of gold, the pavements of silver, the gates ornamented with precious stones.'[10] You get the sense that he glimpsed such glorious abodes and didn't just make things up. He had no need to.

The sightings continued as he matured, which he later said was key as, for others, the seeing fades and ceases. During his late teens, he worked for a while in Westminster Abbey, which enchanted him. The building is medieval and gothic, not neoclassical as was the favoured Georgian style, and Blake loved the architecture's 'living form,' as he put it; amidst the criss-cross of aisles and reaching up of arches, he detected the 'livid twilight of past days,' and in the Abbey his clairvoyance spontaneously kicked in.[11] He saw long-dead monks and priests, choristers and censer-bearers processing around the royal tombs. Personally, I'm unsurprised at this particular instance of strange espying as I was once myself locked into Westminster Abbey after hours. I play the organ and the evening is the time a novice can practice. I longed to feel the marvellous power of the instrument at my fingertips, but as I pulled out the stops and reached forward to strike a crashing cord, a fear gripped me. Who or what might such a terrific noise disturb in the shadows?

Blake clearly enjoyed his visions and could joke about them. One day, he showed a picture he had made to his great friend, Johann Fuseli, another visionary artist. Fuseli spotted that Blake was proud of it and said as much, to which Blake replied: 'Yes. The Virgin Mary appeared to me, and told me it was very fine,' then adding: 'What can you say to that?' Equal in wit, Fuseli retorted: 'Say! Why nothing, only her ladyship has not an immaculate taste.'[12] I imagine Blake chortled. Another droll incident captures the practical reality of living with spirits. The story relates how Blake was busy working when there was an unexpected banging on the door. He rose patiently to attend to the interruption; he never knew whether a disturbance might be an angel calling. Only this time, he was met by no gleaming being but a grimy coalman humping a great sack.[13] Sometimes a knock at the door is just a knock at the door.

Some of Blake's reports do test credulity, given that those I've cited so far have not already slipped from the intriguing to straightforwardly dubious. There was a lady who happened to sit next to him at a tea-party or soirée, whom he turned to and asked, 'Did you ever see a fairy's funeral, madam?' She instantly retorted, 'Never, sir!' At which point Blake continued by saying that he hadn't either,

> not before last night. I was walking alone in my garden, there was a great stillness among the branches and flowers and more than common sweetness in the air; I heard a low and pleasant sound, and I knew not whence it came. At last I saw the broad leaf of a flower move, and underneath I saw a procession of creatures of the size and colour of green and gray grasshoppers, bearing a body laid out on a rose leaf, which they buried with songs, and then disappeared. It was a fairy funeral.[14]

Wow—or should that be, what? Or maybe the existence of garden fairies seems as likely as the existence of heavenly spirits, with the upshot that once you admit one, you admit the lot. Only there is a serious issue attending these marvels and a question of discernment.

The novelist Salley Vickers, whose bestseller *Miss Garnet's Angel* features said beings, argues that we need fairies, to resist 'the reign of those grim twin isms, reductionism and materialism.' She continues: 'We once inhabited a world that was animate, in which humans were creatures who not only perceived but were themselves perceived.'[15] The world could answer back, not least in the form of nymphs and sprites, who have designs of their own and are resistant to human control, will and desire. Cross the little people and you can expect to find they aren't so little. Blake would have agreed that fairies and angels are expressions of immaterial intelligences that elude narrowed perceptions. If not seen, they no less press us by their company.

*Mind Expanding*

Fairies, angels, prophets, God. If you are not going to opt for either glib dismissals or assertions of madness, and also not for uncritical, unthinking acceptance, then what of Blake's visions? I'm trusting that their meaning and significance is revealed by not deciding too quickly, either with an easy affirmation or accounting for them in such a way that a materialistic worldview is left safely beyond question. Blake would insist that visionary sight must be developed before a judgement can be made and this plea is fundamental to learning from him. He offers both an invitation and a challenge. Can you too see more?

Here is an analogy. Consider the multidimensional aspects of awareness that must emerge in order to understand a language. Think first of a child, aged about two, and imagine saying to them, 'I am a tiger.' The toddler would be confused; if you repeated the remark, insistently, they might become upset. But if you said, 'I am a tiger' to a child a year or so older, aged about three, they might think your statement funny. They might giggle and retort, 'Don't be silly! No you're not!' A child at that age can push back. A shift has occurred.

If you say, 'I am a tiger' to a child about the age of five, they may wonder what you mean. If I myself said it, a youngster might think that I were referring to my ginger hair, which might be said to look a bit tiger-like. A slightly more mature child could countenance something further, an inner meaning: might I mean that I've a fierce temper *burning bright*, analogous to a tiger's growl?

As a child becomes agile with language, further dimensions of the same phrase would emerge, which is also to say that previously hidden aspects of reality start to reveal themselves through the phrase. Maybe it is a reference to being tiger-like in a particular context, when a passionate fire burns in the eyes? Or could it be a reference to a dark side of the human psyche, a *fearful symmetry*, in marked contrast to a calm exterior? This might then lead to the realisation of a truth about human beings in general: one person can have several sides to them, which often exist in tension or conflict. A young person who hears 'I am a tiger' in this way is starting to see that humans can be seized by tiger-like demons, as if possessed by *deadly terrors*. They might ask, *In what furnace was thy brain?*—to cite once more Blake's probably most famous poem, 'The Tyger.'[16]

The reflections needn't stop there. Someone on the cusp of adulthood might ponder whether human individuals are ever really a coherent unity or, rather, whether they are more like an erratic burn of character flares and quivering instincts? And then further: do the things that affect us come equally from outside as inside our psyches, forged in scattered furnaces, driven by alien imperatives? This further possibility is available for consideration not because of literal-mindedness or naivety, but because of a capacity to contemplate complex features of existence. Blake certainly had such a high-quality intelligence. He was to become immensely, subtly perceptive.

What matters when it comes to sightings of angels and the like, then, is the quality of the mind making the assertions. With what level of sophistication do they speak or conversely, if they are straightforwardly against the supernatural, what assumptions may limit their sight? That Blake was no fool is implied in another anecdote. He was relating an incident in which he had seen what, at first sight, looked like an ordinary bucolic scene transform into a ravishing sublime tableau. One of his listeners, gripped by the tale of the metamorphosis, thought that she would like to take her children to see the spectacle, as it would entertain them. So she asked Blake where he saw the glorious display. He replied, 'Here, madam' and tapped his forehead.[17] They might go to exactly the same spot and see nothing untoward.

Gilchrist, who records this exchange, uses it to insist that Blake did not hallucinate as if unhinged, nor was he like a medium who impresses by channelling. There was plenty of table-turning and panel-knocking going on amongst the Spiritualists of Georgian England, and Blake was not one of those. Rather, his capacities of sight were coupled to wit and discernment, like a person advanced in the nuances of speech and language. What he encountered were 'phenomena seen by his imagination: *realities* none the less for that, but transacted within the realm of mind,' Gilchrist continues. What might be accomplished by this imaginative agency was a central concern for Blake. He did not seek to disregard such experiences but to examine them, on occasion questioning them quite directly.

This happened, on another day, when exasperated he sighed, 'who can paint an angel?' He muttered the question to himself and, perhaps not entirely surprisingly, heard an answer: 'Michelangelo could.' Being Blake, he decided to address the voice. The story continues:

> 'And how do you know,' I said, looking round me, but I saw nothing save a greater light than usual. 'I know,' said the voice, 'for I sat for him: I am the archangel Gabriel.' 'Oho!' I answered, 'you are, are you: I must have better assurance than that of a wandering voice; you may be an evil spirit—there are such in the land.' 'You shall have good assurance,' said the voice, 'can an evil spirit do this?' I looked whence the voice came and was then aware of a shining shape, with bright wings, who diffused much light. As I looked, the shape dilated more and more: he waved his hands; the roof of my study opened; he ascended into heaven; he stood in the sun and beckoning me, moved the universe. An angel of evil could not have done that—it was the archangel Gabriel.[18]

Blake tested what happened, which is a venerable response to visions. In the ancient Greek world, for example, when a lucky pilgrim received a message from the oracle at Delphi, their next task was to question what had been said. Hence, when Socrates heard that the priestess had said that no one was wiser than him, he went about Athens seeking someone who was. He couldn't find anyone and only then did he realise what Apollo was communicating to him: he was wise because he was conscious of the limits of his knowledge. Similarly, when Jesus was baptised and heard God's voice in blessing, he immediately went into the wilderness to work out what the voice might mean in practice. Or again, after the prophet Mohammed had received his first visitation from the angel Gabriel, which initiated his receipt of the Quran, he was terrified and only began to realise what was happening with the assistance of his wife, Khadijah.

Blake was active in his engagement with these experiences; he made much of them, not in a crazy way, but creatively. For this reason, his otherworldly encounters are not adequately addressed by attempts to treat them as deluded symptoms of an underlying malaise. This approach seeks medical or diagnostic rationales. For example, temporal lobe epilepsy is frequently invoked to account for people who have religious experiences like Blake's and Blake scholars nowadays have regularly presumed this condition affected him. Only, the hypothesis can never be tested because of the impossibility of knowing whether he had such seizures. It is also a mistake to presume that irregular brain states cause unusual experiences, rather than merely correlating with them: the explanation is a case of the tail wagging the dog.

Hyperphantasia is another condition cited in scholarship grappling with Blake's supernal tales. For people suffering with hyperphantasia, thoughts spontaneously turn into vivid images, with the upshot that sufferers become overloaded with impressions unless they derive means to moderate the cinematic deluge, such as by becoming an artist. Was Blake flooded with fantasies and so painted, described and drew them to get them out of his head? I doubt it—partly because there is also aphantasia, which is almost the opposite of hyperphantasia, that other scholars prefer. This condition is living with an inability to produce images, and these individuals, the argument goes, have to develop artistic skills so as to stimulate their imaginations, which it is then proposed Blake did copiously. Another theory is that he suffered from migraines and interpreted the associated sight of zig-zag lines as rips in the fabric of reality, through which could tumble all manner of entities.

The theories multiply, much as the lists of mental disorders in psychiatric manuals lengthen. The syndromes and disorders are really just alternative ways of grouping symptoms and might, therefore, continue indefinitely replicating. But could Blake, who repeatedly stressed the necessity of clear-sightedness for any creative work and spent a lifetime arduously refining his art, have been so persistently fooled? Wouldn't he have suspected he were mad and, if he were, discounted his experiences as delusions? He certainly knew people who were insane and read about the horrors of real craziness. He annotated a book by the phrenologist, Johann Gaspar Spurzheim, entitled *Observations on the Deranged Manifestations of the Mind, or Insanity*. He also knew he could be distressed and troubled, and said so. But that is not the same as elaborate, systematic, life-long self-deception, which is why he rebutted those he suspected of accusing him of such. *Thou callst me Madman, but I call thee Blockhead*, one of his epigrams reads.[19] Further, he was aware that people might dismiss what he saw out of jealousy, as another epigram implies. *'Madman' I have been call'd: 'Fool' they call thee. | I wonder which they Envy, Thee or Me?*[20]

He was fully aware of explanations that explain away. In one place he mocks treating perceptions of God as a *Simulative Phantom of the over heated brain!*[21] The thought is akin to the later observation of William James. The great American psychologist reasoned that if religious experiences are biological by-products then so are scientific theories, because both would arise from the grey matter within the human head. 'Scientific theories are organically conditioned just as much as religions emotions are,' James wryly remarks in *The Varieties of Religious Experience*, 'and if we only knew the facts intimately enough, we should doubtless see 'the liver' determining the dicta of the sturdy atheist as decisively as it does those of the Methodist under conviction anxious about his soul.'[22] A Richard Dawkins is not speaking the truth because he is free of superstitions, but because he is suffering from congested bile; follow the logic and the dismissal cuts both ways.

Such rationalisations of Blake's visions seem either inadequate or self-contradictory. For myself, the conclusion of the psychotherapist Anthony Storr is illuminating, when he argues that the true genius knows how to dismiss distractions in order to see clearly.[23] Their secret is not flirting with insanity but is rather becoming more grounded.

*Engaging Entities*

There's a deeper point. What matters is not what Blake's neurons were doing but what his seeing conveys: what he and others make of it. The desire that people have for Blake tells me something fundamental about his mind because straightforwardly disturbed people are never so engaging or ingeniously prolific. Rather, any appeal they might have is negative, based on revulsion or fright. Moreover, their difficulties spin in ever tighter circles around the same narrow fears that soon become tedious, even boring, no matter how florid. I used to work in a psychiatric hospital and whilst it is true that even the most troubled can speak words of clarity from time to time, these moments of calm are upset by anxiety and delusion. True generativity is marked by the opposite energy, a moving out into ever wider circles of insight, originality and delight. Coleridge put the point well when he made a distinction between what he called mere fantasy, which collapses in on itself, and expansive imagination, which opens onto new worlds that others are subsequently drawn into as well.[24] This is the direction in which Blake allows us travel, walking with him along paths of disclosure.

Perceptual openness is the second fundamental virtue in a Blakean way of life, and discernment is not an optional extra; a discriminating mind is an active agent in the esoteric domain if the weird and wonderful are not to remain merely that. There is another story which suggests as much. It relates the only time in his life that he saw a ghost, which is a remarkable one-off given he so frequently saw other occult beings. The spook appeared at the top of a staircase when Blake, caught unawares, happened to look up. It was a ghastly figure, 'scaly, speckled, very awful.'[25] It seemed to make for him, sallying down the steps at a pace. 'More frightened than ever before or after he took to his heels, and ran out of the house,' Gilchrist records.[26]

Blake later reflected on how it was that he saw the ghost. He explained that ghosts appear as an invasion from the beyond, when an unsuspecting victim is not ready for them. They are uncanny: disturbing because disturbed; shocking because out of joint. The shock they cause is turned into a device in horror movies. Jump scares require the monstrous to remain in the shadows, beyond control, ready to leap out when least expected. That is what caught Blake by surprise on the occasion he saw a ghost. Conversely, his usual experience of spirits was shaped by his readiness to meet them; there was no crashing the boundaries between life and death but a crossing into a third realm where the two can meet harmoniously. This capacity is what his visionary experiences invite us to foster.

The stress on reciprocity is echoed in a further incident. Blake was walking with a friend along Cheapside in London, when he suddenly took off his hat and bowed. 'What did you do that for?' the friend asked, naturally enough. 'Oh! That was the Apostle Paul,' Blake supposedly replied. Gilchrist again tells this one. It is too good to miss—though this time, Gilchrist relates the tale

Fig. 6: Print entitled "Fear & Hope Are— Vision," 1793.

in order to dismiss it as a fabrication. The stories around Blake could proliferate and he judges this one false because, he reasons, Blake would not have bowed to a vision, as if walking by like a human person. Rather, he would have engaged with it, as you would with a dimension of reality that isn't solely a fabrication of your own mind, nor is wholly detached from it. Second sight is like a language; the more fluent you are, the more you are able to enter its domains and so the more you understand or see. Further, the more you can bring your awareness of the moment to the moment, the more fully, more inventively you can respond, and so the unveiling continues. 'The spirits which appeared to him did not reveal themselves in palpable, hand-shaking guise, nor were they mistaken by him for bodily facts,' Gilchrist continues. 'He did not claim for them an external or (in German slang) an *objective* existence.'[27]

That reference to the word 'objective' is also illuminating. Blake lived during a period in which many words were changing meaning. I have already cited 'fact' and 'reason.' The shift reflected the emerging modern worldview and the respect for science that we take for granted beginning to bed down. One aspect of that stands out: the eighteenth century became enamoured with the search for order and laws, inspired by great scientists like Robert Hooke and Isaac Newton who were celebrated for spotting deep patterns in nature, and appreciating how things can be regularly arranged became something of an obsession. For example, the notion that periods of time could be linked by their century was itself an eighteenth-century invention, presumably because no one had previously felt the need numerically to bundle up the years. A corollary of this tidying-up was that more words were needed to express the ways in which reality might be organised. For instance, words such as 'arrange' and 'regular' took on the meanings known to us; before, 'arrange' had been a specialist military term, referring to troops readying for battle, and 'regular' had described monks who live in community. In the poem, 'Windsor-Forest,' the poet Alexander Pope makes the sentiment explicit. He praises the wood he had known in his childhood because it is 'Not Chaos-like together crush'd and bruis'd | But, as the world is, harmoniously confus'd: | Where order in variety we see, | And where, tho' all things differ, all agree.'[28]

'Objective' was another word in transition, which is why Gilchrist refers to it as 'German slang.' In fact, objective is a particularly dramatic case in point because it did not widen its meaning, as happened with 'regular' and 'arrange,' but instead switched its meaning altogether, somersaulting with its seeming opposite, 'subjective.' Such changes fascinated the philologist, Owen Barfield, who was part of the group known as the Inklings, which included J.R.R. Tolkien and C.S. Lewis. Barfield explains that the meaning of 'subjective' developed from 'existing in itself outside of human consciousness' to 'existing only in human consciousness.' Meanwhile, 'objective' made a move in the opposite direction, from 'the observed details of something' to 'the truth of something regardless of what's observed.'[29] The upshot is that 'subjective' and 'objective' came to be seen as contrasting concepts, ideally denoting entirely different realms of knowledge—one inner, the other outer.

Two centuries on, we spontaneously assume that subjective means personal and so doubtful, and objective means impartial and so correct. Only, when you think again, the difference is less clear. Take the so-called objective truths of science. They are actually the ones that keep changing; the history of science is the story of their continual modification. Newton ruled the world of physics in Blake's day, whereas Einstein does now, with contemporary physicists busy building their careers by questioning his reign. That continual questioning is what makes science interesting. And it indicates something further: the subjective and objective are not actually opposites but meet at an in-between zone, as do what is called inner or outer, as well as the seen and not seen. Blake knew that, because of his anomalous experiences, and revelled in the mix, especially when teasingly sharing the stories of fairies and glorious lights. As Peter Ackroyd, one of the great recent biographers of Blake, points out, Blake lived in a moment when 'the imperatives of industry and technology had not yet closed the 'spiritual eye'.'[30] Blake would have us learn to open it again, reflecting on how we parse our experiences because that shapes what we see or don't.

Fairies might help. One of his works that forms part of what are known as the *Lambeth Prophecies* was, he said, dictated to him by a fairy. Blake declares this startling detail at the start of the poem and it's worth asking why. The work is called *Europe a Prophecy* and was written in the aftermath of the French Revolution. The verse begins with a prelude in which Blake describes overhearing a fairy mocking limited human perceptions. *Five windows light the cavern'd Man*, the creature sings, as it sits on a *streak'd Tulip*.[31] The godling lists the nostrils that take in the air, the ears that hear music, the mouth that tastes delights, the eyes that catch glimpses of wonders, and touch that is joyous and sweet. As the fairy sings, Blake sneaks up on it and catches it in his hat, *as boys knock down a butterfly*.³² The fairy doesn't resist; a trickster by nature, it knows when it has been tricked, and so submits.

The poet seizes his chance; he has a request. He might converse with a resident of the Otherworld, which is to say that his mind has entered the in-between zone which can *light the cavern'd Man* with subtler senses than the empirical senses that the fairy was mocking. So he asks the fairy about the world it sees: *what is the material world, and is it dead?*³³ In response, the fairy laughs. It asks Blake to feed it *love-thoughts* and *poetic fancies* that enable it to enter more deeply into the realm in which the subjective and objective blur.³⁴ Then, when tipsy in this altered state of consciousness, the fairy promises Blake that they will see something together. The world is alive and *every particle of dust breathes forth its joy*.³⁵ Seen aright, even humble dirt shines.

Incidentally, the phrase inspired the role of dust in Philip Pullman's great fantasy trilogy, *His Dark Materials*. Much of the action in the novels is driven by the effort to detect dust and understand it, which humans struggle to do because they have become blind to illusive realms seen only with alternative forms of awareness and understanding.

In his poem, Blake continues to press the captured fairy and the fairy obliges. Together, they walk back to Blake's house and enjoy glimpses of eternity in the flowers that they gather on the way. The fairy laughs as the flowers *whimper because they were pluck'd*.³⁶ The allusion is sexual, the blossoms letting out yelps of pleasure rather than pain, all of which extends Blake's openness. But he also doesn't lose sight of his intention; his agency does not flee. By the time they reach his writing desk, he is ready to receive the prophecy, which isn't a set of predictions about the future but is a portrayal of the dynamics, human and superhuman, seen and not seen, active in the present. *My Fairy sat upon the table and dictated EUROPE*, Blake explains.³⁷ He has made the most of the visitation and a poem is born.

The great lengths to which Blake goes to describe his encounter with the fairy unpacks why the poem is called a prophecy; a fairy can initiate the state of mind that the reception of a prophecy requires. He did not want to write a cool analysis of the French Revolution, based on gathered facts, measured reason, and historical expertise. His is an attempt more like an invocation than an essay, to instil in the reader a felt perception of the divisive forces being unleashed across Europe and the resulting *strife of blood*.³⁸ The focus of attention is where events and experience, fact and fiction, meet. There will be more to say about how this deeper perception shaped Blake's take on politics later.

For now, sticking with the fairies and angels: Blake entertains them, both to cultivate innocence and push against the sceptical tide, which had begun actively to educate away such revelatory beings. The seventeenth century philosopher, John Locke, is a key player in this denuding of experience. A massive intellectual presence in the Georgian period, he was, for Blake, responsible for much that was going wrong. On the matter of goblins and sprites, Locke had explicitly argued that schoolchildren should not be told about them lurking in the darkness. Once told, he feared a link between the otherworldly and the frightening would impress a perpetual fear of night-time on young minds. That would be as unhelpful and false as, what he took to be, the superstition that goblins and sprites exist.[39] Needless to say, Blake felt precisely the opposite: keeping the possibility of their existence open might enable more to be seen. Angels, fairies and the like are valuable because they remind us we don't know it all, far from it. We will explore further how that can work when we come to consider more of Blake's philosophy and poetry. For now though, the crucial point is this. The charged world disappears not because it is a fantasy but because the imagination required to see it is lost. Conversely, an empowered imagination can re-open closed doors of perception.

Blake is growing up. His parents had sensed that he was unlike their other children and they weren't wrong. He would have had to help in his father's shop as he was able, but they had spotted his artistic talent and its associated second sight, and so, from the age of ten, they took him out of school and personalised his education. Blake was forever grateful: *Thank God I never was sent to School | To be Flog'd into following the Style of a Fool*.[40] His inner talents were not educated out of him. All people have it, to a greater or lesser degree, he once told the journalist and diarist, Henry Crabb Robinson, 'but it is lost by not being cultivated.'[41] He not only cultivated it, he trusted it and forged it into a complete theory of perception. 'You can see what I do, if you choose,' he promised his friends.[42] The in-between zone is accessible. An attitude of wise innocence can be cherished. Both are, according to him, key to living well in the world. But what else? We must now develop the great theme of the imagination directly.

3

ALL THAT WE SEE IS VISION

William Blake is now eleven or twelve years old and is writing his earliest surviving poem. The verse reflects on his love of walking from the chartered streets of London into the nearby countryside. The opening lines begin: *How sweet I roam'd from field to field, | And tasted all the summer's pride.*[1] The iambic beat conveys an immersion in nature, another experience that he knew drew him into the wider circles of enchanted life. When he came to write another of the *Songs of Innocence*, entitled 'The School Boy,' the start heralds a similar advocacy of what was called retirement—or time away from busyness so as to appreciate more.

> *I love to rise in a summer morn,*
> *When the birds sing on every tree;*
> *The distant huntsman winds his horn,*
> *And the sky-lark sings with me.*
> *O! what sweet company.*[2]

*Learning's bower*, as the poem goes on to put it, is a forest school in which being open to the world enables ways of knowing that abstract information leaves untouched; the coppiced library is unlike the brick classroom— the latter likely a place of dreary cramming, overseen by tired teachers, sapping not inviting a spirit of adventure. The living world can teach a person to see properly, if time is spent in it. Becoming conversant with its *minute particulars*, as Blake often calls the myriad radiant creatures and things around us, is a fundamental aim of a Blakean education—which signals the third element in the fundamentals he urges we need; to a wise innocence and undefended perception can be added an expansive imagination. Beneath *learning's bower* are found the materials with which to initiate this ability.

Direct contact enhances learning in a way that general knowledge cannot because being physically alongside things and others stimulates the body as well as the mind. A specific encounter is tangible, a singular presence presses on the soul, which is why Blake reacted against an idea of knowledge that prefers the sweepingly generic over the pointedly specific. *Some See Nature all Ridicule & Deformity, & by these I shall not regulate my proportions; & Some Scarce see Nature at all. But to the Eyes of the Man of Imagination, Nature is Imagination itself*, he wrote—a vitality awaiting discovery that made him *love to rise in a summer morn*.[3]

The offer is more complex than what would pejoratively be called a romantic education because nature's tutelage includes brutal truths as well. The earliest poem, written when he was not yet in his teens, is remarkable for moving swiftly from a wide-eyed celebration of the delights of *lilies for my hair* and *blushing roses for my brow*, to a gnawing sense that time in these *gardens fair* can simultaneously generate a feeling that full accord is out of reach or easily spoiled.[4] The young Blake goes on to envisage *sunny beams* presaging a dark side: they can spin a silken net that drags him from *golden pleasures* into a *golden cage*.[5] Trapped, he now feels he is being played with, like a caught bird denied flight. These are sophisticated thoughts for a youngster, though maybe not for one who genuinely did see nature as his teacher. This tutor does not protect its pupils from ordeals or worry.

His imaginative development was aided by another decision made by his parents. They freed him from running errands behind the counter and sent him to a progressive drawing school. Plaster ears, cross-hatched eyes, etched mouths and mezzotint noses filled the time he wasn't wandering in fields, as he sat copying an array of prints and casts of Europe's greatest paintings and seminal sculptures.

He had entered the art world of London and the 1770s was an exciting decade to do so. The school Blake attended was run by Henry Pars. Henry had a brother, William, who had been travelling in Italy and Greece, sending back all manner of drawings of classical statues and architecture. Later Blake wanted to take the Grand Tour himself, as several of his fellow students did, though he was prevented for lack of funds. But perhaps the disappointment was a blessing in disguise because whilst Blake learnt from the greats, particularly Michelangelo with whom he developed a strong affinity, he had to be inventive not simply imitative in response to their works. A loss can become a gain to the person of imagination, constraints prompting innovations and leaps. He learnt to capture the spirit preserved in the copies that he studied and developed novel ways of conveying that interiority for himself.

What he discovered was that although he loved nature, a realistic depiction of landscapes, flora and skies was not to be his style. Rather, he sought to portray what he saw with the eye of the mind. *Men think they can Copy Nature as Correctly as I copy Imagination; this they will find Impossible, & all the Copies or Pretended Copiers of Nature, from Rembrandt to Reynolds, Prove that Nature becomes tame to its Victim nothing but Blots and Blurs.*[6] Blake would have us discover the world contained within external appearances. This dimension shows itself with the kind of attention that is alert to the felt impression a bird or bug makes, alongside the details of its physical form. Similarly, the relationship between things matters at least as much as things seen in isolation, which is why botanical art and medical studies are not part of his output, though gyrating bodies amidst meandrous vines are the essence of it. I reckon that part of the thrill of encountering the seeming riot of figures that he typically paints on a page is the dawning consciousness of an experience of entwined roots, reaching souls and billowing clouds dancing as an ensemble; imagination joins those hands together.

The support of his parents did not stop with the drawing school. They were the type who allow a child to develop his or her own instincts and they supplied the money for Blake to start an art collection of his own. He began frequenting the shops of print-dealers and the galleries of auctioneers; the Grand Tour was beyond his means but in London the Grand Tour came to him. One Covent Garden auctioneer, Abraham Langford, called Blake 'his little connoisseur' and offered him reduced job lots, a friendliness that was probably aided by Blake's eccentric choices.[7] Like an uncommon tourist wandering the back streets of Florence or investigating the minor churches of Rome, he searched for the work of artists who were then unfashionable—copies of Raphael, prints by Dürer, Michelangelo impressions. He was laughed at by cultured despisers, a sneering with which he would become familiar, though the sniggering did not put him off. He was clear about the lines, colouring and tints that affected him and he remained faithful to their calling, another facet of an imaginative education: let what one intuits never be lost to what one is told.

Still, a technique must be mastered and the budding artist achieved proficiency in these years. In the summer of 1772, at the age of fifteen, things moved on again when his father, James, presented his son to another

## AWAKE!

James—James Basire, an engraver of some renown. The introduction was astute as the market for books was burgeoning, stimulating in turn a demand for images to illustrate them; for a teenager with talent, engraving might prove a lucrative trade. An agreement was reached and William was indentured to Basire for a term of seven years. In return for instruction, board and lodging, his father paid the sum of just over £50, about £10,000 today, securing a profession for his son which, artistically, was to serve him extraordinarily well. *I defy any Man to Cut Cleaner Strokes than I do, or rougher where I please*, he was later to boast.[8]

There was another reason the time with Basire proved invaluable. His teacher was also a keen antiquarian and the principal engraver to the Society of Antiquaries. That would have appealed to Blake. Antiquarians had a reputation in Georgian England for being eccentrics. In particular, as the historian Rosemary Hill has argued, they attempted to integrate objective study with subjective feeling; for them, field evidence and imaginative interpretation went hand in hand.[9] Further, whilst historians restricted their studies to written records, antiquarians loved all that was not prose. 'Antiquaries, unlike historians, studied architecture and stone circles, pottery, sculpture, coins, bells, armour, textiles and much more,' Hill explains.[10] They sought to dwell amongst the relics of the past, like the pious patron of a medieval painting who asks to be depicted kneeling at the foot of the long-dead saint. They resisted what was to become the gold standard in science—methodical observation at one step removed—and preferred to steep themselves in the waters of history, which echoes Blake's convictions about the education offered by immersion in nature: the heart as chief guide to knowledge, not the head. You can see it in his designs that often have an antiquarian feel, featuring megaliths, chariots and arrows. The antiquarians, like him, knew that dreaming mattered if you seek to be transformed by what you study. Pay attention to the facts, for sure, but don't let them tyrannise the truth found in the fiction.

Blake might have felt at home amongst these frequenters to Basire's workshop for a further reason. Antiquarians had a reputation for being 'bitchiferous,' or contentious, and he could be terse too. Take Blake's references to the famous man of letters, Dr Samuel Johnson, who features a handful of times in his writing. At one point, he likens Johnson to a *Bat with leathern wing, Winking & blinking, Winking & blinking*.[11] That could be a brief for James Gillray, the great Georgian satirist who was a direct contemporary of Blake, also honing his skills in these decades. Blake must have loved the exuberance of the caricaturist when his work exploded into the public domain; Gillray's cartoons were quite as punchy as Tracey Emin, Damien Hirst and Banksy combined, as is pointed out by the historian, Alice Loxton.[12] The sheer weirdness of the images, which might reduce a lampooned celebrity to a giant sphere or disembodied nose, was part of the imaginative sea in which Blake would have us swim, and can act as a warning in our day against too strident a reaction to online attack and mockery. Outright harassment or total fabrication are one thing, but ribbing and humour that might make you gasp fructifies inventiveness. Blake was not averse to the catty, as it goes with the imaginative territory and need not mean losing a capacity to be kind.

## Ideas of Imagination

Imagination is the portal to the in-between zone he inhabited. In fact, it *is* the in-between zone and is sometimes uncomfortably alive. *The Imagination is not a State: it is the Human Existence itself | Affection or Love becomes a State, when divided from Imagination | The Memory is a State always, & Reason is a State.*[13] Imagination is the leaven in the dough, the vital force, the air that is breathed. It resurrects memory, feeds reason, loathes shallows, quickens love. This is the richness of the third Blakean basic, after innocence and angels, and there is no limit to what Blake believed the imagination can reveal or do. *This World of Imagination is Infinite and Eternal.*[14]

He was unusual in this view. The imagination was then and is now typically held in warm though frivolous regard. Inner imagery and fancy can be valued and simultaneously treated as prime sources of error, inclined to misguide through bias and self-deception. The critique treats the imagination as, at heart, an often winning though usually whimsical habit of an individual mind. Consider the sceptical Dr Johnson once more. In his fable on happiness and ignorance, *The History of Rasselas, Prince of Abissinia*, he included a chapter entitled, 'The Dangerous Prevalence of Imagination.' There he wrote of said danger: 'All power of fancy over reason is a degree of insanity.' He might have been exaggerating but only so as to highlight the belief and hope of the Enlightenment Age that a rule of reason would come, in which intellect is installed as the arbiter of knowledge: a piercing torchlight to expose fancy, superstition, error. The condescension is that the imagination undoubtedly aids the human creature in the perennial quest for meaning: think of art, story and music; we can't do without them. But strictly speaking, it cultivates a fabulous representation of reality and offers no reliable content, but instead impressions, moods, mirages. Blake's *blushing roses*, from his early poem, provide a case in point: Dr Johnson might observe that the flowers are not really blushing at all; that's just the poet's conceit.

A robust cosmology lies behind this reductive worldview, which has become dominant in our time. A recent biographer of Blake, John Higgs, encapsulates it in this way: 'The human mind is the one thing that emits imagination into our closed, limited, finite universe. It is we and we alone who are the source of meaning, purpose, love and hate in this otherwise cold, dead cloud of matter.'[15] An austere summary of a widespread view: the imagination as a humanly invaluable but essentially deluded source of invention. The expressive theatre of our minds is presumed as unlike the vast and impersonal cosmos as chalk is from cheese: the split that leads to the disenchantment of nature.

Higgs's description is useful, though, because it expresses the precise opposite of Blake's view. Of course, we can be fooled by fanciful images that confuse what is seen with what actually is; false memories and wishful thinking definitely exist. As Shakespeare intuited: 'The lunatic, the lover, and the poet, | Are of imagination all compact.'[16] But whereas the lunatic may be permanently mistaken and the lover swept along for a time, the poet knows something else: imagination can reveal what is hidden from the detached observer. Further, Blake insisted, imagination as a truth-bearing faculty is a prerequisite for any kind of discovery, advance or epiphany. *If it were not for the Poetic or Prophetic character the Philosophic & Experimental would soon be at the ratio of all things, & stand still, unable to do other than repeat the same dull round over again.*[17]

The imagination is, then, widely treated as a means of adding value and conjuring meaning. But for Blake, someone with imagination is not just a person who can paint from the palette of a colourful mind, or is good with words, or can read the times, or inspire others, though they may well be able in these ways. Blake insists that there is a root cause of a visionary person's abilities: imagination flows not only from them, but also floods into them. The abundance of insights issue from without as well as from within the soul, which is never so detached as the individual might assume, dwelling in the zone that is neither wholly objective nor subjective: theirs and not theirs. If the universe were an ocean of indifference, with only our lighthouse minds able to cast pulses of meaning across it, there would soon be no novelties to enjoy, but rather a fixed stock of ideas on infinite repeat. Distraction or, worse, despair would become endemic—which is, of course, how many do respond to this bleak account of existence. This must, in turn, fuel excessive consumption as a compensation, as well as stoking personal unhappiness and social discontent: a cold, dead understanding of reality is rightly too much to be asked to bear.

This, then, is a first facet of imagination's power: it is the light of everything around us and brings that lustre to us. 'We use our imagination not to escape the world but to join it, and this exhilarates us because of the distance between our ordinary dulled consciousness and an apprehension of the real,' was the philosopher and novelist Iris Murdoch's way of putting it.[18] Affability, fear, strangeness and wonder all swirl in its currents—a variety of perceptions that Blake caught in verse. Take this paragraph from his poem, *Milton: a Poem in 2 Books*, which describes the dawn chorus. Blake imagines the daybreak opening with a solitary lark, whose song stirs all the other birds to sing. The harmony is heard with the imagination.

> *The Lark sitting upon his earthly bed, just as the morn*
> *Appears, listens silent; then springing from the waving Cornfield, loud*
> *He leads the Choir of Day: trill, trill, trill, trill,*
> *Mounting upon the wings of light into the Great Expanse,*
> *Reecchoing against the lovely blue & shining heavenly Shell,*
> *His little throat labours with inspiration; every feather*
> *On throat & breast & wings vibrates with the effluence Divine.*
> *All Nature listens silent to him, & the awful Sun*
> *Stands still upon the Mountain looking on this little Bird*
> *With eyes of soft humility & wonder, love & awe.*
> *Then loud from their green covert all the Birds begin their Song:*
> *The Thrush, the Linnet & the Goldfinch, Robin & the Wren*
> *Awake the Sun from his sweet reverie upon the Mountain.*
> *The Nightingale again assays his song, & thro' the day*
> *And thro' the night warbles luxuriant, every Bird of Song*
> *Attending his loud harmony with admiration & love.*[19]

For Blake, this symphony is a gift of the imagination, which can detect love in one bird's song, amplified by all the birds singing together and further, behind that, an outpouring of divine song. That is what the dawn chorus rehearses, which the rest of the natural world, including the Sun, stands still to appreciate and absorb. The moment is in one way a diurnal event, as dawn turns into day, but in another, it is a timeless pause, as the music carries eternal intimations and boundless beauty, which to the imagination are undeniable. All we have to do is listen. Blake is perfectly aware that his description will appear fanciful to some, perhaps many, and the person who doesn't stand still with the sun, or long somehow to do so, will have no idea what they are missing. *The idiot Reasoner laughs at the Man of Imagination*, he remarks a few lines later.[20] Not that Blake is dismissing reasoning tout court, only reasoning that would judge, rather than serve, the liberty of the imagination and the awakening it brings.

This raises a second point. In truth, even supposedly sovereign reason is indebted to a take on the world determined by imaginative assumptions, including the contemptuous sceptic who declares they trust reason alone. For one thing, a powerful imagination is required to experience the universe as closed, limited and finite—a conclusion that for most humans, for most of history would have seemed ridiculous, and which is why the so-called scientific revolution merits the epithet 'revolution'; it is an overturning. But our ancestors knew something different: they shared in a plethora of unceasing, responsive, intelligent activity. The perceptual narrowing that characterises our age has become possible only through the sustained effort required for a distinctly mechanical worldview to take hold. The shift and the nature of that hard work is portrayed in one of Blake's best-known pictures, featuring the natural philosopher, Isaac Newton.

Blake was unfair on the great scientist, who is now known to have been fascinated by all manner of occult dynamics and divine esoterica, but in this image Blake makes a point. He shows the physicist focused on geometric shapes, a triangle and arc, inscribed on a scroll of paper. Sitting on a rock, seemingly at the bottom of a dingy sea and uninterested in the wafting marine life around him, Newton draws the mathematical forms with a pair of compasses and gazes longingly at them—which is an imaginative act, if one that deliberately refuses any wider contemplations. After all, the triangle and arc he is studying do not exist in the world around him; he is meditating on them in a quest for hidden regularities and elusive symmetries that he is sure govern things. Deducing such verities is a remarkable accomplishment, displaying an ingenuity that delivers tangible results, not least in the form of technology. Only this is an imagination that has come to dominate so as to exclude, as Blake's image depicts. The attention is limited to what is deemed important and is committed mostly to the type of abstract reasoning that Blake called *Single vision and Newton's sleep*.[21] For this self-reliant mentality, the conceptual is most real and the imagination is commandeered to

## ALL THAT WE SEE IS VISION

Fig. 7: *Newton*, c.1804.

serve it. Nowadays, government budgets, international agreements, and dedicated institutions have rallied to the cause; the organisation of the millions who work in science and technology is a remarkable achievement that could have been accomplished only by the power of imagination. Only, with this type of imagination there is a downside—disenchantment, a complex but clockwork cosmos, a dispirited soul—and that is Blake's concern.

### Chickens and Pigeons

In fact, I doubt a scientist who possessed *single vision* alone would be good at their work; they might make a decent jobbing technician but not be a person to progress discoveries. I tried to foster a scientific mindset myself, when studying physics as an undergraduate, and particularly loved staring through a telescope towards our nearest neighbour, the Moon, in a project aimed at measuring the heights of its cragged and serrated grey mountains. This was a clear case in which doing science provokes irresistible wonder, and wonder is the imagination stirring and seeking to burst boundaries. The trouble comes when that mental momentum is constrained by philosophical straitjackets, a constraint that condemns people, Newton-like, to the bottom of the imaginative sea.

And yet, when reason and imagination are working together, wider perceptions and possibilities emerge. One that was much debated in Blake's time concerned the consciousness of animals. Ever since Descartes, in the early seventeenth century, had described mammals and fish as reflex-driven automata, the question of what animals can feel and be aware of had provoked dispute. Descartes himself had performed controversial vivisection experiments on yelping dogs and screaming rabbits to study phenomena such as the beating of the heart. 150 years later, in Georgian England, the general public's horror at such practices was reaching fever pitch; baiting animals was in decline and keeping pets was becoming popular, whilst thoughtlessly slaughtering and killing animals for sport was regularly condemned as cruel. Blake clearly felt keenly about such bloodletting and it was his imagination that fired his feelings and told him his objections were true. *Each outcry of the hunted Hare | A fibre from the brain does tear.*[22] A fibre isn't literally torn from the brain, but you feel precisely what he means.

At one level, the protest is a feature of his innocence: 'The School Boy' references birds that are *born for joy*.[23] But at another, Blake knew that the cooperation of reason and imagination can reveal all sorts of features about the plant and animal kingdoms. Here is a section from another poem, *Visions of the Daughters of Albion*, which celebrates the sophistication of creaturely awareness and asks whether that can satisfactorily be explained without referencing the aspirations and personalities of the creatures concerned—with the implied answer: it cannot. *With what sense*, the verse repeatedly asks, pointing to the presence of an intelligence as active in other creatures as it is in us.

> *With what sense is it that the chicken shuns the ravenous hawk?*
> *With what sense does the tame pigeon measure out the expanse?*
> *With what sense does the bee form cells? Have not the mouse & frog*
> *Eyes and ears and sense of touch? yet are their habitations*
> *And their pursuits as different as their forms and as their joys.*
> *Ask the wild ass why he refuses burdens, and the meek camel*
> *Why he loves man: is it because of eye, ear, mouth, or skin,*
> *Or breathing nostrils? No, for these the wolf and tyger have.*
> *Ask the blind worm the secrets of the grave, and why her spires*
> *Love to curl round the bones of death; and ask the rav'nous snake*

# ALL THAT WE SEE IS VISION

*Where she gets poison, & the wing'd eagle why he loves the sun;*
*And then tell me the thoughts of man, that have been hid of old.*[24]

Human thoughts may be self-conscious in a way that the feelings of the wolf and worm are not, but all creatures thrive because of a sentient engagement with the practical matters of foraging and fighting. The imagination makes that known to us as we share in the business of being alive, and the implications do not stop there. A further suggestion Blake makes is the necessity of ascribing imagination to nature herself. Only then can the inventiveness of her creatures be fully accounted for. This step is a key one to recovering an enchanted conception of things because it suggests that there is a power in nature, not only in the creatures that occupy the natural world.

Put it like this. Living creatures are only able to shape their reactions to the environment to a limited degree. Even animals that are smart enough for human beings to admire, such as crows that use tools, do not display capacities for intuition, but rather are confined to the admirable tenacity of trial and error. 'The birds are not dim,' writes the evolutionary biologist Simon Conway Morris. 'And they observe what is going on, but they do not have insight or imagination.'[25] So the stunning range of animal behaviours which are observed must in large part originate elsewhere, as a shaping energy or spirit of life that endows creatures with their abilities. There is a creative aspect inherent in nature, which living organisms manifest and the human imagination can apprehend. 'The subtlety of nature is greater many times over than the subtlety of the senses and understanding,' wrote the Elizabethan Lord Chancellor of England, Francis Bacon, who in Blake's book is another prime suspect for the crime of disenchantment, though in truth Bacon made observations of which Blake would have approved.[26] For example, he suspected that matter itself is 'laden with appetites and desires.' He detected an animism even in what might be thought brute stuff.[27]

*Trust in Evolution*

Referencing such a restless potential, working within the world like a composer within a piece of music, will raise the eyebrows of those with a knowledge of evolutionary theory. Blake did not know about the ideas of Charles Darwin, which were to burst into world consciousness during the Victorian era, though he did read and provide engravings for *The*

# AWAKE!

*Botanic Garden* by Darwin's grandfather, Erasmus Darwin. A prototype of the popular science book, this poetic celebration of discovery and plants anticipates the later theory in certain respects, not least in arguing that sexual reproduction drives the ferment of nature. Blake was not against that per se, far from it. But he must have been wary of the thrust of the older Darwin who, rather than directly giving words to the inner lives of bell-flowers and holly, conveys a sense of piety towards the plant kingdom; Erasmus Darwin personifies roses and irises to convey the functional purpose of stems that have thorns or flowers that hang down. This is to say that his poetry fosters a spectator-stance towards nature—the observer is admiring but strictly as an onlooker—whereas Blake's observer wonders because of a communion with what is being observed.

In fact, the younger Darwin, Charles, hesitated before describing the inhabitants of the natural world solely by features and functions. In his book, *The Expression of the Emotions in Man and Animals*, for example, he

Fig. 8: "Fertilization of Egypt" from *The Botanic Garden* by Erasmus Darwin, one of the engravings Blake provided for the book, in which Blake can't help but highlight a distinctly animate and supernatural element to the workings of nature.

happily proposes that the behaviour of creatures conveys moods with which he is familiar, too. 'Even insects express anger, terror, jealousy, and love by their stridulation,' he observes.[28] He realised that bees can become as angry as he could, expressed by changes in their humming that resonate with the same feeling in himself. 'Darwin, a country boy living close to animals all his life, very early learnt to understand their forms of communication,' writes the philosopher of science, Mary Midgley. 'He viewed them as intelligible fellow creatures, being akin to him whose attitudes he could often grasp.'[29] That is what the imagination can reveal, with the upshot that Charles Darwin's writings echo Blake's conviction that nature is imagination itself. 'I have, also, often personified the word Nature,' Darwin wrote, 'for I have found it difficult to avoid this ambiguity.'[30] The difference is that Blake would have advised not seeking such an avoidance. The reason why it seems apt to personify the word 'Nature' is that Nature shares in qualities known to persons, not least the power of the imagination.

Incidentally, there are signs that evolutionary scientists are reconsidering the active role played by the interior life of living things, as there has been a quiet revolution in understanding the natural world in recent years that is only beginning to bubble up into public consciousness.[31] The developments are laid out in *How Life Works* by Philip Ball, a prize-winning science writer and former editor of the leading science journal, *Nature*. He seeks to explain the significance of the shift and in particular how the reductive and mechanical account of 'selfish gene' biology has been replaced. 'This new view of biology—which is by no means complete and indeed is still only nascent—depends on a kind of *trust*,' he writes.[32] That word 'trust' refers to holistic and intelligent processes that operate across all levels of life, from microscopic proteins and genes to the organism as a whole and the so-called external environment. Cooperation shapes things as much as competition, with manifold interactions observed across species, too. Simpler organisms show habits of attraction and collaboration that in more complex creatures manifest as altruism and love, suggesting a continuum of instincts and intentions. Further, all these behaviours are forms not only of reaction but cognition, manifesting a practical wisdom spread throughout nature.

Blake captures this active dynamism in his poetry. Here is how he continues his celebration of the dawn chorus as, after the singing birds, the waking plants turn to the rising sun.

# AWAKE!

> *First, e'er the morning breaks, joy opens in the flowery bosoms,*
> *Joy even to tears, Which the sun rising dries; first the Wild Thyme*
> *And Meadow-sweet, downy & soft waving among the reeds,*
> *Light springing on the air, lead the sweet Dance: they wake*
> *The Honeysuckle sleeping on the Oak; the flaunting beauty*
> *Revels along upon the wind; the White-thorn, lovely May,*
> *Opens her many lovely eyes listening; the Rose still sleeps,*
> *None dare to wake her; soon she bursts her crimson curtain'd Bed*
> *And comes forth in the majesty of beauty; every Flower,*
> *The Pink, the Jessamine, the Wall-flower, the Carnation,*
> *The Jonquil, the mild Lilly, opens her heavens; every Tree*
> *And Flower & Herb soon fill the air with an innumerable Dance,*
> *Yet all in order sweet & Lovely. Men are sick with love.*[33]

As evolutionary biology continues to advance and develop, I reckon Blake's portrayal of the dancing order of the living world will cease to be judged charming but outmoded. There will be more to say about how he might contribute to the revival of a more expansive and accurate understanding of living vitalities later. Right now, though, and sticking with the exploration of the imagination, consider this: given that nature is imagination itself, what might nature reveal to us about our imaginative lives? Or to put it the other way around: when we open ourselves to the lives of the creatures around us, what do we gain in understanding ourselves? An example of the kind of thing I have in mind stems from Blake's love of a singularly remarkable phenomenon, which was being newly investigated at the time, namely the way in which a caterpillar transforms into a butterfly or moth. Next time you see one, think on this.

The voracious larva first becomes a chrysalis in which it literally digests itself, before the emergence of the fluttering adult a few weeks later. The metamorphosis is astonishing, from munching grub through fermenting gloop to quivering beauty. The phenomenon had been studied in the century before Blake by the Dutch biologist, Jan Swammerdam, who discovered that within the ooze of a cocoon, the shadows of wings, antennae and legs could be detected. These incipient structures are now known as imaginal disks, from the Latin *imago* or likeness, which the development of the microscope as a scientific instrument in the mid-seventeenth century revealed to consist of small groups of cells that seed the formation of the adult body. The name 'imaginal disks' is apt; the adult is not assembled in the chrysalis as if from a set of machine-like components, but rather emerges as if driven by latencies lurking in the formless goo. Blake wrote, *The wondrous work flows forth like visible out of the invisible*.[34] You might say that the beating wings and flashing colours of the adult are the expression of a yearning for completion in the alchemy of the chrysalis—which must be partly why a butterfly looks so joyful, bobbing purposefully on a summer breeze: it has made it!

For Blake, who liberally deploys bodily references throughout his work, the new science connected to an old wisdom. He knew that for millennia, the marvels of the lifecycle of butterflies and moths had spoken to human beings of the passage through death to life. In ancient Egyptian theology, the immortal *ba* emerges after death from the chrysalis-like mummy.[35] In Platonic philosophy, the butterfly-like wings of the soul enable human beings to rise and pursue an instinctive affinity with beauty and goodness.[36] There is a deep link with the imagination implicit in these correspondences as well. As the chrysalis contains within itself the expression of the mature insect in potential, so too the imagination is an active domain within which an individual can be transformed so as to transcend elementary stages of life.

The imagination is not our possession but, it might be said, possesses us: an active imagination. That includes, for human beings at least,

Fig. 9: *Jerusalem: The Emanation of the Giant Albion*, plate 14, detail showing Albion asleep, chrysalis-like, and Jerusalem, Albion's spiritual form, rising as a moth beneath the promise of a rainbow.

collaboratively and consciously moving towards a remade tomorrow. Imagination, then, is a lively spirit that nurtures the realisation of what was at first shadowy, as the insubstantial 'bodies forth,' to recall Shakespeare's famous phrase.

*Golden Coins and Heavenly Hosts*

So the imagination is a many-faceted thing in Blake. It is, first, the faculty that enables us to see more of reality. Blake's education born of walking in nature convinced him that as a person becomes adept at imaginative perception, the more of the world around them they will see; the imagination is the primary organ of perception and we can work with it quite as carefully as with sight, sound and touch to investigate the world and deepen our awareness of its complexity and truths. He once used an analogy to make the point, comparing eyes with windows. In the same way that no one gazes at the glass of a window but immediately realises that the glass offers sight of what is outside, so too with eyes: it is not the physical eye that sees the world but the mind's eye, aided by the physical eyes. We attend, or 'question' as he puts it, with all the faculties of the mind. Blake writes: *I question not my Corporeal or Vegetative eye any more than I would Question a Window concerning a Sight. I look thro' it and not with it.*[37]

Blake strives to make a richer point, too, to bring to our awareness a more fundamental facet of the imagination; it is not only the capacity to see but is, simultaneously, the source of all that can be seen. The imagination is not, therefore, our own, though we have a rich share in its capacities. Rather, human beings, animals and plants, earth and heavens, are *contain'd in the All Glorious Imagination*.[38] The imagination is the realm within which abundant reality dwells.

This capaciousness comes out when Blake refers to the Sun and also adds a final dimension to what the imagination can see. His starting point is familiar: what you take to the act of looking at our neighbourhood star, as with anything else, fundamentally shapes what you make of its presence. One person, set on flat observation alone, might report that the Sun looks like a round disk of fire, akin to a golden coin, rising steadily above the horizon, Blake notes.[39] Another, informed by an understanding of stars that doesn't disqualify an occasional riff, might add that blazing stars like the Sun fashioned the building blocks of life in their nuclear furnaces, including the essential ingredient carbon; the Sun is therefore, in a way, a proxy parent, for we are made of stardust. A wider imagination steps further when a third person continues with an overtly relational thought; the Sun is radiant, they will venture, even blissful, which is why sunlight feels so good to us: its warmth corresponds to our happiness. They might continue by addressing the Sun: 'Your light falls equally on all, a model of generosity! Your love reaches out to the Moon, who receives it through the night!'

Such an individual may then move into more philosophical territory. After all, isn't the word 'light' used to describe inner as well as external experiences? There must be a reason we talk both of physically lighting the way and of becoming mentally enlightened. That would be because the Sun's light is akin to the mind's light, both being reflections of an intelligence by which the details and dynamics of the world are revealed and known.

Such acclamations are not far from how a fourth person might respond, as Blake himself did when replying to a fictitious questioner.[40] The enquirer asked Blake what he saw when he observed the Sun—a golden coin perhaps or a disk of fire? *O no, no!* Blake retorted. *I see an innumerable company of the heavenly host crying, 'Holy, holy, holy is the Lord God Almighty!'* The heavenly host is not just acclaiming the effulgence of the sunlight that is also our inner light, but is further an angelic sharing in the godly brilliance that sustains and forms all things on earth and in heaven; the primal Light of which all other light is a reflection: the Light of lights. Blake's imagination could join all the dots so that his experience of the Sun was of multifaceted reality, integrated from gilded object to divine presence.

Delight in this solar source and dwelling must lie behind an, at first, odd story about Blake wanting to mingle with the Moon, remembered in a conversation recorded between him and another contemporary of genius, Thomas Taylor. 'Pray, Mr Taylor,' said Blake one day, 'did you ever find yourself, as it were, standing close beside the vast and luminous orb of the moon?' 'Not that I remember, Mr Blake: did you ever?' 'Yes, frequently, and I have felt an almost irresistible desire to throw myself into it headlong.' 'I think, Mr Blake, you had better not. For if you were to do so, you most probably would never come out of it again,' Taylor replied.[41] Blake was celebrating the *All Glorious Imagination* by desiring to cast himself into the silvery Moon, as if a lover. Taylor showed that he knew what his friend meant by wittily acknowledging the ecstasy with a warning; the experience might be so wonderful that Blake would never return.

# AWAKE!

In truth, the rapture is an intensified version of what we tacitly experience every waking moment. We see the natural world in its myriad forms because imagination lights it all. When we relish a sunset, delight in a bird on the wing, or admire that a stately sunflower has turned to track the sun's course across the sky, we are experiencing the effects of an existence that is imagination in action. We are enjoying the power that is within, around and over everything, which we human beings can deliberately spot, as well as extend and magnify—in art, praise and, when not unnecessarily curbed, scientific description. The imagination enables the appearance within the external world of what is detected by an inner eye. *All that we see is Vision*, Blake declared, and whilst what we intuit in this way may be palpably present one minute and seemingly gone the next, what the inner eye saw can be recalled and continually investigated by our minds because it is *Permanent in The Imagination*.[42] We can step into *Worlds of Thought* that are not separate from the material world around us but are implicit in it.[43] Blake argued that these inner dimensions are the fundamental reality, from which empirical observations spring. *Mental Things are alone Real*, he averred.[44]

This is to make a philosophical point and steers us towards a fourth Blakean basic, after innocence, angels and the imagination: fearless critique—which he offers us, too. For Blake was an agile thinker as well as an unimpeded artist, an intellectual with a penetrating mind. He read the savants of the day and developed powerful refutations of their ideas. Further, he saw their principles moulding the perceptions of his contemporaries and realised that, alongside critique, creativity is needed if the flight to disenchantment is not only to be halted but countered. Where they encouraged gazing at triangles on the seabed, Blake wanted to equip his readers with an alternative visionary system. His fourth virtue is a combination of intellectual resourcefulness and courage and these, too, can help us stay awake.

4

CREATE A SYSTEM

Blake completed his engraving apprenticeship with James Basire in 1779. Now aged twenty-one, he enrolled at the Royal Academy of Arts to improve his painting and drawing. The institution was just a decade old and presided over by Sir Joshua Reynolds, champion of the Grand Style of portraiture: noble figures depicted in richly textured oils. Blake loathed the images as a grotesque display of vanity and his considered opinion of the illustrious Sir Joshua is declared in a jotted remark: *This Man was Hired to Depress Art*.[1]

Many of the details of Blake's life survive in the form of such lively asides. They are sometimes disreputable, regularly entertaining and include a sizable proportion possessing an apocryphal feel. A historian on a quest for the real Blake might conclude that the more outlandish anecdotes should be discounted, though they are particularly valuable to my mind. There was clearly something about the man that produced wild tales. He caught people off-guard and in part sought spikey reactions with a serious aim in mind. He wanted his fellows to see more fully and that involved seizing the moments when he could be skilfully provocative. Challenge and eccentricity combined to transmit his spirit.

The effect was aided by his charisma. *I hate scarce smiles; I love laughing!* he wrote of himself.[2] He also approved of the saying: 'Keep him at least three paces distant who hates bread, music, and the laugh of a child.'[3] But the joining of eloquence, charm and daring in his character had a consequence: he tended to divide the people he met—who at this stage in his life were often notable. 'He knew every great man of his day,' an admirer reflected later in Blake's life and Blake might reasonably have hoped to join them.[4] At about this time, he received high praise from George Romney, one of the most celebrated English portrait painters, whose muse was Emma Hamilton, Nelson's lover. Romney publicly compared Blake to Michelangelo. 'Such praise from such a man could have been enormously influential,' remarks Blake's biographer, G.E. Bentley.[5] But note the conditional tense. The trouble was that Blake didn't care to be clubbable, which is a major part of getting on.

*Seeding Nihilism*

Take his relationship with Thomas Paine. Blake found himself to be partly in sympathy, partly not, with the revolutionary thinker. Blake admired what he called Paine's *Energetic Genius*.[6] He would have shared many of the principles proclaimed in Paine's bestseller, *The Rights of Man*, which when it appeared in 1791 sold an extraordinary 50,000 copies in its first weeks; the poet agreed with the activist that the mark of civilisation is the poor being happy, meant in the spirit of Gandhi's famous remark that such a civilisation would be a good idea.[7] Here is the opening verse of Blake's bitter poem, 'Holy Thursday.'

> *Is this a holy thing to see,*
> *In a rich and fruitful land,*
> *Babes reduced to misery,*
> *Fed with cold and usurious hand?*[8]

Blake would similarly have been inclined to affirm some of the sentiments that Paine expressed in his next publication, *The Age of Reason*. 'My mind is my own church,' the pamphleteer declared, continuing: 'it is necessary to the happiness of man that he be mentally faithful to himself.'[9] I can imagine Blake nodding when he read that.

His alignment wasn't just ideological but also practical because, on one occasion, he possibly saved Paine's life. They were at a dinner party, at which Paine's talk turned seditious. When he rose to leave, Blake warned, 'You must not go home or you are a dead man!'[10] Blake realised that the authorities were eager to arrest the author. He was right. Paine followed the advice and left England that night, never to return.

However, Blake also profoundly disagreed with elements fundamental to Paine's creed. For example, Paine labelled Christianity a fable, which was doubly wrong to Blake, first because he held Christianity to be essentially true if regularly distorted and, second, because he believed that within the clouds of fancy with which fables are wrapped verities shine. 'Mr Paine you are in error,' Blake would have tried to explain as they talked, 'roundly so on the work of God.' And this critique highlights the problem that Blake had with Paine, alongside other Founding Fathers of the United States. He agreed that society needed root and branch reform; he could recognise the bravery with which these figures championed their discontent. But he rejected an underlying assumption of the agitators.

The issue was that they were deists—a way of interpreting God's relationship to the world rationally, as if God were a distant designer and judicious craftsman. Blake blamed this theological tenet on a triumvirate of natural philosophers, whose names ring out like a death knell across his works: *Bacon, Newton, Locke*.[11] Bacon stood for the mechanical over the imaginative, Newton for rigid principles of cause and effect, and Locke for insisting that human beings are processors of sense data not receivers of revelations. Three fatal doctrines, Blake was sure.

The beliefs render God's presence in the world indistinguishable from natural processes, which for Blake means God becomes a blundering *Nobodaddy*: a stiff issuer of diktats. *Why does thou hide thyself in clouds | From every searching eye | Why darkness & obscurity | In all thy words & laws*, Blake writes capturing the loss, which is not only a crisis of devotion.[12] As naturalistic explanations gain pace, the whole world is increasingly presumed to run on embedded code, rendering a deity increasingly superfluous—which is why nowadays belief in God can be treated as an optional extra for those so mistakenly inclined. Blake felt so strongly about what he regarded as the *fatal & accursed* consequences of deism that he called advocates of naturalistic explanations, *Enemies of the Human Race*.[13] The move presages nihilism, a word coined during his lifetime. Default scepticism was coming. *If the Sun & Moon should doubt, They'd immediately Go out*, he jeered and could not have been clearer about his objection to the enlightened mindset that steadily undermines meaning.[14] He titled his own first pamphlet, printed in 1788, *There Is No Natural Religion*, and clearly maintained this conviction throughout his life—without, as I hope to show, any loss of subtlety and sophistication in his account of religion. He was sure that if humanity becomes uncoupled from real transcendence on the grounds that deities are conjured out of all-too-human hopes, fears and superstitions, then humanity is in real trouble.[15]

There are a number of reasons to be concerned about deism, not least that Blake believed it is not true, but a key one is its political ramifications. The idea that God might be a marvellous engineer was supercharging the socially progressive hope that things, for the most part, tend to get better when similarly rational human beings are in charge. As Paine proclaimed: 'We have it in our power to begin the world over again. A situation, similar to the present, hath not happened since the days of Noah until now. The birthday of a new world is at hand.'[16]

The logic runs like this: as Newtonian physics reveals the world to have been constructed beneficently, so society can be reformed to conform with the grain of that bounteous pattern, growing happier as a result. But Blake would have spotted an irony. It was not only the progressive revolutionaries who claimed Newton's system as their own. So did their conservative opponents; the King and other establishment figures invoked the same cosmic regularity to justify their high rank and authority. 'God and the Georges were the constitutional monarchs respectively of the universe and the nation,' summarises the historian Roy Porter, noting that Queen Charlotte, the consort of George II, made a garden in Richmond that featured busts of Newton and Locke because they embodied 'the Glory of their Country'—much like the King and Queen, in fact.[17] A plague on both your houses, Blake might have muttered. Both sides worshipped *Nobodaddy*, which was tantamount to worshipping themselves—another fast track to nihilism.

He was ideologically apart, though there was an upside to his isolation. In his nuanced disagreements with the social revolutionaries as well as the King, he was forced privately to work on the articulation of more radical transformational possibilities. *I must Create a System, or be enslav'd by another Mans | I will not Reason & Compare; my business is to Create*.[18] That clarity is his real value now, I believe. He saw *dark Satanic Mills* on the horizon, which became literal features of industrial society but, more profoundly, are an expression of the atheistic mentality that begets such a world: the cosmos conceived as a great machine.[19] He would forge a wholly different imaginary.

### Engineering the Future

One of the places in which he began to work out his critique is in an unpublished parody of the fashionable salon. Entitled *An Island in the Moon*, Blake probably has the Lunar Society in his sights, the monthly gathering of Georgian high-achievers which included Erasmus Darwin, James Watt, Joseph Priestly and Josiah Wedgwood. The said island is an analogy for the highbrow get-together, which to Blake, increasingly an outsider, looked like a smug bubble. *The people are so alike, & their language so much the same, that you would think you was among your friends*, he writes, tongue firmly in cheek, because the conversationalists are not really friends as he understood it.[20] Rather, they gather to parrot modish opinions and make a show of their acumen, not to challenge or test each other. They are *thinking of nothing*, Blake continues, bar the stylishness of their dress or of their status and fame.[21] That is worth little because, as he averred, *Opposition is true friendship.*[22] No tension, no growth.

From the perspective of the twenty-first century, Blake's ridicule of the Lunar Society might seem churlish at best and possibly foolishly mistaken. Watt, Priestly, Wedgwood: are these not heroes of the Industrial Revolution? Watt perfected the steam engine. Priestly discovered oxygen and put the fizz into carbonated water. Wedgwood was an innovative designer and prosperous manufacturer of the elegant crockery that bears the family name. (Moreover, Blake briefly benefitted from Wedgwood's success when, later in life, he executed some designs to decorate bedpans and teacups.) These were some of the paragons of the day, which the biographer and historian, Jenny Uglow, described as 'The Friends Who Made the Future,' in her book on the club, *The Lunar Men*.[23]

But at the time, science and industry had yet to ascend the thrones that they have today. The economy and people's ways of life were only beginning to reorganise around the infrastructure required to make everything from railways and internal combustion engines, to electric lightbulbs and telephones. The word 'scientist' had not yet been uttered, let alone freighted with cultural cachet, and there was suspicion of the vigour of these philosophers, as they were called, because of the methods that they deployed. Their advocacy of trial and error—a phrase first promulgated in the Georgian period—looked to many like a big-headed waste of time as each savant, another eighteenth century coinage, championed their theories and experimental obsessions. The pursuits were mocked in *Gulliver's Travels* by Jonathan Swift, the tale of an adventurer who meets, amongst other peoples, indefatigable investigators trying to turn marble into pillows and cucumbers into sunbeams. Gulliver witnesses them building a computer-like device called an engine that uncomprehendingly generated strings of words as a simulacrum of learning: a large language model AI *avant la lettre*.

Swift is satirising the self-congratulatory Age of Reason and was not alone in regarding the phrase as a cliché to be ribbed. Other thinkers, notably the Scottish philosopher, David Hume, asked whether reason is not really post hoc rationalisation and so secretly 'the slave of the passions.'[24] Appetite and preoccupation are the true drivers of invention and commerce, the critics suspected, which is partly why Blake

# AWAKE!

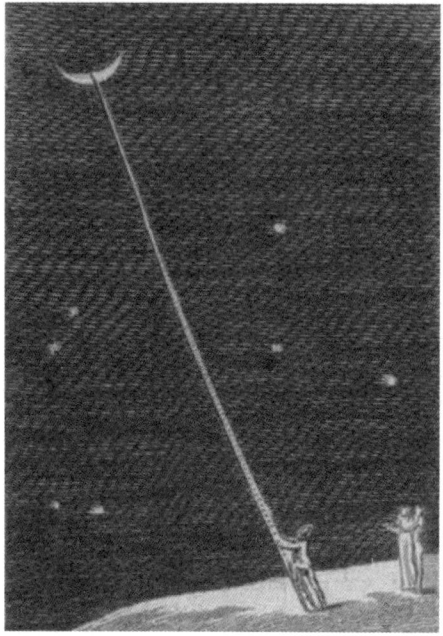

Fig. 10: "I want! I want!" from *For the Sexes: The Gates of Paradise*, 1793.

concluded that progressive philosophy has a shadow; it was as likely to breed exploitation as advance. *Pity is become a trade, and generosity a science, That men get rich by*, he noted.[25] He spotted the self-deception that comes with worldly success and the destruction that material growth leaves in its wake. Consider the airy Midlands towns in which the Lunar Society met to cogitate. They have since become vast and grey: Birmingham, Derby, Stoke. From the perspective of the twenty-first century, Blake's suspicion was not unfounded.

## Confronting Originality

He was becoming the rare type of individual who can be called *atopos*. This word was first used to describe the ancient Greek philosopher, Socrates, and means out of place. The gadfly of Athens, as Socrates was called by the people whom he bugged, irritated because of his quizzical inquiries. His probing would call anything into question, which is to say that Socrates had offbeat views, as if he popped out of a parallel universe. People often didn't understand what he was driving at, or couldn't be bothered to ask, and so lazily put him in a box marked 'strange.' If there was one fact that the average, fifth-century BCE Athenian would have known about the city state's most famous son, it would have been that he walked about barefoot.

To meet Socrates was to be 'confronted by the other's originality,' the French cultural critic Roland Barthes notes. Commonly, such a person is not wanted.[26] And yet, at the same time, if the temptation to attack or envy the eccentricity is resisted, another option can emerge: encountering a Socrates, or a Blake, sparks questions otherwise hard to conceive, let alone ask. They offer a rare form of education. What in them

# CREATE A SYSTEM

Fig. 11: "Job Rebuked by his Friends," from *Illustrations of the Book of Job*. Blake's portrayal of Job being accused by his friends might be partly inspired by the story of Socrates being accused by his fellow Athenians.

is at first unsettling can become intriguing and then positively desired. That's why figures like Socrates and Blake divide people, simultaneously causing upset and inspiring devotion. It is also why the anecdotes about Blake are remembered. Colourful tales, even if exaggerated, are better than blank reports. Falling in between objective records and subjective impressions, they can relay what it was like to meet him and, as a result, he can continue to live.

Here is another remark of Blake's that conveys this deeper value. It was recorded by Henry Crabb Robinson, the journalist who knew Blake and repeatedly asked whether his acquaintance was a genius, a mystic or mad.[27] That confusion deepened when, one day, a thought of Blake's particularly shocked. Blake announced: 'I do not believe that the world is round. I believe it is quite flat.'[28]

Blake a flat-earther? Robinson reacted as many reasonable souls might, wanting to protest. He tells us that he was about to retort, 'But the globe has been circumnavigated!' However, the dinner bell rang and he was left pondering what on earth Blake was driving at—or teasing him about;

what was it about the Earth that 'this remarkable man' sought to affirm in his confrontational way?[29]

After all, Blake knew that, physically speaking, the Earth is a sphere. In one of his early *Poetical Sketches*, written just before he joined the Royal Academy, he describes human beings walking on *the steadfast globe*.[30] He also drew the Earth as a sphere in one of his late projects, the illustrations to Dante's *Divine Comedy*. But Blake realised something else. When the Earth is not just described but experienced as a globe floating in space, there are consequences. The blunt fact can trounce the humanising fiction by insisting that our planet is nowhere in particular and nothing remarkable, merely one of countless heavenly bodies, spinning in a colossal vacuum. To habitually think of Earth as a minor body orbiting a minor star in a minor region of a negligible galaxy is to become distanced from our home as we otherwise spontaneously know it—replete with significance, and definitely not just one planet amongst millions, for us. The enchanted Earth is the one we inhabit, which is why people haven't stopped talking of dramatic sunrises and glowing sunsets, for all that the Sun doesn't rise or set as it is the Earth that turns; or of the broad sky as a sapphire dome, which again presumes the Earth is flat and the firmament above a veritable *paved heaven*.[31] Blake wants us to return to the Earth we can love, the one before and around us, and be glad to be living here:

> *And every Space that a Man views around his dwelling-place,*
> *Standing on his own roof or in his garden on a mount*
> *Of twenty-five cubits in height, such space is his Universe.*
> *And on its verge the Sun rises & sets, the Clouds bow*
> *To meet the flat Earth & the Sea in such an order'd Space.*
> *The Starry heavens reach no further, but here bend and set*
> *On all sides, & the two Poles turn on their valves of gold.*
> *And if he moves his dwelling-place, his heavens also move*
> *Where'er he goes, & all his neighbourhood bewail his loss.*
> *Such are the Spaces called Earth & such its dimension.*
> *As to that false appearance which appears to the reasoner*
> *As of a Globe rolling thro' Voidness, it is a delusion of Ulro.*[32]

It might seem pedantic but he was speaking with intent. He was insisting that this plane of existence is the place where we belong and can find belonging, if we know it aright. We must close the gap prised open by descriptions of the planet that sideline its meaning. The Earth is a globe, fine. But don't lose contact with *ten thousand thousand springs of life* and how, when spoken with, they speak.[33]

His stance was not a romantic gesture of complaint; it was part of his creative struggle with the deism and scientific naturalism that were emerging in his times and have fully seized ours. Newton's laws were not only being used to enforce social attitudes, conservative and radical, but were also being used to drive a wedge between the natural and the supernatural, with the latter then being dismissed. David Hume, for instance, defined a miracle as 'a transgression of a law of nature.' But as he also believed that laws of nature rule every eventuality and are not transgressed, his aim was to ridicule miracles and any supernatural source altogether. He was being reasonable in the pejorative sense to which Blake was alert: a rationality that doesn't know what it can't see. Blake would have spotted that Hume conveniently overlooks that the idea of laws of nature originally rested on the deistic belief in a deity who regiments the world, excluding a presence that might be detected in forces more akin to sympathies, surprises, acts of spirit.[34]

Blake undertook a programme of reading in which he scrutinised the essays and treatises propagating this *Newtonian Phantasm*, which to him was an *impossible absurdity*, given the way it denuded lived experience and deployed questionable logic.[35] He was an intellectual against the intellectuals as he tells us himself in typically strong words:

> *I read Burke's Treatise when very Young; at the same time I read Locke on Human Understanding & Bacon's Advancement of Learning; on Every one of these Books I wrote my Opinions... They mock Inspiration & Vision. Inspiration & Vision was then, & now is, & I hope will always Remain, my Element, my Eternal Dwelling place; how can I then hear it Contemned without returning Scorn for Scorn?*[36]

Their disdain for the charged world he perceived would be matched by his derision of their flatland. *I will not cease from Mental Fight, Nor shall my Sword sleep in my hand*, is his famous summary.[37]

That said, it is worth stressing that he was not against science per se. Far from it. Scattered throughout his writings, there are ringing endorsements of a systematic way of investigating things, which is what science so brilliantly achieves. *What is the Life of Man but Art & Science?*[38] *The Primeval State of Man, was Wisdom, Art, and Science.*[39] *Arts & Sciences are the Destruction of Tyrannies or Bad Governments.*[40] Richard Dawkins could not have said it better.

## AWAKE!

In fact, Blake was something of a working scientist himself. Knowledge of materials was key to his trade and, further, part of what distinguishes his art is his habitual experimentation with media and materials, which he saw as integral to cooperating with inspiration. His workshop therefore resembled a laboratory, stacked with sheets of copper and plates of iron, alongside slabs of marble and bottles of *aqua fortis*; there would have been an acrid smell hanging in the air, produced as acids wash over metals. Piles of paper and tubs of ink would have been stacked on benches, alongside pots of gum and glue, watercolours and the ingredients for tempera, plus burners for heating plates and screens for protecting eyes. Tools were Blake's instruments, each kept in its own place: the wooden rolling-press, the gravers, burnishers, brushes made of camel hair which he preferred over sable, hammers and etching-needles and the oil-stone to sharpen them. He needed magnifying glasses to see details and had drawers of chalks, varnish and candles for treating copper plates. These were the materials with which he drew, etched, painted and printed, after which the works were placed on shelves or hung from lines to dry. All in all, his metier was as technical as his vocation was visionary; they were two sides of the same coin. His workplace would have looked like a cross between an alchemist's lair and a laundry, with science manifest on every surface and bench.

But therein lies the difference: science is not an impartial, academic pursuit for him. His relationship with pigments and chemicals was personal. He had to work collaboratively with them to know how they responded and what they liked. His materials were living substances to him, conveyors of spirit, which is a big part of the reason he formulated such powerful objections to *Newton's sleep* and the detached direction science was taking. He was like the Luddites of the early nineteenth century, whom Blake does not mention in his own writings but with whom he can be conceptually linked.[41] They were to trash the automated looms and spinning jennies proliferating around them not because they were against machines but because, as skilled machine operators, they knew when a machine was no longer working with them and they were being forced to work for the machines. They perceived a tipping point: the technology was remaking them, not they it. A stand had to be taken, which Blake took, too. A vignette records someone showing Blake the first edition of a new publication entitled *The Mechanic's Magazine*, presuming that Blake would welcome this sign of the times. That was a

# CREATE A SYSTEM

mistake. 'Ah, sir,' Blake replied, somewhat haughtily. 'These things we artists hate.'[42] He was voicing what the essayist, Thomas Carlyle, was to express definitively: 'Men are grown mechanical in head and in heart, as well as in hand.'[43]

## *Causes and Correlations*

The crux of Blake's objections can be put like this. When science claims superior, possibly exclusive, access to truth, a compliant wider culture tends to take the appearance of things as the truth of things, marginalising the in-between zone of the imagination and with that the innately meaningful and symbolic. Humanity is enticed along a pathway that overlooks the felt and relational, being led instead by the utilitarian and efficient; personal experience is doubted, as opposed to discerned and prioritised. The light of the Sun or the touch of a breeze does not invite us to 'see into the life of things,' as Wordsworth puts it in 'Lines Composed a Few Miles above Tintern Abbey.' Instead, experts reach for a measuring device. Alternatively, a declaration of something's beauty is regarded as merely an opinion, signifying one thing to one person and another thing to another, or an impulse of love is not a participation in a cosmic tendency because, 'At its most basic level, love is biological bribery. It is a set of neurochemicals which motivate you,' to quote evolutionary anthropologist, Anna Machin.[44]

Reductive redescriptions have come to be treated as self-evident truths in a thousand newspaper articles and public debates and get everything the wrong way around. When genes and atoms are treated as what really exists, experience is treated as a source of data-points to evidence abstractions: the human environment is depleted, the natural world devalued, as a result. The mentality replaces choiring birds and waking flowers with zombie organisms and colliding particles. *You accumulate Particulars, & murder by analyzing. But General Forms have their vitality in Particulars*, Blake observes, countering the great reversal, which he realised is bad for both the arts and the sciences.[45] The attitude fosters ignorance of that which it purports to study, *Generalizing Art & Science till Art & Science is lost*.[46]

The double tragedy is that, two hundred years on, if you quietly ask a scientist what these brute forces or dancing atoms might be, they will likely confess that the idea of them has been surpassed. I remember the first lecture we had as physics undergraduates. 'Everything you have learnt up to this point is likely wrong,' the lecturer teased, as he mocked the principles and equations we had mastered to secure our A-levels. The assertion was at once humiliating, exciting and daunting, but he might have had Werner Heisenberg in mind. One of the founding geniuses of quantum theory, Heisenberg argued that the new physics not only dissolves the assumption that phenomena such as matter, space and time are real in the way Newton had assumed and people still do, but also highlights that science does not provide a good description of life as we know it. Heisenberg implicitly affirmed Blake's realisation that the scientific method abstracts because scientific concepts require precise definitions tractable to mathematical analysis. 'But through this process of idealisation and precise definition the immediate connection with reality is lost,' he continued, stressing that the way we can keep in touch with reality is not, therefore, through science but through tried and tested human intuitions about consciousness, the soul or God: 'they touch reality,' he said, in a way that scientific concepts do not.[47] Likewise, the philosopher of science, Richard Gunton, argues that scientific objectivity is always at least one step removed from reality; it derives useful representations of what is studied but at the cost of removing things from their natural relations and functions.[48]

Similarly, and though he didn't always agree with Heisenberg, Albert Einstein consistently referred to the theory that light consists of particles called photons as a 'heuristic.'[49] *Blots Indefinite*, Blake accurately called them, and his poetry, which holds together scientific imagery and the wider human imagination, might help us better see the actual strangeness of the physical world. *Every particle of dust breathes forth its joy*, the fairy had told Blake and he agreed.[50] All life comes from the dust of the earth, for sure, and returns to it, in its mortal aspect. But that must mean that even humble dirt is alive, in some sense, not inert and subject solely to laws but possessing potentialities, tendencies and habits. *Each speck of dust to the Earths center nestles round & round | In pangs of an Eternal Birth*, was another way Blake saw the omnipresent, striving energy.[51]

He was alert to the connections between the infinitesimal and the infinite with which modern cosmology, in fact, concurs. *Wonder seiz'd all in Eternity, to behold the Divine Vision open | The Center into an Expanse, & the Center rolled out into an Expanse*, he wrote.[52] His poetry might also facilitate the uncoupling of biology in the popular imagination from the robotic determinism of selfish genes so as to perceive the remarkable involutions of entangled life.[53] *One Law for the Lion & Ox is Oppression*.[54]

## CREATE A SYSTEM

His lines invite us to remember that hypotheses are useful but they come at a price, that of drifting from nature and straying from reality which isn't, in fact, as uniform as the hypotheses imply; you only have to look. *The apple tree never asks the beech how he shall grow, nor the lion the horse how he shall take his prey*, Blake suggested.[55] He loved nature's diversity too much to see otherwise and detected an absolutism in thinkers who insist that universal laws governing all things should have the last word. As he puts it with typical punch: *To Generalize is to be an Idiot. To Particularize is the Alone Distinction of Merit*.[56] And he would have chuckled at the irony of tilting at generalisations with a generalisation.

Blake longed for *sweet Science*, as he called it, in continual dialogue with what is actual—and I do know scientists who agree.[57] A friend of mine, Pauline Rudd, who is a professor of biochemistry, explains that her work on viruses, say, involves identifying with the microscopic organisms in the sense of imaginatively aligning with their movement and behaviour. Then, intuitively, the processes they might use come to mind. Blake would have agreed, as is suggested by another anecdote featuring his friend, Thomas Taylor. On this day, Taylor decided to teach Blake some mathematics. Taylor was gaining a reputation as a Platonist devoted to ancient wisdom—philosophical and esoteric—so their enthusiasms crossed. But when Taylor decided to guide Blake through Euclid's *Elements*, Blake brought the exercise to a halt at only the fifth proposition. It describes the properties of isosceles triangles, arising from the equal angles at the base. 'Taylor was going thro the demonstration,' the historian, William George Meredith, noted in his commonplace book, 'but was interrupted by Blake, exclaiming, 'ah never mind that—what's the use of going to prove it, why I see with my eyes that it is so, & do not require any proof to make it clearer."[58]

Taylor believed mathematics exhibits a sacred beauty as well as possesses a practical power and so he would have realised that his friend was not against the proof. Rather, in that moment, Blake was saying, let's stop the lesson and appreciate the symmetry by looking. That is the crucial element not to lose sight of: visibly elegant harmonies. Indeed, even in abstract calculations active impetuses can be felt. Why else would 1 + 1 imply 2? The flows that inhabit generalisations are given to humanity by God too, Blake said, and discerning practitioners can witness *mathematic motion wondrous along the deep, | In fiery pyramid, or Cube, or unornamented pillar square*.[59] I imagine Taylor forgiving his friend's impatience, knowing that it sprang from a love of direct perception and, moreover, a fear that when people forget it, they are at risk. *Thus were the stars of heaven created like a golden chain | To bind the Body of Man to heaven from falling into the Abyss.*[60] Stop seeing the stars of heaven as a golden chain and instead as indifferent pinpricks in the silence of space: start that steep decline.

The implications of Blake's fearless critique, applied both to the political and scientific revolutionaries of his age, shows why this fourth virtue so much matters: without the takedown, nihilism looms. As a young adult, he formulated a far-reaching agenda to unpack in the years that lay ahead. It was as substantial and informed as it was passionate and redemptive. The intellectual Blake was now fledged, as was the imaginative, visionary and cannily innocent. During his time at the Royal Academy, he not only muttered against those he deemed mistaken, he worked hard to clarify his objections and, in so doing, discovered his vocation. He came, he said:

> *To cast off Bacon, Locke & Newton from Albion's covering,*
> *To take off his filthy garments & clothe him with Imagination,*
> *To cast aside from Poetry all that is not Inspiration,*
> *That it no longer shall dare to mock with the aspersion of Madness*
> *Cast on the Inspired.*[61]

He would show that humanity can recover divine sight, for the revelatory makes us human. Science alone cannot save us, but science charged with imagination might help. Having identified the values that inform a Blakean way of life, we can now turn to how these manifest in practice. We will begin with a matter about which creatives nearly always complain, as it was also causing a revolution in society: the mushrooming of money.

# PART II

# ENERGY

5

MONEY IS USELESS

As a man, Blake cut a striking figure. He was 'short, but well made, & very well proportioned' with a 'large head and wide shoulders. Elasticity and promptitude of action were the characteristics of his contour.'[1] The aura of energy that surrounded him was manifested in sparkling eyes and flame-like hair that 'looked at a distance like radiations.'[2] A charged presence may have been why he had a rough time when it came to finding a wife with whom to settle down: it seems that he attracted potential partners easily and as easily frightened them off.

In the summer of 1781, he had completed his time at the Royal Academy and was looking to establish a household from which to work as a commercial engraver. But he found himself so affected by love's trials that he became ill. The experience was grave enough for him to retreat to Battersea to recover. The village, as it then was, clung to a rickety wooden bridge that crossed the River Thames a couple of miles west of London. It enjoyed acres of common land and copious fresh air. He lodged with a householder who was a family friend or possibly a relation; a market gardener who went by the name of Boucher. Boucher had a black-eyed, open-hearted daughter called Catherine and she became interested in the wounded guest from town. And this time it was to be different. One evening, as Blake mourned in a corner, she blurted out that she felt sympathy for him. 'Do you pity me?' Blake replied cautiously. 'Yes! I do, most sincerely.' 'Then I love you for that!' he exclaimed.[3] The bright beam of his affections turned to her and she welcomed the excitement.

They were married a year later, after Blake had persuaded their respective families that his trade could provide for them both. The ceremony was conducted in the new church at Battersea, rather than in his parish at the church of St James's, Piccadilly. That was irregular, even illegal, though perhaps William wanted the luck he found along the river

# AWAKE!

Fig. 12: St Mary's Battersea from the north side of the River Thames.

to bless their lives together. If so, it worked. They were to spend forty-five years in each other's company and be apart for just five weeks.

Catherine came from a large family of ten surviving children and meagre means, with the result that she had no education. When they met, she was probably working as a maid earning no more than a subsistence wage. But she was smart. He taught her to read and write, which is no mean undertaking for an adult. He simultaneously tutored her in the skills required for engraving so that, before long, she became an invaluable assistant, helping him with the mechanics of producing prints as well as the arts of colouring. Her middle name was Sophia, wisdom, and she brought forethought to the marriage, soon becoming indispensable to him, as life with him proved transformative for her. Blake's later patron, William Hayley, reckoned that Catherine was 'perhaps the only female on this Earth, who could have suited [Blake] exactly... she draws, she engraves, & sings delightfully & is so truly the Half of her good Man, that they seem animated by one Soul, & that a Soul of indefatigable Industry & Benevolence.'[4]

A moving portrait in pencil which he drew of her survives. The soft, clear graphite lines speak of his luminous affection. He captures the energy of her soul in the shape of her eyes, mouth and cheeks, as well as details like eyelashes. The image is a testament to their union and his habit of sketching her. I imagine it was a form of therapy: her presence calmed him when he became agitated. Sometimes he even hit writer's block. 'What do we do then, Kate?' he was once heard asking. 'We kneel down and pray, Mr Blake,' she replied, revealing their practised custom.[5] Theirs was a marriage of close partnership and profound affection.

Which is not to say that they didn't quarrel at times, as the anecdotes recall. One features William's beloved younger brother, Robert, who had moved in with them partly as a member of Blake's family, partly to learn the engraving trade as well. William had set up shop with a friend he had met whilst they were both apprentices, James Parker. The atmosphere in the busy household and workshop was mostly happy, though one day, Catherine became cross and snapped at Robert. The altercation caused William to lose his rag and, pulling rank, he told her to kneel and beg Robert's pardon, under threat of never seeing him again. When she retold the story, she insisted that his response was harsh, particularly as Robert was at fault, not she. Only, it turned out that Robert saved the day. As Catherine made to confess that she was mistaken, he interjected: 'Young woman, you lie! I am in the wrong.'[6] It was an ugly moment, casting William in a poor light, but there is another side to the incident. It speaks of Catherine's fieriness, which could match that of her husband's, and it tells of the confidence she had gained in the marriage—evidenced by her willingness to relate the story as she saw it.

She managed the household, looking after the money. This somewhat went against convention, as the man might have been expected to control the purse strings. But Georgian gender roles were shifting, with longstanding assumptions easing as part of the progressive spirit of the age.[7] So, when William admitted that financial matters distracted him and he would prefer to have little to do with balances and budgets, Catherine was free and willing to step in. One person's burden is another's increase of liberty.

## Money Matters

Just what William disliked about money is worth contemplating because it takes us from the principles that shaped his life to the way of life those foundations supported: how to live in the modern world as he saw it. 'Blunt,' as the Georgians called cash, was another major factor in the reshaping of the times and, as such, was a force that disturbed him and might still give us pause. The reason why comes to the fore by considering his near contemporary, the economist Adam Smith, whom Blake would have known about as the Scottish professor's works came to prominence from the mid-1780s. Smith offers an astute description of the emerging cash economy and its repercussions on increasing numbers of people. The discussion comes in his book, *The Theory of Moral Sentiments*, which he considered a crucial scene-setter to his subsequent and far better-known, *An Inquiry into the Nature and Causes of the Wealth of Nations*. In the earlier work, Smith argues that, for many, the consequences of a growing economy are not straightforwardly good. He spots people becoming weighed down, literally and psychologically, by the possessions that the new money tempts them to buy and, more perniciously, encourages them to want, whether they buy the stuff or not. '[People] walk about loaded with a multitude of baubles… of which the whole utility is certainly not worth the fatigue of bearing the burden,' Smith writes.[8] He laments that acquiring bejewelled snuff boxes and elegant pocket watches brings suffering under the guise of bringing happiness. Money is equated with value in more ways than one and the person who has the appurtenances that others envy is attempting to secure an aura of success and feeling of wellbeing. Nowadays, it is a rare person who isn't seduced in the same way.

But, Smith concludes, people are tacitly agreeing to a scam, remembered in the cliché that money doesn't buy happiness. Everyone knows that. And everyone—or nearly everyone—ignores it. Which is just as well, Smith reckons, for the personal anxiety and, on occasion, individual ruin that comes with the cash-based way of life is a price worth paying. 'It is this deception which rouses and keeps in continual motion the industry of mankind,' he explains.[9] And with industry comes the purpose of the exertion: progress.

Smith concluded that the ambivalences inherent in this new mode of living are worth it. Blake was not so sure. He agreed, in one way, that his hometown was driven by ambition and was becoming a marvel of change, lifting many out of poverty and connecting peoples who had been strangers. The place could pride itself on being increasingly lively and cosmopolitan; that is the gain of empire, which Blake recognised and celebrated. *In the Exchanges of London every Nation walk'd | And London walk'd in every Nation mutual in love & harmony. | Albion cover'd the whole Earth, England encompassed the Nations, | Mutual each within others bosoms in*

*Visions of Regeneration*.[10] Economic activity has an upside and Blake hoped to be a beneficiary. His surviving correspondence shows that he would ask to be paid well for his work and begrudged artists who were paid more, particularly if he thought their output inferior, which it often was. *Peace & Plenty & Domestic Happiness is the Source of Sublime Art*, he affirmed. *Enjoyment & not Abstinence is the food of Intellect*.[11] As they began to build a life together, William and Catherine were not without material aspirations and they had grounds for such hopes. Looking back on the time, he later wrote to a friend:

> *It is very Extraordinary that London in so few years from a City of meer Necessaries or at least a commerce of the lowest order of luxuries should have become a City of Elegance in some degree & that its once stupid inhabitants should enter into an Emulation of Grecian manners. There are now I believe as many Booksellers as there are Butchers & as many Printshops as of any other trade.*[12]

The culture of the energetic Lunar Men was one that loved booksellers and printshops and that was good for Blake.

But there was a downside. A society dependent on money reminded him all too clearly of both a science in love with abstractions and the delusions of self-made men. Much as proposals like billiard-ball atoms alienate the soul by placing human beings in a cosmos considered fundamentally dark and dead, so money readily replaces true riches with clinking pennies and crowns. *To the Eyes of a Miser a Guinea is more beautiful than the Sun & a bag worn with the use of Money has more beautiful proportions than a Vine filled with Grapes*.[13] Money is like reason, Blake intuited: unchecked, both become masters when they should be servants in the service of higher goals. In particular, money carries this danger: it rationalises desires by converting hopes and wishes into an amount; the freedom rooted in a love of life morphs into a slavery of experiences and achievements.

That's the mentality of money infecting the soul, and Blake held the opposite view, that the best things in life are free: *For every Pleasure Money Is Useless*, he wrote.[14] *Artificial riches | They give to scorn, & their possessors to trouble & sorrow & care, | Shutting the sun, & moon, & stars, & trees, & clouds, & waters, | And hills.*[15] He was too alert to the preternatural power of the *fair moon*,[16] *overflowing stars*[17] and *clouded hills*,[18] believing money 'misenchants,' which is to say that its ability to enthral conjures a false sense of what's sacred.[19] And that, again, contributes to despoiling the world. *I see a Cave, a Rock, a Tree deadly and poisonous, unimaginative… I see | Pits of bitumen ever burning: artificial Riches of the Canaanite | Like Lakes of liquid lead: instead of heavenly Chapels, built | By our dear Lord: I see Worlds crusted with snows & ice.*[20] Money is indeed the root of all evil when it separates us from felt relationships in a teeming world.

Ecological destruction is all too familiar now; Blake spotted its antecedents and diagnosed the core problems—the cosmological system devised by Newton and its soporific effect on people; the imagination, so key to a spirited connection with the rising sun and the chorusing birds, diminished by thinkers like Locke. In a mechanical cosmos, it is much easier to treat rivers as resources and land as a storehouse of commodities; it becomes close to an automatic assumption. The imperatives of efficiency and utility take hold and this means that callousness takes hold, too. Ways of treating the natural world that would have seemed sacrilegious to our ancestors become so normal that devastation spreads almost unnoticed.

Blake felt the pressure himself and 'feared nothing so much as being rich lest he should lose his Spiritual riches,' reported a later friend and advocate, the painter, John Linnell.[21] The association is an old fear, caught in Jesus's remark about the dangers of trying to serve God and Mammon, a biblical terms for riches. The two become easily confused, doubly so when material gain shapes the culture. The human birthright and desire to know life's plenteousness becomes narrowed into a scramble to manufacture stuff and accumulate things. Blake wrestled with the confusion and wrote about it in a poem, presenting the issue as a daily challenge and constant struggle.

> *I rose up at the dawn of day-*
> *Get thee away! Get thee away!*
> *Pray'st thou for Riches? away! away!*
> *This is the Throne of Mammon grey.*
>
> *Said I, 'this sure is very odd.*
> *'I took it to be the Throne of God.*
> *'For every Thing besides I have:*
> *'It is only for Riches that I can crave.*
>
> *'I have Mental Joy & Mental Health*
> *'And Mental Friends & Mental wealth;*
> *'I've a Wife I love & that loves me;*
> *'I've all But Riches Bodily.*

## MONEY IS USELESS

*'I am in God's presence night & day,*
*'And he never turns his face away.'*[22]

The poem continues and by its end, Blake is reminding himself not to fall for *Mr Devil*, who threatens him with the thought that if he doesn't pay homage to Mammon, he'll have to *eat coarser food & go worse shod*. That's the economic treadmill that Blake knew to resist. He observed what was happening in the world around him and had the measure of his soul's enemy, *the accuser of sins*. 'And so you may do the worst you can do: | 'Be assur'd Mr Devil I won't pray to you,' he resolutely concludes.[23]

### Escaping the Rat Race

The point is that consumables and appurtenances, including luxury items like books, certainly stimulate and can inform, but they do not satisfy; the owner of volumes may remain resolutely foolish. More broadly, the risk is that once the treadmill has started to turn, it doesn't stop, consuming people as they consume—to reference an old word that took on its modern meaning at about this time as 'consumers' and 'consumer desires' were born. Riches can bring another kind of poverty, Blake reasoned, sheltering the well-off beneath *a Tree of Misery*.[24] He saw coming a gilded cage built of mortgages and pension plans.

And yet, he did not want to be piously puritan in response to the worry that *Riches* might supplant *Mental wealth*. He was clear that the mercantile energies swirling round him, and the bewitching psychology that Smith had identified, were precisely that: a seductive perversion of the glorious longing that human beings have for *the Throne of God*.[25] He recognised the dangers of being swept along by the spirit of consumerism, but simultaneously recognised that to react by disciplining desires or limiting wants was to risk weakening the impulses that can propel human beings to worthwhile delights. There is a good energy at work in industriousness, even if it is readily bedevilled by the demands of growth and progress, and it is better to act on desire and suffer the consequences than neuter it, he felt, for without desire we are too much reduced. *The road of excess leads to the palace of wisdom.*[26] What, then, to do? What manner of life to foster?

Some might say that Blake needed to strike a balance. As he and Catherine settled into married life, they might work out how to be in the commercial world, as his trade required, but not unthinkingly of that world. What must be sought is a happy medium, with work that provides amply without stifling more fulfilling endeavours. There is something in that, though the Blakes discovered that trying to sustain a balance is an endless task with assessments required almost daily, as is revealed in a touching domestic habit. They developed a code. When he had spent the day absorbed in a visionary idea or promising design, which was inspired but not productive, she would place an empty platter on the table at dinner. He took it as a signal to spend the next day making prints that could be sold: one day honouring God, the next acknowledging that Mr Devil had a point and nodding to Mammon. She had another recourse, as well, which was secretly to keep a guinea in reserve. The coin would be enough for them to live on for about a week, should needs be. Her thrift meant that whilst they were sometimes poor, they were never impoverished. Money certainly has its uses.

Compromises are a feature of adult life. But still, Blake found them irritating. Committing to a lifetime seeking a balance between inner desires and outer demands risks inadvertently opting for stasis; 'happy medium' is a contradiction in terms. He was convinced that prudence must play second fiddle to the creative drive in each human heart, yearning for expression. He needed another principle with which he could align earnestly and he found one. His solution was not an accommodation but a fusion: the clash of personal values and worldly enticements could itself be a source of vigour. The mix of loving and loathing the mercantile spirit could beget a tension that he would allow to agitate him. *Energy is the only life*, he concluded and it was to be his passion, that elemental enthusiasm marked not by a refusal of daily life but a seizing hold of it.[27] His innocent spirit, engaged imagination, searching mind and atopological character would be guides.

He captured the stance in a pamphlet printed after he had been married to Catherine for a few years, wittily entitled *The Marriage of Heaven and Hell*.[28] The marriage he discusses in it is not contracted by a man and a woman, but by the opposites within oneself. He would accept the mood that darkened the *burden'd air* and *Hungry clouds* of London, and transmute it.[29] *Those who restrain desire, do so because theirs is weak enough to be restrained*, he declared.[30] No: he would seek to live well not with, but through the pressures of modern life, holding out for the rediscovery of dimensions consumerism forgets.

One section of *The Marriage* states the aim in a pithy summary: *Without Contraries is no progression*, it insists.[31] At one level, that much had become evident from having to make a living in a period organising itself around industriousness. But at another level, the observation is a rejection of the happy medium or sensible balance approach. It is an affirmation of the necessarily messy dynamism needed to flourish. *Attraction and Repulsion, Reason and Energy, Love and Hate, are necessary to Human existence*, he continues.[32] The development of the soul is fostered by positively cherishing dilemmas—or to put it the other way around, insights inevitably bring errors, deeds misdeeds, desire envy, and striving means struggle. But errors, envy and the like can also signal a way forward, properly discerned, and that's where the energy should go: not towards anxious puritanism or careless indulgence but lasting enjoyments.

The creed embraces both/and rather than treating life as a series of either/or choices, though Blake's contraries are not equal and opposite but asymmetric. This is crucial. One pole is prior, namely the one that taps more fully into the wellsprings of life. This means that the contrary energies can maintain a movement that avoids viciously spiralling down and rather, when well engaged, opens onto a wider awareness. Blake was not trying to have his cake and eat it; life is inevitably compromised but don't let that compromise your embracing the whole of life. Living is not mastered by moralising, any more than swimming is learnt from fluid dynamics; you must get in the water. With splashing about comes the art of staying afloat, followed by the skill to paddle and glide. *Virtue is not Opinion*: it is a practice.[33] That is crucial to remember because when people seek to feel self-righteous, intolerance and hypocrisy inevitably follow. *The Moral Virtues are continual Accusers of Sin & promote Eternal Wars & Dominency over others*, Blake contended, two centuries before the trend named woke.[34] The risk is that token groups, deemed beyond the pale, are adopted as substitutes for the fault lines that, in truth, run through everyone.

'Out of the crooked timber of humanity no straight thing can ever be made,' lamented Immanuel Kant in an essay published in 1784, though Blake was inclined to think kinks are good.[35] *Improvement makes strait roads; but the crooked roads without Improvement are roads of Genius,* he wrote in *The Marriage*, presumably correcting the German philosopher.[36] He grew fond of phrases such as *the Wastes of Moral Law*, believing that a spotless soul, should one actually exist, is actually a lifeless soul, bleached of what delineates and defines it.[37] Far better to love our flawed condition and be ready, often, to forgive. This mingling is what *infernal wisdom* understands, Blake continues, knowing that a better way is to reject vain simplifications

AWAKE!

and appreciate the subtleties of nuanced truths.[38] *The man who never alters his opinion is like standing water, & breeds reptiles of the mind.*[39]

## Uneasy Reflections

This is not to say that individuals shouldn't examine the nature of their passions and virtues. If they are serious, they most certainly should, as Blake demonstrates in the annotations he made to a book that he was reading at this time. Entitled *Aphorisms on Man*, it is a collection of maxims and observations written by Johann Kaspar Lavater, a Swiss poet and thinker. Blake loved the text for the way it searched his own soul. Inside the cover of his copy, he inscribed his name alongside that of Lavater and encircled both with a heart. The warm gesture must have been because Lavater spoke precisely to the issues with which Blake was contending. His guide was particularly insightful about human foibles and contradictions, not so as to condemn them, but spot them and learn from them. Blake read the book as an exercise in self-analysis.

Some of the time, he felt affirmed, as when Lavater wrote: 'He who reforms himself has done more toward reforming the public than a crowd of noisy, impatient patriots.' *Excellent!* Blake wrote in the margin, perhaps recalling the Gordon Riots of 1780.[40] These were a week of protests in London, prompted by anti-Catholic sentiment, that ran violently out of control. Days of looting and arson reached a furious climax when the mob burned Newgate prison, freeing hundreds of prisoners. Blake unwittingly found himself in the front line of protestors. He faced being fired on by soldiers charged with restoring order and could further have been hanged alongside the children and men who were subsequently arrested had he been similarly identified and caught. When he later wrote of *thunder smoke & sullen flames & howlings & fury & blood*, he spoke from direct experience—having also learnt the lesson that any social reformer must: be doubly convinced of the need to reform yourself.[41]

Lavater's *Aphorisms* also frequently challenged him. Don't trust the desire for fame, the Swiss writer remarks in another paragraph, adding an extended metaphor: 'If from the stream of occasion you snatch a handful of foam, deny the stream, and give its name to the frothy bursting bubble.' The image is an exposé of the tendency to grasp at the transient effervescence of acclaim, which risks addiction to flattery. Blake read the lines and admitted: *Uneasy. This I lament I have done.*[42] In

## MONEY IS USELESS

other comments, too, he found an honest appraisal of his own cravings and behaviour. Whilst reading Lavater, he wrote *Uneasy* dozens of times in the margins.

Passions can seed violence, desires can fuel vices, though honesty is a candid guide. *Reason is the bound or outward circumference of Energy*, which is to agree that an unexamined life is not worth living, but scrutiny must not swamp energy or all will be lost.[43] The exploration in *The Marriage* continues with some of Blake's most famous adages, collected as *Proverbs of Hell*.[44] Many of the aphorisms express the conviction that impulse, movement and zeal are supreme and should be held invaluable. The lines are worth reading because the energy they themselves convey instils the attitude Blake sought.

> *He who desires but acts not, breeds pestilence.*
> *The busy bee has no time for sorrow.*
> *No bird soars too high, if he soars with his own wings.*
> *If the fool would persist in his folly he would become wise.*
> *The cistern contains: the fountain overflows.*
> *One thought fills immensity.*
> *The tygers of wrath are wiser than the horses of instruction.*
> *Expect poison from the standing water.*
> *You never known enough unless you know what is more than enough.*
> *Exuberance is Beauty.*[45]

The boldness acclaimed is also on display in the imagery with which Blake surrounded the words, many of the pictures and designs being notably sexual. The title page features numerous couples—some of the opposite sexes, some same sex—walking, embracing and flying, amidst flames and bending trees. Successive plates show nudity, birth and combat.

What is being advocated is not licence but a directed freedom known in the body, tried in life and prioritised by the fervent soul. Blake is not celebrating antinomianism, which is simply chaotic, but what might be called a transnomian attitude to life: a state of being in transit and at least partially glad of difficulties and crises because they bring vital pivot points. Energy is loved not for energy's sake but because, when well engaged, it brings illumination. To embrace contraries is to dwell in-between, neither wedded to old convictions, nor too quickly seizing what is only beginning to emerge. There is a direction of travel and inner progress but probably not much certainty because the imagination is where advances are made. *What is now proved was once only imagin'd.*[46] The

# AWAKE!

Fig. 13: *The Marriage of Heaven and Hell*, plate 21, detail showing a man looking up to heaven.

attitude to foster is one that develops faith and attends to potentials. And faith is worth having because, ultimately, the imagination can always be trusted. *Every thing possible to be believ'd is an image of truth.*[47]

The triangulation of impulses, always ready for the unexpected alternative, is akin to his encounters with spirits and fairies. They are similarly transnomian as communications from a culturally illicit world, found in the space between the subjective and objective, bringing awareness of novel currents. The invitation is to be playful and audacious. The man who conversed with prophets and angels found he could revel in this spiritedness, to the point of risking outrage. Further Proverbs of Hell reach this level. *Drive your cart and your plow over the bones of the dead*, he writes, presumably alluding to Jesus's gritty proverb: 'No one, having put his hand to the plough, and looking back, is fit for the kingdom of God.'[48] Keep driving forward; don't lose your edge. Or there is this: *Sooner murder an infant in its cradle than nurse unacted desires.*[49] Yikes! Though I think this most edgy of edgy maxims is again born of profound insight. A life of frustrated desire is one that might well surreptitiously seek release in sexual distraction—which Blake would have witnessed. He saw the prostitutes on London's *midnight streets*.[50] The escape they offered led, in turn, to unwanted pregnancies and the death of infants, which was alarmingly high in London during the mid-eighteenth century, at up to four out of every ten births.[51] *Arrows of desire* bring life, but misdirected, also distress.[52]

But again, he warns against simple repression, a theme that defines several of the *Songs of Innocence and Experience*. This is the approach of religions that default to the preaching of moral creeds. Nowhere is Blake's objection to this habit of churches clearer than in 'The Garden of Love.'

> *I went to the Garden of Love,*
> *And saw what I never had seen:*
> *A Chapel was built in the midst,*
> *Where I used to play on the green.*
>
> *And the gates of this Chapel were shut,*
> *And 'Thou shalt not' writ over the door;*
> *So I turn'd to the Garden of Love*
> *That so many sweet flowers bore;*
>
> *And I saw it was filled with graves,*
> *And tomb-stones where flowers should be;*
> *And priests in black gowns were walking their rounds,*
> *And binding with briars my joys & desires.*[53]

Repression denies but also distorts. Another poem, 'A Poison Tree,' tells the tale of a person who became annoyed with another and how that irritation, concealed within upright behaviour, festered silently inside, metastasizing into a murderous rage.

> *I was angry with my friend:*
> *I told my wrath, my wrath did end.*
> *I was angry with my foe:*
> *I told it not, my wrath did grow.*
>
> *And I water'd it in fears,*
> *Night & morning with my tears;*
> *And I sunned it with smiles,*
> *And with soft deceitful wiles.*
>
> *And it grew both day and night,*
> *Till it bore an apple bright;*
> *And my foe beheld it shine,*
> *And he knew that it was mine,*

# AWAKE!

> *And into my garden stole*
> *When the night had veil'd the pole:*
> *In the morning glad I see*
> *My foe outstreach'd beneath the tree.*[54]

Repression is bad: point well made. But where might transnomian energy propel us? Can we gain some sense of where Blake's advice might lead?

### *Infinite Desire*

The true nature and end of our desires is captured in another couple of extraordinarily perceptive lines from the pamphlet entitled, *There Is No Natural Religion*. This short booklet can be read as a companion piece to *The Marriage of Heaven and Hell*, with the particular lines I have in mind being these:

> *If the many become the same as the few when possess'd, More! More! is the cry of a mistaken soul; less than All cannot satisfy Man.*[55]

The words take a little unpacking, which I think is part of Blake's aim when he bundles up his wisdom. To have to work out what he is saying increases the chances of being roused by what he is saying, which is fundamental to discovering the way to which he points.

Take the opening clause: *If the many become the same as the few when possess'd*. 'The many' refers to the goods, trinkets and delights appearing in London's shops and arcade windows. The chance to have such things, by earning the money to buy a 'few,' is the promise made to and pursued by the consumer. What is never quite given is the lie: the promise is a trap because the human soul is not fulfilled by possessing a token few of the many things. So much is so familiar after 200 years of the experiment. But Blake's analysis next takes the surprising turn, which is the one we have been tracking. He does not recommend buying less or stopping shopping, which as moral injunctions would be an attack on desire. The finger-wagging is futile because it is pitched against the enormity of human hungers, which are in a crucial sense valid and good. But if you can't check desires and shouldn't, you can educate them—which takes us to the second clause: *More! More! is the cry of a mistaken soul*. Rather than discipline, there can be discernment so as to perceive more deeply what is going on. Yes: seeking more and more, in cycles of work and accumulation, is an error—typically a dispiriting one, sometimes a disastrous one. But the misunderstanding is forgivable because the human soul does long for something tremendous: unbounded life. Hence the third clause and punchline: *less than All cannot satisfy Man*. The error is the belief that satisfaction comes with *the few when possessed*, because the truth is that human desire is, at heart, infinite. No end of goods and trinkets will assuage that well of longing. But there can be a realisation: what human beings really want is the 'All.' And this, he implies, we might find.

Blake spotted that human beings are unlike other creatures, who do tend to stop when their immediate needs are met. We, though, have an inner life that can, in principle, reach out indefinitely and so it is crucial to cultivate the means for that fullness to be recognised in activities that can match the immensity. He saw that the cruel genius of the materialistic culture arising around him was to channel these great longings into trivial appetites. Mercantilism has a secret plan: to direct the enormity of human love into a narrow greed for things. The progressive world was in the process of driving the soul's divine yearning into a cul-de-sac, condemning people to an addictive, anxious need for stuff, for distraction, for satisfaction: misenchantment replacing genuine enchantment.

Much of Blake's future work was set on exploring this imprisoning of desire and the ways it closes imaginative horizons under a pretence of opening them up. The analysis is another reason why Blake so much matters today; he was sure that answering the human cry for the All is essential. Nothing less than our happiness depends upon it. *If any could desire what he is incapable of possessing, despair must be his eternal lot*, he reasoned, adding the key insight: *The desire of Man being Infinite, the possession is Infinite & himself Infinite.*[56]

The need inside us is untold, unending. That's just the way it is for we humans. So what on earth are we to do about that? The question takes us to the second of Blake's crucial practicalities: how expansively to desire and, in particular, unconditionally to love. For if our yearning is immense, it can, guided by the imagination, find release.

6

LOVE! LOVE! LOVE!

In the autumn of 1785, William and Catherine had been living for a couple of years with William's business partner, James Parker and James's wife, Anne. Another member of the household was Robert Blake, William's brother. But William, Catherine and Robert decided to move. Their new home was 28 Poland Street, just around the corner. The house itself has since been demolished and replaced by commercial buildings. The last time I looked, number 28 was home to Cut and Grind, a modish barber-coffeeshop combo. And yet, right next door is a print shop, as if keeping the memory of William and Catherine's industry alive.

The practicalities of commercial engraving and printmaking undoubtedly occupied much of their time, though something else apparently troubled them. The concern, relayed by some of Blake's biographers, was a personal matter, and is captured in a second anecdote about life in the Blake household. The story focuses not on quarrels but on sex which, like money, can inveigle its way into people's lives, commandeering their imaginations. It seems that in the house at number 28, William was working out how to channel the flames of love and desire.

Alexander Gilchrist, who records the earlier story of Catherine's outburst and Robert's magnanimous apology, hints that there were 'stormy times' in these years of their marriage.[1] But does that euphemism point to markedly male appetites posing a threat to their peace? To cut to the chase: there is a report that William decided he wanted to take a mistress. The excuse was a desire to model his life on the Hebrew patriarch, Abraham. According to the Bible, Abraham slept with both Sarah, his wife, and Hagar, their servant, to make up for what Abraham didn't obtain from the marriage: a child. Moreover, Abraham had Sarah's blessing for the affair. Apparently, William sought permission from

Catherine to do likewise, only the proposal made 'Mrs Blake cry,' as the anecdote records, and so William didn't.[2]

The presumed strife has been doubted to the point of dismissal by recent Blake scholars because the earliest account of it appears not until decades after William and Catherine's deaths. Nonetheless, due to the titillating subject matter and some circumstantial details, notably that he and Catherine did not have children, the tale has captured the imagination, to the extent that free love is often attributed to Blake as a matter of fact. But if that conclusion is overblown, the tale raises a good question nonetheless: why might he be associated with polyamory and what does the inference misunderstand? There is something subtler to tease out about the conduct of love in a Blakean way of life and that can be pursued by once more returning to Blake's affinity with the esoteric.

*Christian Tantra*

Amongst some of the dissenting churches and secret societies of London, which Blake knew well, sexualised sacred verse and meditations were not uncommon and presumably led, sometimes, to intimate nights of holy experimentation. His mother had been a member of the Moravian community, which had something of a reputation for sexual scandals, in part because Moravian devotions ranged from the straightforwardly pious to the distinctly erotic. For example, the group's collective prayer-life stressed the value of singing hymns that actively contemplate the suffering of Jesus in ways that could foster sexual fervour. One reads:

> What Pleasure doth a Heart perceive, that rests in the precious Hole, lives there, loves and sports, works and praises the little Lamb... I kiss with the greatest Tenderness the Scars on his Hands and Feet... I lay myself in the Hole made by the Spear... I have licked all over that Rock Salt! O how well did it taste, on that Moment my little Soul is transported into the little Side-Hole.[3]

Lines like these are eye-catching, possibly repulsive, or maybe just plain confusing: tasting the 'Side-Hole'? However, for Blake, there was something of value in this erotically-charged mysticism because it can engage another energy, imaginatively to allow and follow. *Energy is the only life, and is from the Body*, he had concluded in *The Marriage of Heaven and Hell*, which means that the passions of the body matter quite as much as those of the soul when it comes to *Eternal Delight*.[4] And that makes sense. In erotic pursuits, we humans, often unconsciously, seek the All, through losing ourselves in another. There must be, therefore, a path from the sexual to the heavenly that Blake wouldn't shy from tracking. Venturing along that way will be part, too, of discerning the temptations of a sexualised consumer culture, which utilises sexual feelings because they misenchant equally as effectively as money. The challenge is to become familiar with these powerful stirrings within us, not simply to indulge them, but rather so as to discover the infinite: the true object of their longing which might also bring lasting satisfaction.

One of the Proverbs of Hell makes the connection explicit: *The lust of the goat is the bounty of God.*[5] The issue is how to use that bounty well. *The nakedness of woman is the work of God* declares another, a celebration of the divine fecundity in human form that includes the nakedness of men as well; Blake celebrates the two by drawing numerous muscular nudes of both sexes dancing and stretching across many of the pages of his prints. Erotic desire is powerfully felt by all. But how healthily to live with it?

Fig. 14: "I found him beneath a tree," from For the *Sexes: The Gates of Paradise*, plate 3. In this image, Blake depicts a woman pulling a child out of the ground, which looks odd, until you wonder if the scene reflects a tryst under the tree that had longer-term consequences for the women than the absent man.

## AWAKE!

He was not alone in musing on these matters. Georgian England has been called an 'openly sexualised culture,' featuring indulgence, moral panics, abuse, and earnest examination.[6] James Boswell delightedly recorded his unplanned alfresco liaisons and when Mary Wollstonecraft finally found happiness with William Godwin, she wrote of the felicities of the bedroom with an almost religious excitement. 'I have seldom seen so much live fire running about my features as this morning when recollections, very dear, called forth the blush of pleasure, as I adjusted my hair.'[7]

Sex is important to Blake because its affections and frenzies agitate a set of contraries with which we must wrestle if we want to live well: the animal and the human, the relational and the fantasised, the base and the sacred. Foreplay and intercourse are complicated because whilst sex clearly has a biological dimension, our mating is never mere coitus. It is invariably entangled with efforts to express love or release a murkier mix of emotions. The erotic contains wheels within wheels because sexual pleasure, at least for us humans, is not just about the stimulation of organs and instinctual satisfaction. It is about the presence of another person, actually or imagined. Maybe the same is so for other animals: Charles Darwin was sure that some female birds, for example, carefully study the displays of males, selecting who to admit by criteria of elegance and beauty, not just stamina or strength.[8] But whatever is going on in avian and other minds, for the human creature, the erotic response of one person to another is undoubtedly determined by all manner of factors, from barely controlled spasms to the deepest yearnings of the soul.

The subtleties of this quickening potency become clear when considering touch—one of the senses that Blake contemplated as he felt it could circumvent the machinations of the mind and cut through to what's immediate and basic: physical touch can put you psychologically in touch. Consider, say, what happens if a stranger brushes your hand; the contact may prompt a note of surprise or jolt of shock. Conversely, if a friend does the same, a welcome wish of goodwill is communicated. A third scenario is when a potential lover reaches out with what, on the surface, might appear to be exactly the same gesture, though with this charged touch, an utterly different set of feelings is unleashed; as their hand touches yours, sparks fly. And of course there is a dark side to sexual touch, too, when it belies obsessional or abusive motives: a pat masks a grope. Blake described the manifestations of calculated lust like this:

*here the affectionate touch of the tongue is clos'd in by deadly teeth | And the soft smile of friendship & the open dawn of benevolence | Become a net & a trap, & every energy render'd cruel.*⁹ For humans, intention is all, which is why, alongside the thrills, the erotic provokes feelings including aggression, anxiety and shame.

This electric aspect of human experience drew Blake's interest for philosophical reasons, as well. Notice how sexual desire is always directed towards a specific individual or act. For example, when it comes to love, as opposed to just sex, suggesting that Alex is as lovely as Ashley, to someone who is infatuated with Ashley, would probably be offensive—and, when you think about it, the fact that one person can't be exchanged for another in matters of love is fascinating. The belief is that by being with this person and this person alone, not any other, longing itself might cease. Paradoxically, the beloved who cannot be substituted for any other connects us with something universal, which is part of the reason that Blake valued *minute particulars* over abstract generalities. Only the actual and specific touches the All. That's a telling clue about how to know the infinite, which Blake expressed in famous words:

> *To see a World in a Grain of Sand*
> *And a Heaven in a Wild Flower.*
> *Hold Infinity in the palm of your hand*
> *And Eternity in an hour.*¹⁰

Seen aright, the humble grain of sand and the simple wildflower make the boundless tangible; the modest space of your hand and the passing passage of an hour accommodate that which is free of containment. These things become sacred, as can a loving touch, and that awakening of holiness is a major sign that desire is connecting with an immensity that might satisfy.

The erotic piety that Blake would have encountered with the Moravians seeks to deploy this range of feelings; it is a kind of tantra that is, in fact, a longstanding aspect of Christian desire for God. Take the Ecstasy of Saint Teresa of Ávila. The scene has been represented numerous times in religious art, not least in the marble masterpiece by Bernini, which shows a youthful angel, face aflame, about to plunge a golden dart into the saint's heart and entrails. The mix of extreme pleasure and pain precipitated by the vision left Teresa moaning and 'utterly consumed by the great love of God,' as she described it.¹¹ Held by the exquisite contrary of delight and torment, Teresa felt her own self annihilated and so supremely open to the divine—and that is another sign of the direction in which an erotic feeling

# AWAKE!

Fig. 15: Image of the Transverberation or Ecstasy of Teresa, by an unknown seventeenth-century artist.

is headed. If the will of the individual is inflated then self-indulgence is indicated; if quietened, self-transcendence becomes possible.

Blake understood these conjunctions and loved Teresa's writings, often quoting them to friends.[12] And why wouldn't he? In the same paragraphs in which Teresa recalls 'the sweetness caused by this intense pain,' she also discusses the ways in which she sees angels: rarely in tangible form, more usually as apparitions.[13] He must have valued the reflections of this spiritually intelligent mystic who similarly dwelt in the in-between zones.

A further point of comparison must have appealed. Teresa explains that she did not seek these episodes, but found them happening to her as a gift from God. I think this is significant as a further indicator. Blake frequently and freely deploys erotic imagery in his work. He sketched genitals conflated with gothic structures and angels reaching out to pudenda; the vaginal and phallic were living symbols of contact to him, not taboo body parts. But I think it unlikely that he cultivated sexual sensations in the hope of glimpsing God, as a seeker keen on erotic mysticism might. For one thing, he didn't need to—the marvellous and strange happened anyway—and for another, he understood that this energy, in its contrary forms, was something better to wait on than grasp after. The pursuer of peak experiences delivered sexually or otherwise, risks becoming addicted to them and that is imprisoning.

*Heroic Love*

As with money, consumerism and progress, Blake sought liberty by understanding erotic impulses, not attempting to crush or morally proscribe them. His way is to artfully engage the spirit they bring to lead to something more: a transnomian way that follows moments which are particular, sacred, self-transcending and gifted. What this means in practice is mapping the intricacies, confusions and messiness of sexual energy, which he did too.

The results appear in the form of a poem that dates about the same time as *The Marriage of Heaven and Hell*, the late 1780s and early 1790s. The eleven-plate-long composition of verse and pictures is entitled *Visions of the Daughters of Albion*, a phrase that might be glossed as 'what is perceived by the women of England.' The gender specificity is deliberate: Blake knew the philosophy of Mary Wollstonecraft, who in these years was writing her mature work. His wary engagement with her ideas had begun a few years before, when the women's rights advocate sanctioned his illustrating an edition of her educative stories for boys and girls, which she had penned earlier in her writing career. Entitled *Original Stories from Real Life, with Conversations Calculated to Regulate the Affections, and Form the Mind to Truth and Goodness*, the tales were designed to prompt a child to reflect on kindness, cruelty and mercy. 'Good habits, imperceptibly fixed, are far preferable to the precepts of reason,' she wrote in the preface, following the educational theories of John Locke, which treat children as amenable to influences that impart what is good. That is regrettable to Blake. He certainly wanted people to value what is good, but moralising even when benign was objectionable to him: desire may be supressed and feared, not released and understood. His alternative to Wollstonecraft's stories is found in his poems about boys and girls being lost and found, which he published in *Songs of Innocence and Experience*. Take 'A Little Girl Lost.' It opens with lines which, if Wollstonecraft ever read them, would have made her wince, as Blake celebrates what to her would have been a risky and indulgent attitude to love:

# AWAKE!

*Children of the future age*
*Reading this indignant page*
*Know that in a former time*
*Love! Sweet love! was thought a crime.*[14]

Of course, Wollstonecraft had very good reasons for her approach. She argued rightly that men can be seized by an 'indulgence of vice' that is injurious to women. She therefore felt that women must not passively rely on men but take responsibility for their safety themselves, which included checking their desires.[15] Blake does not dispute the fact that some men are a real threat. But what do the women of England see by his lights?

The poem has a heroine, Oothoon, a young woman on the threshold of adult sexual experience. She is innocent at first, though in Blake's sense, insofar as she realises the encounters she seeks will prove a mixed blessing. On the one hand, making love can bring joy, liberty and the comfort of togetherness with another; on the other hand, sexual desire

Fig. 16: *Visions of the Daughters of Albion*, title page.

will expose her to the vicissitudes of relationships with other floundering human beings: her male lovers.

Her name imparts the tension. Oothoon is vulnerable: open-minded, open-hearted, as the shape and repeated letter 'o' in her name implies. Simultaneously, the fourfold 'o' evokes what she seeks: the completeness for which sexual yearning hopes, symbolised in the wholeness of a circle. But if to discover the wonder of the erotic is to open yourself to another, the character of the other to whom you are opening is crucial. Her name carries notes that are both guileless and ominous.

The epigraph with which the poem begins expresses the exposure: *The Eye sees more than the Heart knows*.[16] The heart is the primary guide but in pursuing love, the eyes will be opened, perhaps forced open. Blake tells Oothoon's story to examine this jumble of surprise, delectation and distress, and convey what might be learnt from her experience. My guess is that he needed to write the poem; he is working out what sex means to him. *Visions* is about the sexual awakening of Oothoon and is also a presentation of Blake's erotic philosophy.

The title page is dominated by Blake's flowing italic announcing its name, *Visions of the Daughters of Albion*. That is set against the backdrop of a rainbow shining through clouds. Within those clouds, various figures can be seen. Some dance, others lounge, but in the centre and low down, runs a woman, as if coming out of the page. Her arms are raised, her hair flying. She is fleeing from a bearded man, who looks like he is caught in a cloud of fire or miasma of lust.

The individual looks like an abuser, though might simultaneously be one of Blake's other creations, making here a first, brief appearance: the personification of trapped vitality that he called Urizen. The name sounds like 'your reason,' which, when treated as sovereign, is what Urizen is trapped by. The name also sounds like 'horizon,' a word that comes from the Greek for bounding, limiting, dividing and separating—all things Urizen does when uncoupled from faculties like imagination and love that enriched reasoning can serve.

The frontispiece follows and develops the sense of foreboding. It shows three people—one is Oothoon—crouching in the mouth of a cave that looks like a human skull seen side-on, opening onto an inky sea. In the sky hangs a blood-red sun, breaking through bruised-purple clouds. Two of the figures, Oothoon and a burly man, are chained to each other, back to back. The man is looking up, his hair waving, his mouth open in a cry. Oothoon is kneeling, her hair falling, her eyes cast to the ground.

# AWAKE!

Fig. 17: *Visions of the Daughters of Albion*, frontispiece.

The third figure, another man, squats beside them. His arms are wrapped around his head in bitter distress, apparently refusing what he might see or hear. Oothoon will meet these two men in the poem and the way Blake depicts them in this opening image offers interpretative clues about the meaning of the encounters.

First, there is the skull-shaped cave that engulfs them.[17] This can be taken as a reference to the skull-bound understanding of the imagination as just your private fantasies which, if right, would leave the three—and all of us—trapped in our heads: your truth is yours and mine is mine would be one contemporary summary. Hence, too, the squatting man, holding his head; he shows how it feels like to be psychologically isolated. As Oothoon will put it: *They told me that I had five senses to inclose me up, And they inclos'd my infinite brain into a narrow circle.*[18] She is complaining about a widespread assumption of our times, which her experience is going to challenge.

A second clue comes from the two bound together, Oothoon and the first man. They recall a story that Blake would have heard from his friend Thomas Taylor: the myth of Aristophanes—a tale that appears in one of Plato's seminal dialogues on love, the *Symposium*. It offers a tragicomic account of why people long for sexual partners. Way back in the mists of time, it says, human beings were cut in two. Ever since, they have gone around looking for their 'lost half'—an expression that originates with the story. This is the meaning of sexual longing, Aristophanes explains: 'It tries to make one out of two and heal the wound of human nature.'[19] Only, it doesn't. For one thing, the impulse can lead to abuse. For another, even when a coupling is characterised by love, the two will still be seeking far more than sex alone can bring. Another person can't save you but, as Plato adds, the delight of discovering a lover can initiate the search for a wider communion. That transcendent possibility begins to disclose itself by enduring the mistaken hankerings of desire. The advice that Plato conveys in his story is akin to Blake's realising that he must bear the often uncomfortable energy of contraries and resist promiscuously reacting to them—which is another way of saying that free love would bind not liberate him.

## *Holding Out for More*

The question of just what a more boundless love might look like is asked by Blake in a third illustration. It shows Oothoon kneeing again, only this time in joy. Behind her is a marvellous sunrise, filling the horizon with blazing yellows and oranges. She is before a flower and kissing a diminutive humanoid creature, who turns out to be a nymph leaping from the ground, arms outstretched, as if launching on a flight to the heavens. That looks good, only there are words above the blissful pair. The lines announce *The Argument* of the poem, meant not in the sense of a statement of its main points, but as a summary of the dilemma that Oothoon faces: the contention with which she must battle to discover what love can bring. Moreover, her predicament looks bleak.

> *I loved Theotormon,*
> *And I was not ashamed,*
> *I trembled in my virgin fears,*
> *And I hid in Leutha's vale!*
>
> *I plucked Leutha's flower,*
> *And I rose up from the vale;*
> *But the terrible thunders tore*
> *My virgin mantle in twain.*[20]

The final line goes to the heart of the matter. She will be raped. The poem will tell how her erotic desire—*I loved Theotormon*—was interrupted by another's, and look unflinchingly at how she responded, for therein lies the lasting hope.

There is a further facet of the complexities of the erotic that we modern people must wrestle with, intimated by the new name in *The Argument*: Leutha. I like the proposal that 'Leutha' echoes the surname of Martin Luther, the charismatic leader of the Reformation whose

# AWAKE!

Fig. 18: *Visions of the Daughters of Albion*, "The Argument."

troubled inner life seeded revolution in Christendom via the religious upheavals that swept through Europe in the sixteenth century. 'I was a sinner before God with an extremely disturbed conscience,' Luther wrote in a brief autobiography, a personal observation that became an assumption amongst his many followers as true of themselves; much of the self-concern that occupies modern minds stems from Luther's self-obsession.[21] Needless to say, confidence in the role of the imagination plummeted as self-preoccupation grew, a result of presuming that the imagination really produces fantasies springing solely from said self.

Blake belonged to these Protestant traditions, though as part of a pushback that particularly showed up in attitudes to sex. He agreed that sexual desire is profoundly affected by the fallen state of human beings and that sexual difference is a concrete manifestation of division within humanity; he calls biological sex a *Cloven Fiction*—not as an advocate of trans rights *avant la lettre*, but because he believed biology does not disclose the fundamental truths of who we are and can, in fact, mightily confuse us.[22] But sexual desire is no less a positive sign that human beings long to overcome their mutual estrangement, which is to say that it is not only a product of the Fall, but simultaneously an anticipation of the day when the Fall will be overcome. *Soft sexual delusions* speak of an energy that can lead aright as well as astray.[23] Congress per se doesn't ultimately satisfy, but when understood as part of the in-between world humans inhabit, people can become wise to sex's limitations, learn from what happens, and so reach out for more. Which is what Oothoon must do and, painfully, does.

We come to the poem itself, which opens by describing what was happening to her in the image with the flaming sunrise, the flower and the nymph. The flower is a *bright Marygold* and in its gilded colour, she detects an attractive though, as yet, unclear prospect.[24] So she asks it a question: '*Art thou a flower? art thou a nymph?*'—which is noteworthy as not everyone would make that link.[25] Oothoon does because she has a capacity for seeing more than one thing at once; she can see both a flower and a nymph in the bloom's living presence—nymphs being agents within the material world. She can see layers, which will turn out to be crucial for her, as it was for Blake: *For double the vision my Eyes do see | And a double vision is always with me.*[26] Much as Oothoon could see flower and nymph, Blake once saw *a Thistle across my way* that was also, inwardly, *an old Man grey*. Or there is the way he could see the sun as an object in the sky and as reflecting the light of God. *My face in fierce flames in my double sight | Twas outward a Sun: inward Los in his might*—Los being the Roman sun god's name, Sol, spelt backwards.[27] With this capacity, the many things in the lovely world can be heard calling and, so, the flower-nymph hears Oothoon's inquiry and replies. '*Pluck thou my flower,*' it insists. '*Another flower shall spring, because the soul of sweet delight | Can never pass away.*'[28] Oothoon is enchanted and places the bud between her breasts *to glow*.[29] She has embarked on her sexual adventures.

But what of the warning in *The Argument*? The flower grows in *Leutha's vale*, a shadowy state of mind in which double vision can collapse because of self-concern. Oothoon is not wholly unaware of this self-centred state of affairs and unlike Thel, in the earlier fairytale poem, she is more able to relinquish her fears and embrace a wider life. '*And thus I turn my face to where my whole soul seeks,*' she declares.[30] It's a brave moment.

What her whole soul seeks is Theotormon, the skull-hugging man of the previous images. He has an abundance of feeling, which might be good, only his name sounds a warning. 'Theotormon' is a combination of Theo, or God, and tormon, short for torment, making him 'God-tormented' or unsatisfied with existence because he feels cornered by his desires, not invited by them to know more. You meet people like this, whose erotic fantasies have been so honed and heightened by indulgence that they become incapable of desiring a real human being. Loneliness is the result and Theotormon is such a man. Stuck in his own head, his hope of love has not only disappointed but enraged him; he has become depressed and envious of what he feels so powerfully he is missing. He is Oothoon's choice, though his name does not presage her happiness and, indeed, when Oothoon draws towards him, *in wing'd exulting swift delight*,[31] the second, burly man in the poem's pictures intervenes.

He is Bromion the brute, a shockingly nasty man, happy to indulge his vices for a thrill, which include sexual pleasure boosted by fantasies of slavery and violence; his name may derive from a nickname for Dionysius, the brawling ancient Greek god: *bromius* means boisterous. And he rapes her. *Bromion rent her with his thunders; on his stormy bed | lay the faint maid*, Blake informs us, bluntly, bleakly.

The remarkable Oothoon is, though, far from defeated. She hopes that, in spite of her ordeal, she might still find love with Theotormon. But Theotormon reacts badly to the situation. He can't bear what he regards as her defilement: *he roll'd his waves around | And folded his black jealous waters round the adulterate pair*.[32] In his mind, Oothoon and Bromion are now joined together, for all that the sex was not consensual. He is tortured by seeing her molested; he is locked in by what he has witnessed, unable to get over what has happened. His disgust overwhelms him and he rejects her. Such things happen.

Oothoon, in response, remains fearless and calls on eagles. These are creatures that Blake associates with genius, which is to say an ability to look up and out and thereby see beyond the confines of the preoccupied mind; eagles can help her *awake the sun that sleeps too long*.[33] Their presence reminds her that her love is not changed by Bromion's attack and, now the brutality has passed, *the night is gone that clos'd me in its deadly black*.[34] She hopes that Theotormon will agree, too, '*that I may reflect | The image of Theotormon on my pure transparent breast*.'[35] He, though, takes a perverse pleasure in the descent of the eagles, imagining their presence in a very different way—as a purification ritual in which they *prey upon her flesh*.[36] She, in return, is willing to tolerate his fantasy, hoping it will enable him to come to her. The situation grows worse though when Oothoon next promises to procure lovers for Theotormon, which he might enjoy whilst she looks on; if she can't be his lover, she might take solace in his loving. Young love can go to extremes and the lines are hard to read, as she says: '*I'll lie beside thee on a bank & view their wanton play | In lovely copulation;*

*bliss on bliss, with Theotormon: | red as the rosy morning, lustful as the first born beam, | Oothoon shall view his dear delight, nor e'er with jealous cloud | Come in the heaven of generous love, nor selfish blightings bring.*'[37] These are desperate measures; this is the complexity of sexual desire that must be untangled. The path is not for the faint-hearted, though there is a gain in following it: a perception that would otherwise be lost.

There is a light in Oothoon that she will not let die. She is a heroine and, alongside the written account of her plight, Blake offers another side of the story that stresses the value of double vision. Accompanying the verse are images that reveal a contrary reality, and reading the poem as Blake printed it is to be exposed not only to pain and horror but a possibility, which her awakening imagination begins to see.

For example, where the text tells us about the eagles, a picture on the facing page shows a golden bird kissing Oothoon's exposed body; the image affirms her hope of connection. On the next page, above the lines in which Blake describes Theotormon's *wave shadows of discontent*, Oothoon can be seen rising in a flame-like wave above the jealous man.[38] She is shown linked by a chain to Bromion—the rape is not simply forgotten— but she is able to transcend her immediate predicament and contend with what has happened with dignity. In the midst of the mess, abused by one man and despised by another, she keeps her mind and preserves her capacity to love. Hers is an alternative response to the harassment women face; they needn't temper their desires to protect themselves, as

Fig. 19: *Visions of the Daughters of Albion*,
plate 3, detail showing the eagle and woman.

Wollstonecraft had sensibly advised, but embrace their desires and keep faith with what they most deeply seek.

But where is the justice? The poem revolves around a rape. Isn't Oothoon entitled to be morally outraged? She is, and Blake gives voice to that, not least in telling the brutal story. He also never forgets the scars of her experience. For instance, he records three times that Oothoon's sisters are with her: *The Daughters of Albion hear her woes, & eccho back her sighs*, they intone like a Greek chorus.[39] However, in so doing, I believe Blake also shows that she needs more than justice. Justice is rightly demanded following abuse. But justice is not enough; relationship must be restored. In fact, Oothoon goes a step further: she is a Christ-like heroine, one who suffers without demanding redress and, like Christ, she thereby discovers a liberty and way forward that does not depend upon recourse.

She finds a power in continuing to love, realising that her love can grow. Her mind reaches out and she detects something remarkable. She returns to what her double vision discloses. There is more. Her desire for Theotormon continues but to it is added an excitement that looks with a wider yearning into the world around and beyond her. This lights a new path and, remarkably, she begins to sing of the longings and fears of other creatures, who have their own instincts and desires,

Fig. 20: *Visions of the Daughters of Albion*, plate 7, detail showing a woman in a wave above a man.

noticing something crucial. Each is unique, though also an expression of a sacred, transcendent life principle, known in myriad forms of love. This diversity appears to her like a boundless gift, which she celebrates as she sings lines we have encountered before:

> 'With what sense is it that the chicken shuns the ravenous hawk?
> 'With what sense does the tame pigeon measure out the expanse?
> 'With what sense does the bee form cells? Have not the mouse & frog
> 'Eyes and ears and sense of touch? Yet are their habitations
> 'And their pursuits as different as their forms and as their joys.'[40]

The comparisons can seem odd at first, given what has happened to her. But she is realising that the real danger for her, following the assault of Bromion and the rejection of Theotormon, is falling into the isolation that binds them. The attack on her love becomes its moment of transformation. Her hellish experience broadens her desire beyond the human world, thereby becoming open to more: much more. Her pain, even shame, morphs into a selfless ability to wonder.

## A Different Kind of Power

Oothoon has discovered that sex and the desire for it are really symptoms of *eros*, that form of love which at heart is a yearning for communion with all creatures and life itself. Individuals in the prime of youth, like her, typically awaken to that wider pull when, at first, they feel a sexual itch. But that is just a start. For love to be fulfilled, it must grow because it can become far more than the search for another person to unite with, but an energy and passion that can join us to the world. 'Its existence is the unmistakable sign that we are spiritual creatures, attracted by excellence and made for the Good,' wrote Iris Murdoch. 'It is a reflection of the warmth and light of the sun.'[41]

Love's increase explains why Oothoon sings of being *open to joy and delight where ever beauty appears. | If in the morning sun I find it: there my eyes are fix'd | In happy copulation.*[42] That references an ancient sense of *happy copulation*, captured in the phrase used in older translations of the Bible: 'And Adam knew Eve,' as it says in the book of Genesis.[43] To make love is to know someone by feeling into their being, as they reach into yours; it is to unite, with the soul of both parties enlarged by the meeting. Oothoon has felt that expansion within herself and so she makes love with the morning sun. She now knows of an intimacy with the more-than-human and that love is not just about finding another but awakening to the holiness in all things, which is the infinite.

She still has hopes for Theotormon and puts it to him that what has happened has not ruined her, quite the opposite. But he lacks her commitment to love and continues to be self-absorbed, seeking consolation not transformation. '*Tell me where dwell the joys of old,*' he says, '*That I might traverse times & spaces far remote, and bring | Comforts into a present sorrow and night of pain?*' Bromion chips in too, mocking her claims to see more. He has absorbed the narrow Newtonian dogma and is convinced that the mind lacks access to knowledge via any route other than reason: the imaginative awakening of which she sings is fantastical. He thinks that the human task is to explore the materiality of existence, *spread in the infinite microscope*, governed by laws of nature. And indeed, a microscope can help him see more in one sense, but only more of essentially the same kind of thing, in more intricate detail. Those *minute particulars* do not convey the infinite, but are corralled to confirm a worldview.

A narrow pedantry has seized those around her, Oothoon realises; they are driven by their devotion to trapped Urizen. He prioritises the *cold floods of abstraction* that a reductive imagination seeks, a sterilising spirit active to this day when, say, the presenter of a TV science programme discusses sex in nature. The dazzle of a peacock's tale, the iridescence of a butterfly's wings, or the mimicry of an orchid's flower will be described, often with enthusiasm and wonder; the accompanying images will be astonishing. But then the entire rich pageant is put down to selfish genes or sexual selection. The generalisation supplants the particulars as illustrations of a theory, flattening reality. '*How can one joy absorb another?*' Oothoon asks bemused: '*are not different joys | Holy, eternal, infinite? And each joy is a Love.*'[44]

She also objects to moralising, the attempt to govern sexual desire by absolute rules and inflexible codes, and sees that, ironically, this gives sex a perverse form of power. Sexual ethics can foster an exclusive focus on sexual acts; an obsession with pinning down what is right or wrong overlooks the role of love and the yearning for relationships. The effect is to make it more likely that an individual will turn in on themselves, to entertain either masturbatory fantasies or anxious preoccupations: am I attractive enough? It is not love *that drinks another as a sponge drinks water*, Oothoon insists in a neat encapsulation of what masturbation can encourage, before adding a remark about the dangers of worried narcissism: *such is self-love that envies all.*[45] Jealousy as a way of life, you might say. That's a great driver of consumption; it is not good for the lonely soul.

The heroine has discovered a different form of power. This is the power of love, experienced as a desire to commune with multiple beautiful things. Blake would have known that in ancient Greek, there are two words for the one English word, power. *Exousia* is patriarchal power, exercised when one person commands another. *Dunamis* is the power of presence, experienced as a loving that attracts. Oothoon sides with the latter and it has instilled in her an unanticipated knowledge of what erotic desire can reveal; she now knows that *trees & birds & beasts & men behold their eternal joy* and she wants to join them in it. They are filled with the energy that carries them towards the All and she readies herself for that fullness. She sings once more: *Arise, and drink your bliss, for every thing that lives is holy!*[46] She is guided by the particular, the sacred, the self-transcending, the gifted.

'Nature is painting for us, day after day, pictures of infinite beauty if only we have the eyes to see them,' wrote the Victorian polymath, John Ruskin, who similarly spoke of opening sealed eyes.[47] Oothoon has discovered this key to re-enchantment: her hard-won awakening to a transcendent presence within all things. That is how her story might suggest a way of satisfying infinite human desires and longings. The process has been brutal, which is not to justify what has happened, though it is to offer an unexpected turn: instead of finding the one man she presumed her whole soul sought, she has discovered a world; her longing for the face of one other, Theotormon, has become a capacity to see the divine face in all manner of creatures and beings. Everything has become the beloved, for everything that lives is holy. She finds a magic in life, available to those who know the power that does not seek to possess but loves the radiance of what is. She can imaginatively commune with beauty wherever and however it appears.

Blake's sexuality, too, must have been tormented at times, which is why he can write about such harrowing and liberating discoveries. But there was no need for him to look outside of his marriage because, as his clairvoyance had long shown him and his imagination increasingly revealed, the springs of infinite being are omnipresent. There is a divine touch within every affection, rightly conceived; an unearthly effulgence lighting the diverse souls that inhabit Earth, be they human or other than human. This is the heart of the Blakean approach to the art of loving. He advocates not free love, but large love. '*I cry, Love! Love! Love! happy happy*

# AWAKE!

*Love! Free as the mountain wind!'* Oothoon exclaims, because mountain winds are not trapped but range widely.[48] The vision sounds appealing. It is. This is where erotic desire can lead us, properly discerned and cultivated. But truly lived this way, love has an unsparing side, no less. Oothoon had borne that and Blake was soon to experience its agony in a relationship with another person he loved.

7

WHY DOES THE RAVEN CRY?

Robert and William Blake were intimate, probably the closest of the seven children born to their parents. William referred to Robert as his 'affectionate companion' and so must have been glad that Robert was working alongside him and Catherine in the mid-1780s. A time of productive, seeming happiness beckoned them, she as an able assistant, he a promising apprentice. Only, one of the sketches that Robert made in his notebook conveyed not joy but foreboding, and it particularly impressed William. Entitled 'The Approach of Doom,' the drawing shows a group of men and women gripping each other in fright as a comet looms overhead, arching across a grey-black sky.

Comets were in the zeitgeist. The astronomer Caroline Herschel, who studied the skies with her brother William through their homemade telescopes, was in the process of discovering several. These periodic visitors from the further reaches of the solar system have long been associated with disaster and so it was natural to use one to evoke the portentousness of *the troubled air* that William, Catherine and Robert sensed around them.[1] The edginess partly came with the regular news in London of conflict abroad: during these years Britain continued to be in an almost permanent state of war with France, the Dutch Republic and others, arising from disputes over trade and sovereignty. Plus, Blake the prophet detected the diseases of progress infecting the souls of his peers and contemporaries. And then, as it turned out, the darkness directly entered their home.

Robert must have developed signs of the consumption that was to kill him soon after they moved into 28 Poland Street. As the bloody hacking grew worse, William nursed him. 'Mr Blake told me that he sat up for a whole fortnight with his brother Robert during his last illness,' recalled the painter and later associate John Linnell.[2] Robert's suffering was

William's trial, too, and it exhausted him. Following his sibling's passing, William slept for a full three days and nights. He didn't make the funeral on 11 February 1787.

Awareness of mortality presents us with the greatest of the contraries we face. If Blake is to speak to fundamental human concerns and guide us towards a transformation, dying is the most basic matter of all. And he does help. Life and death were familiar bedfellows to him and our forebears. People knew of the abyss into which life can quickly slide. In the first decade of their marriage, Catherine was to lose her mother, father and a sister; William his father, mother and a brother. Existence is fragile: innocence entwined with experience. Death is absolute, a point of no return, and regularly alarming and tragic. Blake knew that and frequently qualifies the word 'death' with another, 'eternal,' which makes the point. In the poem that reflects on the bloodshed of the times, *Europe a Prophecy*, he personifies the mortal side of our material existence, who howls about *roaming on dark and desolate mountains | In forests of eternal death, shrieking in hollow trees*.[3] The figure is terrifying, a fear that Blake knew. And yet, at the last moment of Robert's life, as his strained breathing ceased, William saw a remarkable thing. Alexander Gilchrist records the sight: 'The visionary eyes beheld the released spirit ascend heavenward through the matter-of-fact ceiling "clapping its hands for joy".'[4]

William undoubtedly mourned his brother's loss; he kept Robert's notebook with its sketch of approaching doom close to him for the rest of his life. But if the passage of death is one-way, it can also be known as an entrance to another dimension that is also here, a conviction that Blake was increasingly to articulate. He knew that the contraries of life and death speak of more. What this meant, in the case of his brother's death, was not that there is no suffering or loss; quite the opposite in fact, because with a sixth sense came a vulnerability that often left him exposed to what he called his *Nervous Fear*: the clairvoyant can intuit too much and be overwhelmed; they know indisputably that their lives are not in their own hands and so are denied the psychological props available to most of us mortals, the strategies of distraction and denial.[5] But his permeability did mean that Robert remained a companion to him, from the other side of the grave. Gilchrist continues:

> Though Blake's brother Robert had ceased to be with him in the body, he was seldom far absent from the faithful visionary in spirit. Down to late age the survivor talked much and often of that dear brother; and in

Fig. A: Portrait of William Blake made by Luigi Schiavonetti after the picture by Thomas Phillips.

Fig. B: Frontispiece to *Jerusalem: The Emanation of the Giant Albion*, showing possibly Blake stepping over the threshold, carrying a light, through the door of perception.

Fig. C: *The Marriage of Heaven and Hell*, plate 3, in which Blake presents lines that were to guide him in life, 'Without contraries is no progression'.

Fig. D: *Jerusalem: The Emanation of the Giant Albion*, showing Los being seduced by his Spectre, which is what Blake called the sense of self that believes we are individuals and isolated.

Fig. E: *Milton*, plate 42, showing a couple having made love. Blake advocated not free love but cultivating a love of all things, which I've called "large love", symbolised here by the eagle who sees across boundaries.

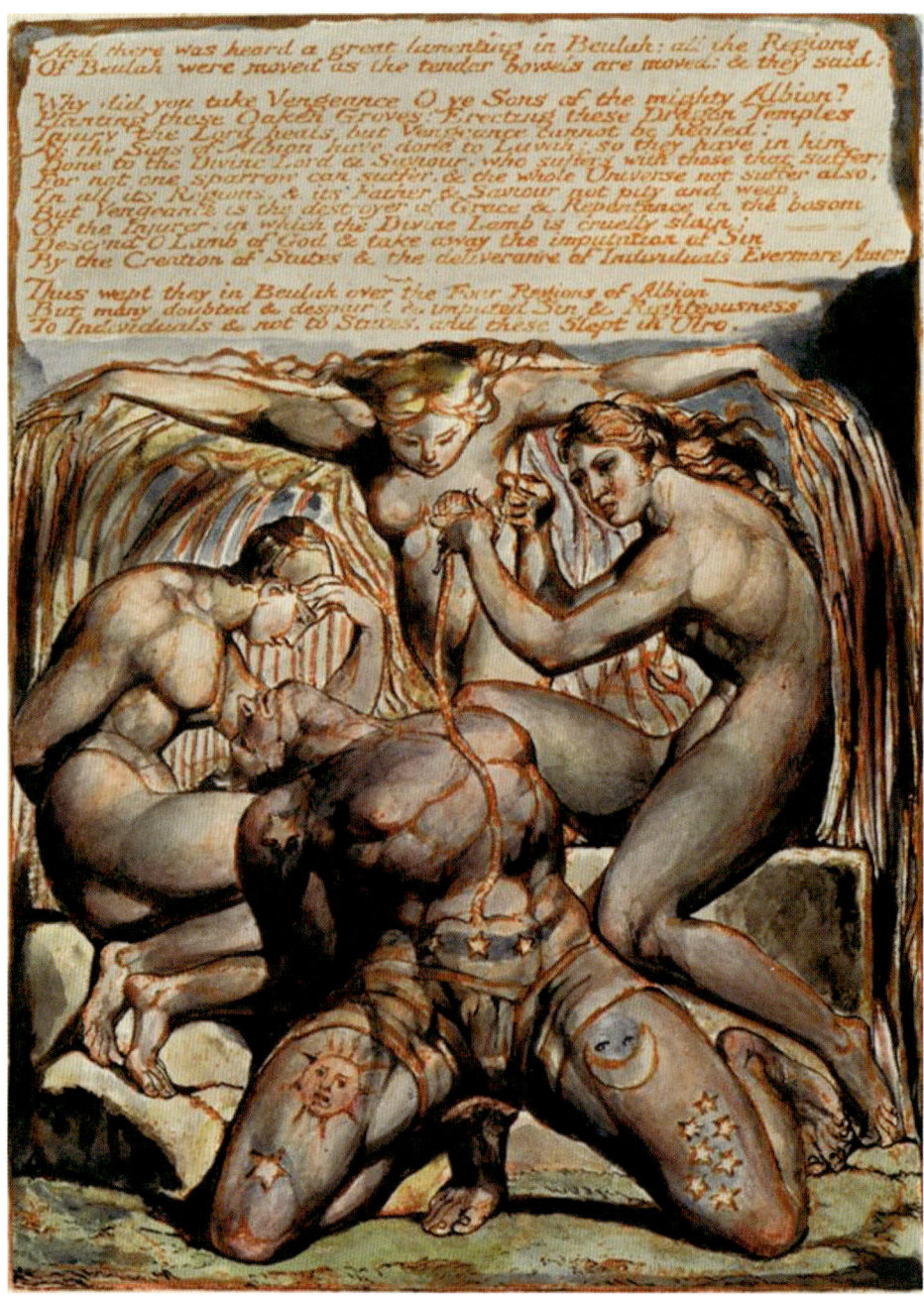

Fig. F: *Jerusalem: The Emanation of the Giant Albion*, showing Albion having his sense of connection with the cosmos stripped out of him by the daughters of memory who, unlike the daughters of inspiration, don't know of that connection directly.

Fig. G: *There Is No Natural Religion*, final plate, which summarises Blake's understanding of Christianity.

Fig. H: "Virgin and Child" painted by Blake after 1810. The image is clearly indebted to icon painting, indicating that Blake was influenced by Eastern Christianity and the Greek Orthodox Church in London in particular.

Fig. I: *Jerusalem: The Emanation of the Giant Albion*, showing a pivotal moment in Blake's epic poem when his superhero, Jerusalem, rediscovers her divine life.

hours of solitude and inspiration his form would appear and speak to the poet in consolatory dream, in warning or helpful vision.[6]

What Blake saw when Robert died is a vivid version of what many testify having witnessed a death: someone left, they didn't just pass away. The attitude of courageous sensitivity that can contemplate such experiences is captured in a letter that Blake wrote a decade later to William Hayley, a poet and writer who was to become an important patron. The occasion for writing was a merciless death which struck Hayley: that of his son. Blake wrote about the immensity of loss. He knew bereavement's agonising misery and bleakness. But he offered Hayley a complementary observation, fostered by his ability to step into the darkness and detect light.

> I know that our deceased friends are more really with us than when they were apparent to our mortal part. Thirteen years ago I lost a brother & with his spirit I converse daily & hourly in the Spirit & See him in my remembrance in the regions of my Imagination. I hear his advice & even now write from his Dictate.[7]

Regions of imagination: the in-between zone in which we live.

Blake continues by asking for Hayley's forbearance; any expression of hope at a time of desolation might offend rather than console. But, Blake explains, hard experiences can point to deeper dimensions of life, a testing of usual assumptions that he captures in one of his awe-inspiring aphorisms, penned at the end of the letter: *The Ruins of Time builds Mansions in Eternity*.[8] The line is so resonant that even the most hardened sceptic might momentarily pause at its ring. 'Ruin' is a layered word, carrying echoes of what has fallen, that which is falling, and also that which is flowing, because the word in its root links to ancient terms for tumbling and teeming. A sure dwelling place discerned amidst what is unstable can be intimated by the imagination when, through the transient, is detected a splendour and foundation set on rock not sand. The agony of love can reveal what remains untouched, the pain arising because love lasts. Vulnerability can bring connection; cracks can let the light in. Do you want, Blake implicitly asks, to turn your back on that promise?

### Breakdowns and Breakthroughs

The insight about the path of suffering is not new; the religious adepts whom Blake read stressed the same. Teresa of Ávila spoke of the gift of tears. Dante had to traverse through Hell before entering Paradise. Arjuna

## AWAKE!

in *The Bhagavad Gita*, which Blake read in the first English translation when it was published in 1785, is visited by the god Krishna as the warrior is having a catastrophic personal breakdown. Jesus intentionally followed the way to the cross. Blake knew what the saints were driving at and aimed to communicate the conviction in his imagery and verse. Lamentation is not an experience to be forgotten or bypassed but embraced. These lines, from the poem *Milton*, can help us feel and bear the softening, metamorphic heartache.

> *Why does the Raven cry aloud and no eye pities her?*
> *Why fall the Sparrow & the Robin in the foodless winter?*
> *Faint! shivering they sit on leafless bush, or frozen stone*
> *Wearied with seeking food across the snowy waste; the little*
> *Heart, cold; and the little tongue consum'd, that once in thoughtless joy*
> *Gave songs of gratitude to waving corn fields round their nest.*
> *Why howl the Lion & the Wolf? why do they roam abroad?*
> *Deluded by summers heat they sport in enormous love*
> *And cast their young out to the hungry wilds & sandy desarts.*
>
> *Why is the Sheep given to the knife? the Lamb plays in the Sun;*
> *He starts! he hears the foot of Man! he says, 'Take thou my wool*
> *But spare my life,' but he knows not that winter cometh fast.*
> *The Spider sits in his labour'd Web, eager watching for the Fly.*
> *Presently comes a famish'd Bird & takes away the Spider.*
> *His Web is left all desolate, that his little anxious heart*
> *So careful wove; & spread it out with sighs and weariness.*
>
> *This is the Lamentation of Enion round the golden Feast.*
> *Eternity groan'd and was troubled at the image of Eternal Death.*[9]

But breakdown can lead to breakthrough, which is why wisdom is often associated with trouble or trauma. The deeper knowing is not about the increase of learning or accumulation of facts but the passing away of an inadequate mindset or worldview. In that transition, our perspective can be transformed, which is why Blake grew angry and distressed when artists and thinkers, revolutionaries and authorities focused solely on trying to make Heaven a place on Earth. If, instead, Earth is a portion of Heaven, what difference might that make to human aspirations, as well as the trials of death and dying? This world does not have it all, but it can show the All.

He recommends not treating sharp divides, of which the paramount case is life and death, as mutually exclusive. They are real states, distinct states, but not contradictory states. Blake insists that perspectives which seem irreconcilable can converse, as contraries. Then can come the awareness of a *tertium quid*, that third thing, discovered and known through sustaining the tension. Oothoon had discovered that everything which lives is holy, having maintained her hope for love through brutal experiences. A comparable trinitarianism explains why death can be both unremittingly grim and a gateway. The seemingly intractable two elements precipitate an unexpected third: new life that was at first impossible, whilst grieving arrives with a love that is extended, alongside convictions that are humbled and become more open.

The same triangular process applies to the other contraries Blake examined. Take the trouble with the scientific method when it falls into single vision. That takes one pole of reality, the quantitative that is amenable to measuring, and excludes another: the qualitative and felt. But if the two are held together wider perceptions of reality surface. *To create a little flower is the labour of ages*, Blake reflects in *The Marriage of Heaven and Hell*.[10] From the imaginative pole, which is the sublime elegance of a commonplace bud, he intuits a material pole, what is now known to be tens of millions of years of fortuitous evolution, and from the two is expressing a third; a delicate bloom is nothing short of a natural miracle and, in its own way, quite as dazzling as reports of angels or visions of eternity.

That may be so, you might agree. But it is one thing to be amazed with Blake at the sanctity of nature and a world that circles like a great organism from *winter dire, Til fir'd with ardour recruited in its humble season, | It rises up on high all summer, till its wearied course | Turns into autumn.*[11] It is another thing entirely to see the dead rise through the 'matter-of-fact ceiling.'

*Penning Poetry*

Blake's riposte would be not to treat the paranormal as abnormal. Rather, stay open to what currently is hard to envisage and new impressions will come. Blake's recommendation is to see the world as it is, infinite, by living daily so as to have it revealed as such. The imagination can grow, the senses penetrate more deeply, in the first instance by noticing how the ordinary is marvellous.

The natural world is replete with that strangeness hidden in plain sight. Blake saw it and wrote of it frequently, and gave us another readily accessible example: the literary element of his craft and, in particular, his use of words to form proverbs and poems. For the art of a poet is, in a way, an everyday miracle, too: arranging units of sound in such a way that reverberations form, releasing associations that catalyse revelations about the nature of things—from vocalisations to visions.

Blake is particularly good at this kind of transporting composition—too good, in a way, because his lines can be so appealing that couplets, quatrains and whole verses can take on a life of their own. To reference one well-known example: a process of eager extraction has meant that the famous verses which begin, *And did those feet in ancient time,* have been sung and owned by everyone from suffragettes to nationalists. But then again, that only points to the power of poetry and its magic.

The energy of a line is crucial. Consider again the charming verse which opens the *Songs of Innocence.* The *Introduction* features a piper who is persuaded by a laughing child to pause, sit and write the pieces that make up the collection. Here are the crucial two stanzas:

> *'Piper, sit thee down and write*
> *In a book that all may read.'*
> *So he vanish'd from my sight,*
> *And I pluck'd a hollow reed,*

> *And I made a rural pen,*
> *And I stain'd the water clear.*
> *And I wrote my happy songs*
> *Every child may joy to hear.*

The two lines of genius are these: *And I made a rural pen, | And I stain'd the water clear.*[12] Take the first and that combination of 'rural' and 'pen': a rural pen. The association is, at first, baffling; what might be meant? 'Rural' has geographical connotations; what can the countryside or the agrarian have to do with a pen? If he had written 'rustic' that might have made more immediate sense, the pen being crafted from a hollow reed. But Blake cannot merely be remarking vacuously that the pen is not of the town. We are reading a poem and the verbal oddities generate an air of expectancy. What intuition, previously out of sight, may be conveyed by the artful juxtaposition of words? Through attending to the energy the pairing creates, a third thing emerges: meaning.

*And I made a rural pen.* This device is able to bring the charm of the countryside to our awareness, not as a bucolic scene but as a buzzing presence. The instrument the piper has whittled from a reed is as like a magician's wand as a tool for writing. In combination with 'I made,' which alludes not only to crafting but also an active imagination, the line becomes an undertaking: that of re-enchanting. A rural pen can lift veils and revive eyes as well as inscribe words. Reading the poems drafted by a rural pen restores a forgotten consciousness. Awoken, we, too, might stain the water clear, inking pens of perception and speaking again of what was occluded. Lilies might breathe. Trees might weep. Stones might speak. Fairies might tease. Have a read of the verses again and feel the activating power.

My choice of these particular lines is prompted by the Inkling Owen Barfield, who recognised their power.[13] He reflected extensively on how poetry shifts consciousness, having noticed in himself that poems can have a peculiar effect. 'What impressed me particularly was the power with which not so much whole poems as particular combinations of words worked on my mind,' he writes.[14] 'It seemed that there was some magic in it; and a magic which not only gave me pleasure, but also reacted on and expanded the meanings of the individual words concerned.' He offers an example by considering the difference between 'old prophets' and 'prophets old.' The first arrangement is prosaic: 'old prophets' brings to mind an image of aged figures, probably men with beards, living in times long past, irrelevant now. The second arrangement is poetic: 'prophets old' invites a presence of timeless sages, with a wisdom that is possibly as relevant today as it was in the period in which the prophets first lived. 'Old prophets' are of the past. 'Prophets old' matter still.

Barfield likens the effect such a switch can make to moving a wire between the poles of a magnet. The action

Fig. 21: *Songs of Innocence*, frontispiece.

generates something entirely unexpected: electricity, flowing through the wire traversing the field. A *tertium quid*. 'So it is with the poetic mood, which, like the dreams to which it has so often been compared, is kindled by the passage from one place of consciousness to another.'[15]

Barfield went further. He did not allow himself only to enjoy poetry for poetry's sake but pressed at the question of what else the power of coupled words might generate and what the revelation means. He noticed this: 'The face of nature, the objects of art, the events of history and human intercourse betray significances hitherto unknown as the result of precisely these poetic or imaginative combinations of words to which I have referred. I found I knew things about them which I had not known before.'[16] Poetry brings an enhanced apprehension of reality: conveys an otherwise hidden significance. Blake knew this, and urges his readers to test the experience for themselves by reading some poetry, if possible out loud.

Another reflection additionally unpacks things. Like any craft or practice, writing poetry relies on a calibrated mix of effort combined with receptivity, as a writer listens to the effects of words. A similarly double task is asked of a good reader: too much effort overthinks the poem; too little and the magic fails. There needs to be a focus on the immediate business of words, meanings and grammatical structures, but this concentration must not be so strong that it obscures the subtler music of the composition, which needs a more diffuse attention to detect. A poet does not require more words than a prose writer, often far fewer, but they do need to be able to convey more in the words deployed. Prophetic vision is the same, the prophet seeing the world that you or I see, but with a freer apprehension, a shrewder acumen. Words, images and actions can be trusted to have an impact beyond what might be immediately grasped; 'that combination felt right' the poet will say, open to an ingenuity working within them and beyond them. Imagination has them, more than they have imagination.

### Dining with Prophets

A witty section in *The Marriage of Heaven and Hell* examines these things. *The Prophets Isaiah and Ezekiel dined with me*, Blake opens one of the *Memorable Fancies* that form part of the discourse.[17] The two figures from the Hebrew Bible supped with him at the table of wisdom and this gave Blake the chance to ask them about the manner in which they were prophets. *I asked them how they dared so roundly to assert that God spoke to them; and whether they did not think at the time that they would be misunderstood, & so be the cause of imposition.* He wants to know since he suspects God is speaking to him, too.

Isaiah answers first, affirming that he did not see more things than anyone else, but detected more in what he saw. '*I saw no God, nor heard any, in a finite organical perception; but my senses discover'd the infinite in every thing*,' he explains. As to feeling misunderstood, Isaiah reports not caring about the consequences of what he said and did: he was free.

Blake is sceptical. Just because Isaiah felt confident does not mean that he was right, though Blake makes the point not to dismiss the prophet but to understand more about his rationale. Isaiah replies with some psychology, roundly refuting the skull-bound doctrine that perception is a matter of passively receiving sense impressions onto the *tabula rasa*, or blank slate, of the mind—as John Locke had put it. Blake agrees with Isaiah, having long concluded that Lockean solipsism is wrong.

What Blake calls *Poetic Genius* is entirely different. He recalls the etymologies of 'poetic' and 'genius': 'poetic' comes from the Greek for maker or composer; 'genius' comes from the Latin for a guardian spirit and also refers to an ability or power, hence the link between 'genius' and 'generate.' Genius is therefore a spirit within a person that originates from outside of themselves—which is why a person with *Poetic Genius* must have faith in themselves to make something with the inspiration they have received. Blake first used the expression in relation to the divine within us: *He who Loves feels love descend into him & if he has wisdom may perceive it is from the Poetic Genius, which is the Lord.*[18] The awake individual discerns divine activity within them as the essence of their humanity: *The Poetic Genius is the true Man*,[19] Blake frequently writes, which means that someone who loses touch with the way they are 'fearfully and wonderfully made,' to quote the psalmist, loses touch with their humanity.[20]

Ezekiel spells this out in the conversation. He says that the way the imagination enables human beings to perceive the world was first identified by Indian philosophers who developed a science of perception. They talked of *maya*, the anti-imaginative illusion that the world of appearances is all that is. That clouds awareness of the true, divine self. This concern was then taken up in the Hebrew tradition, Ezekiel continues, where the source of all true inspiration was recognised as the one God of the monotheistic faiths: *we of Israel taught that the Poetic Genius (as you now call it) was the first principle*, he says.[21]

# AWAKE!

The dinner party continues with Blake asking about the oddities of being a prophet. Why, for example, did Isaiah wear no clothes for three years?[22] Or why did Ezekiel eat dung and lie on his left and then right side?[23] The answer both prophets give is similar: to awaken people. Isaiah references Diogenes the Cynic, the ancient Greek philosopher who abandoned cultural conventions in Athens so as to foster direct experience of *the true Man*.[24] Ezekiel references indigenous Americans who enjoy, he says, an awareness of the infinite as he did. The link to native American traditions might seem a jump but for the fact that Blake lived during the period in which Europeans were being challenged by indigenous Americans, traveling across the Atlantic from the colonies. In Blake's mind the so-called 'noble savage' was prophetic, too, the inheritor of longstanding, respected practices. When first encountered, the shaman or crone may look odd, even repulsive, though ancient Hebrew prophets probably were, as well, and certainly did apparently crazy things to make others sit up. Strangeness is only to be expected when in the company of those who see more, though the seeming bizarre is not outlandish to them: it is what is real.

Notice something else about Isaiah and Ezekiel. They do odd things but in a quotidian setting: no clothes; lying down. The everyday is where the most enduringly remarkable is found and there is no need to induce altered states of consciousness or meditative fugues or seek anomalous experiences. Blake is clear: cultivating a broader awareness is best done amidst the minutiae of everyday life, for all that the modern world works hard at making the ordinary uneventful. In fact, the manner in which you live day by day can kill Blakean revelations.

## The Radiance Within

Consider Adam Smith's famous example of what it is like to work on a production line making pins, which he writes about in *The Wealth of Nations*. 'One man draws out the wire, another straights it, a third cuts it, a fourth points it, a fifth grinds it at the top.'[25] The point is well made (no pun intended); each step is expedient and efficient but monotonous, thereby pacifying and dulling the worker's mind. And that has ripple effects. As tasks narrow, so does the capacity for experience; as work becomes loveless, so does life. Blake similarly describes the mechanics of manufacturing and expands upon its psychological implications: *that they might file | And polish brass & iron hour after hour, laborious workmanship, |*

## WHY DOES THE RAVEN CRY?

*Kept ignorant of the use that they might spend the days of wisdom | In sorrowful drudgery, to obtain a scanty pittance of bread, | In ignorance to view a small portion & think that All.*[26] The consequence of such employment is that the desires of individuals become cramped and addicted to consumables, ruining the desire for the boundless.

An entire society may, thereby, lose touch with the infinite. This corrosive process explains why modern secular people do not for the most part stop believing in God because they have been argued out of belief. Rather, they conclude that the divine is superfluous because their way of life excludes a felt presence or need of God.

Blake could not arrest the wider trend but could protect his own augmented senses by thinking carefully about the manner of his labour. In the period after Robert's death, he ruminated on the problem of his pattern of work for weeks, and then months. The issue was fundamental. If he did not get things right, his eyes might become clouded, his vision lost.

Then, one night, Robert helped. His form appeared to tell Blake about relief etching. The next morning, William took the half-crown that was in Catherine's purse and stepped out to buy the materials needed. The copper plates suggested by Robert were familiar enough. William had been incising them since his training as an apprentice. But instead of cutting grooves and lines that could be filled with ink to make prints, Robert told William to raise letters and images from the metal by painting onto it and dissolving away what was left exposed, so that the designs appeared in prominent outline. These reliefs could then be printed by applying the required tint, followed by painting the printed pages with washes and colours. The first image that William produced by the new method was one of Robert's: 'The Approach of Doom.'

The process was technically revolutionary and a multifaceted triumph, at once an artistic process and a personal practice: a means of work and a prayer. *Illuminated Printing*, as he came to call it, meant that he could remain involved with all aspects in the production of his art, from conceiving and composing, to painting and publishing, thereby avoiding the division of labour that removes love from the making of things.[27] The new method also combined removal and revelation, another pleasingly conversing contrary; the extraneous copper was eaten by acid, the image thereby appeared. Further, whilst he could produce multiple copies of works, each one was also unique, preserving the value of the particular.

The significance of his mode of production is expressed in some of his best known lines from *The Marriage of Heaven and Hell*.

## AWAKE!

> [T]he notion that man has a body distinct from his soul, is to be expunged; this I shall do, by printing in the infernal method, by corrosives, which in Hell are salutary and medicinal, melting apparent surfaces away, and displaying the infinite which was hid.
> If the doors of perception were cleansed every thing would appear to man as it is, infinite.
> For man has closed himself up, til he sees all things thro' narrow chinks of his cavern.[28]

The leap from a method of making to a statement about the human condition—melting copper surfaces as a remedy for being spiritually closed up—can appear large. But it shows that Blake knew that how we live frames what we see. He no longer needed to fear the prison of the caverned mind.

Moreover, the process had commercial promise. He reckoned that relief etching could prove profitable, since the method could produce attractive books and plates more cheaply than had previously been possible. In a prospectus, which he published in the forlorn hope that his work would become better known, he discusses inventing *a method of Printing both Letter-press and Engraving in a style more ornamental, uniform, and grand, than any before discovered, while it produces works at less than one fourth of the expense.*[29] Catherine may have looked after the money, but William still had an eye on costs. He didn't reject progress but progressivism, the ideology that was so demeaning; he did not want to resign his poetic genius, fearing spiritual depletion, but he never felt tainted by having to earn a living, as some of the Romantics who were to follow him did.

The way one lives matters, and where you live can help, too. In the autumn of 1790, William and Catherine moved south of the river, to the market gardens and boatyards of *lovely Lambeth*.[30] They could afford to rent a whole house there and 13 Hercules Buildings gave them the space of perhaps ten rooms, ranging over four storeys including a basement. The newbuild included a garden that was said to contain marigolds, vines and a fig tree. The Blakes had become relatively prosperous and they kept a servant for a while, although let the maid go when William realised that managing domestics takes too much time. His vocation was, as ever, his priority.

The terrace is the setting for a delightful incident that sounds a tad apocryphal and so must speak of the freedom they enjoyed in this period of their lives. It concerns a visit, one day, from their friend and great patron, Thomas Butts. The summer was at its height and Butts made his way into the garden, at the end of which was a summerhouse. The couple were sitting out but, to his surprise, they were lounging in the suntrap 'freed from those troublesome disguises which have prevailed since the Fall.'[31] They were naked, without clothes like Isaiah, though Blake cried: 'Come in! It's only Adam and Eve, you know!'

Butts would have known William well enough to suspect that the poet was half joking, half intimating that Lambeth spoke of Eden. And they must have felt safe there; Blake wrote that *There is a grain of Sand in Lambeth that Satan cannot find*, meaning that in *Lambeth's mild Vale*, sight of eternity had not yet been lost to modern work practices.[32] But their little paradise was also the vantage from which the Blakes were to witness a fall from Eden which, during that decade, brought more threat: more comet-presaged doom.

8

A MIGHTY & AWFUL CHANGE

Blake's revolutionary way of printing chimed with the times, for revolutions were in the air, almost becoming a way of life: as the period has subsequently come to be called, this was the 'Age of Revolutions.' Across the Atlantic, the American War of Independence had officially concluded in 1783. Across the Channel, the French Revolution was about to explode, with the bloodshed that began in 1789 morphing into the Napoleonic wars that wrecked Europe for years. Blake was partly enthralled and more often disturbed by the turbulence. For a time, he sported the *bonnet rouge* of the sans-culotte, poorer classes in France; I imagine he wanted to try one on for size, better to know what it was like to be a 'Liberty Boy.'[1] The red cap fitted briefly, but he tore it off at the outset of the Reign of Terror. From then on he brooded on the *dark horrors* and *thick clouds* and how *a mighty & awful change threatened the Earth*.[2]

The poetry of his Lambeth years was, in large part, an effort to respond to these events, simultaneously extending his reflections from the personal and mercantile to the political and, even, civilisational. His counsel about managing the energies that grip an individual had been to bear the contending contraries and, like a drawn *Bow of burning gold*, use the tension to reach for targets beyond what an increasingly materialistic culture prized and perceived.[3] But was a similarly prophetic suggestion adequate to the greater energies that were being discharged between nations?

British freethinking had been radicalised ever since the Founding Fathers signed the Declaration of Independence in 1776. England had regarded itself as enlightened and now the flame was burning brighter amongst the Thirteen Colonies. Blake was wary of the excitement though he, in part, shared the dreams. On the plus side, the American revolutionaries saw prospects for humanity that, in addition to constitutional reform

# AWAKE!

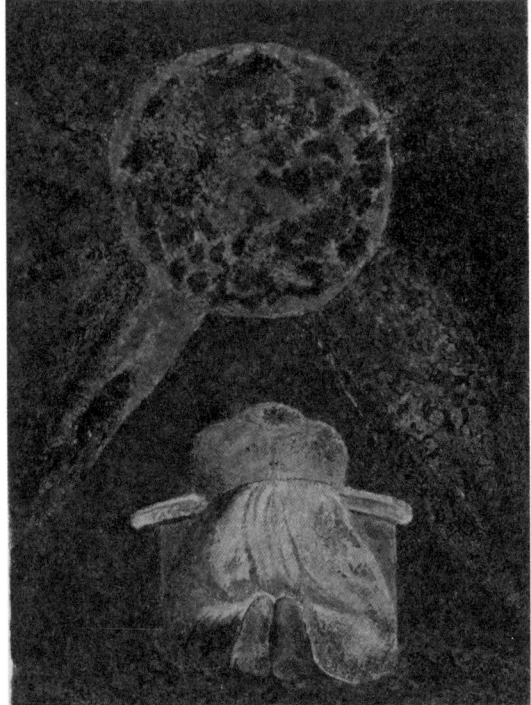

Fig. 22: *The Song of Los*, frontispiece.

and rights, included a regeneration of self-understanding and moral ambition. There was much to inspire. In one of the runaway bestsellers of the time, *Observations on the Nature of Civil Liberty*, the Welsh-born Presbyterian minister, Richard Price, wrote: '[Liberty] is the foundation of all honour, and the chief privilege and glory of our natures.'[4] The soul loves freedom not to speak out or accumulate more but because, at base, that is the condition which allows people to pursue higher things; Blake had concluded *The Marriage of Heaven and Hell* with a section entitled 'A Song of Liberty,' which spoke of awaking from *eternal sleep, For every thing that lives is Holy*.[5] That spirit was not absent from the Patriots' rhetoric but the work of Price and others tended to leave Blake feeling cautious because another aspect of their agenda was clearer. Their declarations bore all the hallmarks of his old bugbears: the rationalising and deistic.

For instance, thinkers like Thomas Paine, Joseph Priestly, Benjamin Franklin and William Godwin agitated for equality and that is not a concept in the Blakean canon. For him, equality has flattening, secular overtones; Blake did not primarily seek a meritocracy of citizens rewarded for worldly industry and talent, but more profoundly hoped for a wise culture in which individuals were guided by a yearning for the infinite: *Would to God that all the Lords people were Prophets*, he wrote.[6] Similarly, for Blake, to be 'liberal' meant to be generously spirited rather than socially inclusive, the meaning with which the word became increasingly associated as the cries for justice from America and France grew stronger. The eclipse of the inner meaning of 'liberal' matters because as demands become actions to materialise those demands, generosity of spirit tends to decline. Conversely, social inclusion readily fosters a desire for revenge amongst the oppressed, and an equally unstable mood of fear, guilt and shame amongst those deemed oppressors. Revolution prompts retaliation and retaliation can be quite as damaging as the original tyranny. Societies that become wedded to this aggression forget that friendship is the only sustainable basis for cohesion and crude narratives of oppression can wreck any chance amity has to form. *The bird a nest, the spider a web, man friendship*: remove that, remove ever feeling at home.[7]

The aim of the two poems he printed whilst living in Lambeth, *America a Prophecy* and *Europe a Prophecy*, was in part to resist these shifts by understanding the spirit of revolution. He would extend the reach of his imagery and verse from personal trials to political earthquakes in order better to grasp the energy released and clarify what can go wrong; he was in line with the old adage that the point of prophecy is not to predict the future but to change it by better discerning what's going on in the present.

## *The Energy of Enmity*

His voice grew stronger and he gained confidence with his methods. He became more able to use his art to uncover the shifts of consciousness that drive events and thereby educate the attentive reader. Insight emerges from the resonances that echo across his lines and the vigorous scenes that he wraps around the text on the page. The poems are meant to be provocative, to re-enchant. They challenge a reader, thereby illuminating the issues within a crisis without attempting neatly to resolve them, as does a cool analysis that flatters the reader with an impression of rational clarity. The invitation is to contend with the uncertainty and await the unexpected. Unlearn and reimagine: that's the way something genuinely novel appears. So what might a poem expose of a revolution and oppression more generally?

# AWAKE!

Fig. 23: *America a Prophecy*, title page.

*America a Prophecy* reflects actual events and references historical figures, including George Washington and Thomas Paine; Blake composes speeches as if delivered by key players and presents the twists and turns of the armed struggle. But his goal is not to be factual. Rebellion enlists contraries—violence to secure peace, timeless principles to inspire change, dispute to foster solidarity. But might that energy secure *Eternal Delight* as well as political progress, glimpses of the higher possibilities Blake thought so key? A distant coloniser, George III, was forcefully ejected for sure. But might the inner life of the Patriots be refashioned, too: the soul decolonised of cultural assumptions? Revolution initiates social change but can it welcome the transcendent?

*Introducing the Eternals*

The poem marks a pivotal moment in the way Blake advanced the asking of such questions. He had previously experimented with fairytale to delve into the anxieties of a single human person, in *The Book of Thel*, and then brutal experience to explore another's hopes, in *Visions of the Daughters of Albion*. However, in *America* and the works that were to follow, he adds a further form, giving a central place to characters who are collective. They personify transpersonal forces that powerfully influence groups of people as well as individuals. Calling them *the Eternals* or *Zoas*, from the Greek for 'life' in the sense of life-force, Blake seeks to study them in their own right. This is a way of understanding the energies that seize whole societies, leaving the individuals within them clashing over feelings of disorientation and elation, division and unity.

The Eternals with their forceful verve can be thought of as heroes, in the modern and ancient senses. Today, heroes are energetic individuals who are inspiring because of their commitment to what is good; they will go to the point of sacrificing all for it. Heroes also tend to be known for one virtue or ability—courage perhaps or love—and Blake's Eternals similarly stand for specific qualities: reason, feeling, energy, imagination. To that he adds the ancient notion of the hero, which brings an enchanted dimension into the frame. For the Greeks of Homer and Plato, a hero is a being who is half-human, half-divine—one who inhabits the regions in between the mortal and immortal, the finite and the infinite. They are powerful, so it is wise to fear as well as honour them, and their actions can be destructive as well as creative. A good outcome is more likely when the Eternals are in touch with the divine. They then work together, united, and reveal transcendent, transformative possibilities. Conversely, when they are not in touch with the divine, they become confused, as likely to wreak havoc as harmony amongst themselves and us. Another similarity with the ancient hero is that Blake's Eternals have qualities of poetic genius, meaning they manifest imperatives beyond themselves and the immediate circumstances. They can inspire humans, who may or may not be conscious of being in touch with them.

The Eternals can be said to be rather like modern-day superheroes, in fact. When Blake references Urizen, Los, Luvah, Rintrah, Palamabron, Rahab, Tirzah and others bear in mind Superman, the Mighty Thor, Wonder Woman or the X-Men. The association is surprisingly helpful. (That said, the recent Marvel film entitled *Eternals*, which was apparently named in direct homage to Blake, treats the superheroes as helpers of humankind whereas, as we will see, Blake's Eternals have a more ambivalent effect on their mortal counterparts.)

Blake is using the mythology to invite us into the insights he gained by clairvoyance, so reading about these characters is another way of cultivating the wider perception he thought invaluable. He is inviting us to contemplate the type of stories that might enable us to become sensitised to the spirits that surround and can invade us: to be alerted to the presence of that which we cannot wholly comprehend, and so not remain unconscious of and passive towards these forceful aspects at play. Myth performs this awakening by inviting the reader to embrace the fictitious world conveyed in the narrative, at once familiar and strange, thereby learning intuitively to relate to cosmic currents and energies. Blake is clear that figures like Urizen and Los are not straightforwardly real entities; he never refers to them outside the context of a poem. But they are imaginative entities that make sense within the perspective of the poem, thereby capturing and conveying truths. They come from in-between spaces to speak to us and a wise innocence can hear them.

Blake's prophecies are therefore not about passing moral judgement so much as detecting the structure and features of the present. They are also revelatory because they address the whole person, not only the thinking mind, thereby changing how we see, what we feel, our relationship

Fig. 24: *America a Prophecy*, frontispiece.

to what's happening, and our involvement with it. Blake believed that raising the subliminal to conscious awareness is likely to be genuinely transformative. As he put it: true revolution liberates because it focuses on *Mental Fight*, not literal war—warfare itself being *energy Enslav'd*.[8] The inner is always crucial to the prophet.

## Saviour Complex

The tragedy of war is depicted in the frontispiece of *America*. A magnificent angel sits bound by chains. His mighty knees are raised, a posture that often indicates despair in Blake. A stout head crowned by luxurious hair is bent down. The creature's athletic wings, joined to muscular shoulders, are folded. I think of him as a guardian angel, created to assist humanity, rendered impotent by the dogs of war. He laments on a broken rampart; a cannon lies on the stone pavement before him. In at least one version of the print, a cross can be seen too, discarded on the flagstones; the chief Christian emblem of sacrifice, which for Blake represents the possibility of renewal, has been misplaced in the turmoil. Nearby is a woman with her children. They are free though traumatised, presumably by the violence they have witnessed: naked and vulnerable, alive though fearful. The frontispiece, therefore, raises questions. Liberty can be won, but what does the shock of battle do to people? Ordeals brutalise and lead first to exhaustion and then compromise, the pieces moved but the game fundamentally unchanged.

The title page next, which features the words *America a Prophecy* engraved in bold capitals, includes pictorial allusions to the contraries that might bring more hope. In the top half of the page, amidst the words of the inscription, are two figures—a man and a woman, surrounded by nymphs. They are studying books, perhaps Paine's pamphlet, *Common Sense*, which advocated self-government for the American colonies. Their minds are gripped by the ambition as they think on what they might achieve, represented by the nymphs who stand, sleep and fly around them.[9] Their mood is idealistic though Blake does not overlook the bloodshed. The bottom half of the page shows a woman hugging a corpse lying on a carpet of dead bodies. Dark clouds above her shed driving rain. She knows the other side of what revolution brings and is suffering the loss that ill-considered action leaves in its wake.

The third and fourth pages start the verse itself, telling of the birth of revolutionary zeal with the appearance of a figure who personifies the sentiments that seized Blake's contemporaries and him, insofar as he sympathised with them. This superhuman hero is called Orc.

The name is ancient in English literature, signifying a hellish creature, to which Blake gives a revolutionary twist; sometimes what is associated with the fiery underworld is needed to poke that which has grown lazy and complacent in the supposedly enlightened world above. Scholars have also noted that Orc is an anagram of 'cor,' or heart, and Orc is certainly a mixed up as well as ardent Eternal, quickly moved by impulse and frustrated by constraints. He is a dangerous superhero.

Blake first tells us, in a prelude, about the awakening of Orc at the vigorous but immature age of fourteen. The freshly *hairy youth* was catapulted into adulthood by the presence of a young woman, who was waiting upon him and whom Blake describes as a *Daughter of Urthona*.[10] Urthona has been mentioned before, almost in passing, in The Marriage of Heaven and Hell.[11] Blake will say more about him as he advances his use of the Eternals, but for now Urthona—which sounds like 'earth-owner'—can be said to represent a chthonic spirit, which is to say a good guardian of place. His daughter, the maiden, is longing to escape her *shadowy* half-life as a girl, so as to embrace the fullness of adulthood.[12] She is a rebellious teenager and, unsurprisingly, Orc and she believe they can help each other and they make love, aggressively. *O what limb rending pains I feel! thy fire & my frost | Mingle in howling pains, in furrows by thy lightnings rent*, she cries.[13] There are echoes of Oothoon's rape in these lines, though the maiden welcomes the rapture in this case.

The emotions of Orc and the young woman are immediately elucidating. He feels imprisoned, simultaneously affronted by impediments to his adolescent power and convinced that he and the world need releasing from *these caverns* with the fierce freedom that he believes he can bring.[14] She identifies with the suffering of the oppressed across North and South America and believes that Orc has been sent from God *to give me life in regions of dark death*.[15] Righteousness and hope, outrage and loathing are the feelings that Blake is presenting, and they are more consequential than the careful calculations of leaders and politicians. He implies that those who feel abused by the powerful, and forgotten by their constitutional leaders, are vulnerable to those with a saviour complex—as the young woman is to Orc. *I know thee, I have found thee, & I will not let thee go: Thou art the image of God*, she cries, no small bit crazed.[16] People in despair love one deemed a hero, projecting all manner of hopes onto the skilled manipulator or canny populariser—who may believe genuinely that they can help, though are also swept along by the adulation.

The poem turns to a version of what might have been exchanged between the human antagonists. It opens as *The Guardian Prince of Albion* [George III] *burns in his nightly tent*, anxious at what bodes badly.[17] He reacts by becoming wrathful and dragon-like, readying his fire and armour. George Washington, leading the oppressed and so sure of his cause, speaks words of freedom, in Blake's shortened version of the Declaration of Independence.

> *'Friends of America! Look over the Atlantic sea.*
> *'A bended bow is lifted in heaven, & a heavy iron chain*
> *'Descends, link by link, from Albion's cliffs across the sea, to bind*
> *'Brothers & sons of American till our faces pale and yellow,*
> *'Heads deprest, voices weak, eyes downcast, hands work-bruis'd*
> *'Feet bleeding on sultry sands, and the furrows of the whip*
> *'Descend to generations that in future times forget.'*[18]

They must resist becoming as ones forgotten; they must rise.

It's stirring stuff, only *heat but not light went thro' the murky atmosphere*, as a fearsome force is unleashed.[19] *Intense!* [meaning extreme, explosive] *naked!* [meaning blameless, certain] *a Human fire, fierce glowing, as the wedge | Of iron heated in the furnace*.[20] They have summoned Orc. War is now their song, Mars their deity, though Orc is initially set on good ends—if by terrifying means—which is freedom for the captives. Simultaneously dreadful and inspiring is the cause and the hero sings: *Let the slave grinding at the mill run out into the field | Let him look up into the heavens & laugh in the bright air.*[21] There, this person will find the very heavens celebrating: *'The Sun has left his blackness & has found a fresher morning, | And the fair Moon rejoices in the clear & cloudless night; For Empire is no more, and now the Lion & Wolf shall cease.'*[22] The words are accompanied by an image of Orc sat naked on the earth, legs splayed, his muscular body angled as he gazes up. He doesn't notice the skull on the ground beside him.

The King tries to undermine the righteousness of Orc, though his highhandedness, mingled with fear, undermines the King himself: *'Blasphemous Demon, Antichrist, hater of Dignities, | Lover of wild rebellion, and transgressor of God's Law,'* he shouts, with accusations more likely to please Orc than concern him.[23] When feelings are driving events, events can quickly turn. And sure enough, *The Terror*, which is to say Orc, answers with an oration that is part visionary—*For every thing that lives is holy, life*

# AWAKE!

Fig. 25: *America a Prophecy*, plate 10, showing figure in flames.

*delights in life*—and part deluded—*Fires inwrap the earthly globe, yet man is not consum'd.*[24] This mix of hope and horror is echoed in the imagery around the texts. In one particularly dramatic depiction of Orc, the young Eternal, whom some scholars argue looks like Paine, is shown immersed in a wall of fire, arms outstretched. He blazes with the spirit of right. Blake has been called a master artist of flames and this is why. *What the hand dare seize the fire?*, he had asked in his poem, *The Tyger*.[25] The foolish hand, it might be thought.

### Political Goals

There is next a telling interlude. Blake leaves the adversaries and considers the ocean that stretches between them. The Atlantic gets its name from the myth of Atlantis, the story of a city and civilisation that was consumed by the waves because, according to Plato who is the source of the tale, the people lost their bearings. Atlantis is *archetype of mighty Emperies*, Blake notes—a model because under the great city's governance, when it thrived before corruption set in, citizens were able to live the good life and *pass to the Golden world*.[26]

Blake is raising the question of what politics is for: the securing of rights and sovereignty or the deliverance of the people in time and eternity; to try to make a heaven on Earth or to see Earth as a portal to Heaven? The question answers itself and in his mature thought, Blake presented a vision of politics that must be self-consciously multidimensional: of temporal concerns in the light of eternity. That can absorb the toing and froing, the disputes and shifting loyalties, the partial successes and inevitable failures in any realpolitik of human societies, whilst not losing hold of a transcendent possibility, beyond the issues of who is up and who is down. The ultimate end towards which a political system tends must be serving human beings who are sojourners on earth and *travellers to Eternity*: the quest for the All, infinite and eternal again, now transferred to the political plane.[27] When that larger horizon is remembered, politics can accommodate periods of disruption and decline because renewal is always conceivable. There is space for mistakes, which might make mistakes less consequential because there is never quite the feeling that the game is over and all is lost.

Blake named the imaginative city-state that can manifest this vision Golgonooza—a reference to Golgotha, the hill on which Jesus was crucified, a place simultaneously of dying and new life. Those engaged in the construction of Golgonooza, *named Art & Manufacture by mortal men*, do not lose heart.[28] Such a community is one that can hold off degenerating into the horrors of *Babylon, founded in Human desolation*, by keeping open a pathway to the golden world of *Jerusalem*.[29] Conversely, when politics fails that is because the politicians and people have lost a sense of the good life beyond material concerns like health and wealth. Politics then becomes an exercise in promissory notes, with vying leaders competing to secure power through emotive soundbites or raw feeling, and little or no real vision.

Blake is, I think, letting go of his earlier, naive hopes of what the American and French Revolutions might achieve. The confusions of war and the presence of Orc, who is really much more interested in overturning than building, do succeed in removing what bars liberty: *& their bolts and hinges melted*, Blake notes.[30] But the telling question is what happens next? Does revolution become a reflex habit, suspicion of government a national characteristic, overthrowing the establishment a perpetual, involuntary impulse?

# AWAKE!

The answer that is emerging to those questions in *America a Prophecy* is yes, as is intimated by further images with which Blake wraps the text. Positively, there are scales of justice and scenes of paradisal happiness; youngsters straddle snakes and swans, clearly enjoying their youthful energy, whilst others rise on flames that bring life. But there are also figures lost in dark waves and an old man walking through death's door. On another page Blake depicts corpses rotting on the seabed. The figure of argumentative, trapped Urizen makes a reappearance, too, looking entirely lost. Blake lambasts his obstinate pride and identifies him with the superannuated *Ancien Régime* of the British: *His stored snows he poured forth, and his icy magazines | He open'd on the deep, and on the Atlantic sea white shiv'ring*, Blake writes damningly.[31] The tragedy is that Urizen is unable to exercise his capacity to bring order because he can't descend from his high horse, hear the good aspirations of his foes, and so work out how to construct a Golgonooza from the ruins.

Blake is expressing a profound scepticism about the politics of his time and is well on the way to becoming wholly disillusioned. The British government and American Orcish dreams had both been shown to lead mostly to heartache and bloodshed. *The Wisdom of this World is Foolishness with God*, he wrote,[32] concluding that what is needed is a turn from politics to that which is sometimes called the 'pre-political': the renewal of what politics is for and, in particular, re-establishing a vision that can incorporate the dimension of the *Golden world, built in the forest of God*.[33] The mistake that much political rhetoric makes is deistic, presuming that mortal life can be perfected, or at least that an attempt should be made to reach such heights. Only it cannot.

What is not grasped, according to Blake, is that mortal life is a vantage from which an unbounded, unlimited life can be perceived; progress is not only about economic and political change but knowing the limits and conditions of this life as thresholds through which the more-than-material can be enjoyed and known. A politics premised on indefinite material growth is unsustainable, not because the Earth has limited material resources, but because material growth doesn't satisfy people, who want not more but the All.

In order to re-establish this lost horizon, Blake increasingly withdrew from politics in the latter years of the 1790s, cutting ties with the radicals. He needed space to tend his vision, away from inflamed opinions fanned by current events. *God does & always did converse with honest Men. Henceforth every man may converse with God & be a King & Priest in his own house*, he reckoned.[34] This kind of disengagement is necessary at times and Blake was following in the footsteps of other prophets. Socrates had said that his *daimonion*, or divine voice, told him not to engage in Athenian public life. Jesus had advised his followers to render to Caesar what is Caesar's, so as to remain free to render to God what is God's.[35] Blake would do likewise, and I think there is good reason to consider this as an option for today, the argument being this. Politics needn't be about highlighting what is going wrong, and either idealising the future or using it to paint apocalyptic pictures of tomorrow, but can instead be about re-envisioning the present moment. Blake's Golgonooza, *continually building & continually decaying desolate*, is a state in which people are thoroughly in the world, serving the good, but resolutely not of the world, because they know that something more than what is currently at play is needed.[36] A poverty of politics is beneficial, less enthralled by news-cycle-driven policy problems and a quest for solutions, more open to the disclosures of the imagination. Golgonooza would value curiosity about what has been lost or forgotten: spiritual intelligence alongside scientific advance. *The Divine Countenance shone in Golgonooza*, Blake avers.[37]

The rest of *America a Prophecy* deals with the battle of personalities and words, captured in further heated exchanges and bloody descriptions, including a moment when it looks as if the revolutionaries will lose: *Then had America been lost, o'erwelm'd by the Atlantic, | And Earth had lost another Portion of the infinite*.[38] Might they be sunk like Atlantis? But there is a reversal. The afflictions that the King had loosed on the Patriots fly eastward back to England and *Albion's Angels* quake.[39] Britain as a whole starts to suffer, another indicator of political calamity. London's vivacious spirit is sickened and Ireland, Scotland and Wales are filled with *shame & woe*; they are thoroughly demoralised.[40] The arts become wooden and laboured, a telling sign that a nation is atrophying, its spirit failing. As Blake later observed: *Nations are Destroy'd, or Flourish, in proportion as Their Poetry Painting and Music, are Destroy'd or Flourish!*[41] Orc secures a pyrrhic victory.

Blake printed *America a Prophecy* in 1793, a few years after the beginning of the French Revolution or, as he puts it, after *France reciev'd the Demon's light* from America and Orc's *fierce embrace* had mutated into the Reign of Terror.[42] A year later, Blake printed the sister poem, *Europe a Prophecy*, which tells this part of the story so as to understand the brutality further and secure the agenda for his alternative response.

# AWAKE!

*France's Demon*

At one level, the English reaction to events on the other side of the Channel is similar to the response to events on the other side of the Atlantic. Panic leads to a clampdown.

> *In council gather the smitten Angels of Albion;*
> *The cloud bears hard upon the council house, down rushing*
> *On the heads of Albion's Angels.*[43]

The reaction leads to a further darkening of mood and the disappearance of common human care.

> *Thought chang'd the infinite to a serpent, that which pitieth*
> *To a devouring flame; and men fled from its face and hid*
> *In forests of night.*[44]

Fear of civilisational collapse infects the populace, as the violence in France spills over into what became a long period of uninterrupted strife between the nations of Europe: the Napoleonic Wars. Blake describes what life is like, highlighting the inner feeling in his telling.

> *Every house a den, every man bound: the shadows are fill'd*
> *With spectres, and the windows wove over with curses of iron:*
> *Over the doors 'Thou shalt not,' over the chimneys 'Fear' is*
> *written:*
> *With bands of iron round their necks fasten'd into the walls*
> *The citizens, in leaden gyves the inhabitants of suburbs*
> *Walk heavy; soft and bent are on the bones of villagers.*[45]

A few key actors are having a good conflict: there is nothing like war to bring on technology in leaps and bounds. Trained professional soldiers, more secure communication channels, and better armoured warships gave England the advantage over the French, which had to rely on vast numbers of conscripts to feed a continent-wide meat machine. To Blake, England's liberty and France's liberation were simply different forms of horror, both sides efficiently feeding the *clouds of war*.[46] Drawing together references to apocalyptic imagery, the sound of cannon and technical know-how, which he attributes once more to deism and the legacy of Newton, Blake summarises the situation:

> *A mighty Spirit leap'd from the land of Albion,*
> *Nam'd Newton: he siez'd the trump & blow'd the enormous blast!*[47]

The lines are a good example of how Blake had learnt to shift, sometimes within a single sentence, from one level of description to another: an historic detail can prompt a psychological insight, which in turn prompts recognition of a cultural mood, expressed in Biblical or mythological imagery, or by reference to strings of resonant places, from Canaan and Troy, to Greenland and Hounslow. The correspondences are not arbitrary or chosen merely for impact. Blake was capturing what he saw in all its layered complexity. He was writing from the imagination. The rapid switching is what a mythological depiction can do and, in relation to portraying complexity, is therefore more accurate than an attempt at factual analysis. He was alert to the threads that link frightened minds, *shadows of men in fleeting bands upon the winds*, to absolutist politics, *Albion's Angel, smitten with his own plagues*, to a bleak science of existence:

> *Then was the serpent temple form'd, image of infinite*
> *Shut up in finite revolutions, and man became an Angel,*
> *Heaven a mighty circle turning, God a tyrant crown'd.*[48]

'Angel' there is used ironically, angels sometimes denoting for Blake a celestial disregard for the concerns of frail human wellbeing. Remember his comment: *I have always found that Angels have the vanity to speak of themselves as the only wise.*[49] A combination of callous desire, indifferent technology and dictatorial authority was the abyss towards which he felt humanity was plummeting. A death spiral had taken hold, replacing the productive tension of contraries with what Blake called *negation*, which leads to less not more. *Contraries are Positive. A Negation is not a Contrary.*[50] A failure to consider what is going on at all levels is what he felt the Orcist revolutionaries, as much as the Urizenic monarchists, got so wrong. *Thus was the howl thro' Europe! | For Orc rejoic'd to hear the howling shadows.*[51]

## The Wrong Gods

The transcendent dimension of the catastrophe is brilliantly shown in the frontispiece to *Europe* with the image usually called 'The Ancient of Days.' It has become one of the best known of Blake's terrific creations. The design features Urizen—again isolated and controlling—as an old man squatting in the clouds, gazing onto a dark earth, welding a pair of cosmic compasses in his hand. The clouds are parting behind the kneeling hero to reveal a sun-like disc. His resplendent white beard and handsome locks of hair are swept to one side by an ethereal airstream.

Fig. 26: *Europe a Prophecy*, frontispiece, "The Ancient of Days."

A widespread assumption is that this is Blake's picture of God in the form of a 'sky-god,' mocked by modern atheists, offspring of Enlightenment deists. However, the deity is the Eternal of detached rationality, who, when operating apart from feeling, intuition and common sense, inclines to the authoritarian—the ordering principle unchecked by compassion or imagination, incarnate today in utilitarian calculus, overweening bureaucracy and algorithm-based decision-making. Mistaking deluded Urizen for God must be why, in 2019, the image was projected onto the dome of St Paul's Cathedral as part of a collaboration with Tate Britain; there is a memorial slab to Blake in the colossal crypt of St Paul's. The effect was magnificent in an eerie kind of way, but the decision to beam a deadly superhero onto the curves of the famous church roof, with sightlines making it visible across London, says much about how confused people have become about eternal matters since Georgian times. Those now in charge of Wren's marble mausoleum didn't appear to know that Blake loathed the building as a product of fossilized theology. He thought the columns and cornices of its Baroque architecture ossified; he felt that the building's vast interiors were designed to intimidate, not inspire. The dome was, to him, a bung in the sky, blocking the light, not bringing it down as the stained glass in a gothic building can do. *Bleak, dark, abrupt it stands & overshadows London city.*[52] Ironically enough, his feelings about St Paul's were one day confirmed to me when one of the *priests in black gowns, walking their rounds* inside the building turned and said: 'St Paul's is not meant to be prayed in. It's built for processions.'[53]

*Europe a Prophecy* includes other potent images that continue the gloom. In one, an angel-become-devil wears black chain mail and carries a sword, accompanied by two angels in white garb who are powerless to stop him. In a second, a domestic scene shows two weeping women by a fire heating a cooking pot. Alongside them lies a dead child, limp on a white sheet, which some have suggested implies Blake is reflecting reports from France of desperate cannibalism: the body will be boiled. And their agony is not the only image of death that Blake includes. A third picture draws attention to the efforts women might make to

Fig. 27: *Europe a Prophecy*, plate 13, showing the suffering of people in times of war, in this case depicting someone who has died of plague.

stop seemingly inevitable war. This image depicts a Urizen-like man sleepwalking into darkness with a woman, clinging to his knees, failing to stop his fatal advance. The church is not let off either, as a fourth design depicts a Pope with batwings, sitting on a throne. A fifth portrays two lithe human forms, dancing through the air, blowing what look like great swirling trumpets. At first glance, the scene looks life-giving, but the text beneath reveals that the figures are angels of death, spreading plagues: *they arise in pain, | In troubled mists, o'erclouded by the terrors of strugling times.*[54] A contrary has become a negation.

A prelude to the poem continues the story of Orc and his lover that began in the prelude of *America a Prophecy*, describing what has gone amiss. This time she alone speaks, addressing another character who will play a major role in Blake's future works: the Eternal, Enitharmon. Her name is 'zenith-harmony' without the first and last letters, and she brings well-meant but often foolhardy inspiration. She listens to Orc's lover singing a song of lament: *I am faint with travail*, the young woman cries, *Like the dark cloud disburden'd in the day of dismal thunder.*[55] Her love has been dashed and she is overcome with regrets to the point of becoming suicidal: *Consumed and consuming! | Then why shouldst though, accursed mother, bring me into life?* she continues bitterly. *My voice is past*, she concludes, raising the question of what real hope is left.[56] None, Blake seems to have concluded, if you stick with the worldview spelt out in the conversation between Enitharmon and Los, the father of Orc, which frames the main sections of the poem.

Their exchange highlights the fundamental, toxic mistake. Humanity has misconceived the nature of existence; people have forgotten who they are. Blake describes two more of his superhero characters rising up to spread the lie: Rintrah and Palamabron, who in this moment can be said to personify a twisted prophetic and poetic spirit. The imaginative is deluded, they declare, the eternal is an illusion. '*Go! tell the Human race that Woman's love is Sin; That an Eternal life awaits the worm of sixty winters | In an allegorical abode where existence hath never come.*'[57] The heralds are charged with spreading a false gospel that Blake explains has usurped true Christianity. Human beings should know the holiness of everything that lives as mirrors of eternity. But in place of contact with the infinite has come competition and warfare; inspiration has been replaced by calculation. Enitharmon, who should be awake, is asleep, as is the higher consciousness of Thomas Paine and George III, Benjamin Franklin and the other players. *Man was a Dream!* Blake declares, *cavern'd.*[58] He is no longer a prophet of eternity, a friend of God, the seat of *Poetic Genius*. The ramifications are near terminal as the poem closes with Enitharmon sending her children across the face of the earth to tell of mortality and fallenness, deluded fantasy and false ecstasy, perplexity and distraction: *All were forth at sport beneath the solemn moon.*[59] The poem ends bleakly with an invocation of the Reign of Terror.

> *The sun glow'd fiery red!*
> *The furious terrors flew around*
> *On golden chariots raging with red wheels dropping with blood!*
> *The Lions lash their wrathful tails!*
> *The Tigers crouch upon the prey & suck the ruddy tide.*[60]

Enitharmon and Los, the heroes wielding muddled inspiration and flickering light, are floundering. But Blake has grasped what is at stake. Rebellious Orc is, practically speaking, the same as dictatorial Urizen, just with more energy; both embrace a way of life that trades in death. The conclusion seems pessimistic. But Blake's faith never wholly wanes. He understands that where there is movement, where there are contraries, there is energy. The light of our awareness can break out yet; the cosmos is not rule-bound but life-pervading, replete with *minute particulars* echoing the sacred, for everything that lives is holy. The possibility of rebirth and renewal lives still, if the imaginative can be reestablished. Re-enchantment not misenchantment is key, and in his next poems he will turn from the historical to the mythological. Both a spotlight on confusion, and incubator of regeneration, this literary form will enable him to find the means to sustain himself, develop his remedy, and keep *the Divine Vision in time of trouble.*[61] He will press the wisdom traditions and Christianity and present what he felt to be the one thing necessary in his time and ours: revived contact with the weird and wonderous ways of the divine. He will wrestle to re-found Golgonooza, not politically but prophetically.

# PART III

# DIVINITY

9

SYMPATHY CAME FORTH

As the nineteenth century dawned, Blake was in the midst of a drawn-out poetic and philosophical critique of the crises of the times. His verse and imagery had cast an unsparing light across the bloody mess and social paranoia that was the turmoil in Europe. The world was being reshaped by endarkenment as much as enlightenment, charged by clashing sympathies and deism—'a new religion of a rational and technical order,' to borrow the phrase of the twentieth-century philosopher, Jacques Ellul, who saw its grip tightening to this day.[1] Blake had a way of analysing the elements and, simultaneously, honouring what he had identified as crucial to freeing our souls: the vigour of the trustworthy imagination; the transnomian path that is neither authoritarian nor libertarian in search of the All; and ways of relating to a living world that he knew to be genuinely enchanted. Plus, he had that cast of charismatic, conspicuously flawed superheroes with which to relate the subterranean spirits at play.

So much for the social exigencies, but he faced personal ones as well. There grew a nagging concern that people did not want his work.

In the summer of 1794, it had seemed that his and Catherine's financial worries might become a thing of the past. He had hoped to secure a project that would bring substantial commercial returns. A young, ambitious publisher called Richard Edwards approached him to provide the illustrations for a truly grand project: a largescale edition of a popular, lengthy poem entitled *The Complaint: or, Night-Thoughts on Life, Death & Immortality*. Edward Young's blank verse was one of the most respected works of the eighteenth century, cherished by individuals as diverse as Edmund Burke and Maximilien Robespierre. Payment for the marathon effort this undertaking would require was modest, but Blake hoped the prestige upon publication would reap rewards. However, when it finally appeared, after two years' work, the edition hardly sold and was only half-heartedly published. The reason gradually became clear. Edwards had gone bust.

The disappointment after all the labour must have been hard to bear. But Blake never lost hope; he had learnt to wager his future on, one day, there being many who would love his art and seek to understand his message. His *modus operandi*, dwelling in the contraries, might not generate wealth, but it was creating riches and that would be recognised in time. And you don't need much materially to have everything spiritually, at least in principle.

Nonetheless, Blake still wanted to be better known. He had a burning mission as well as a flowing talent. He needed a rethink and took his strife to his art, beginning at about this time to work on another prophecy better aligned with the now post-revolutionary mood. *VALA or The Death and Judgement of the Eternal Man: A DREAM of Nine Nights* is a vast unfinished epic, through which Blake steadily worked out a revived way to express his ideas. He revised the dozens of pages of verse for more than ten years and, although it was never published, thereby found a way from *Death, Despair & Everlasting brooding Melancholy* to a restored awareness that *delights Shall be renew'd*.[2] But it took time, the undertaking not allowing short-cuts or bypassing. If the greatest commercial opportunity of his life had slipped through his fingers, these years became, instead, a period to refine his faith and convictions. After all, calamitous events cry out for far-reaching responses.

His next step was to develop a complete mythology to navigate what was going on. The value of myth or *Spirit of Prophecy*, Blake realised, is not fundamentally explanatory or expressive, though it may offer some of that.[3] More basically, its purpose is to allow a person, or society, to remain in a state of uncertainty and await an alternative to either grasping after half-truths as a substitute for vision, or tipping towards rage and despair, which is the other tendency when in periods haunted by disaster. Myths don't resolve the tensions or dissolve the fears: *the Night, a silver cup | Fill'd with the wine of anguish, waited at the golden feast. | But the bright Sun was not as yet.*[4] But they do sustain hope—perhaps *weak hope*, perhaps *silent hope*—which is not optimism but, rather, a trust that benign spirits are operating beneath the horizons of human awareness and will be alive still on the other side of tragedy: transcendent hope.

Moreover, a good myth is psychoactive; it might actually reduce the chance of the catastrophe it traces. This is because the layered story steadies the heat, neither wantonly fanning the flames like an agitator's conspiracy, nor aiming to quench the fire like a fearful politician's shallow promises. By being neither reactionary nor evasive—not writing *the bitter words Of Stern Philosophy* nor kneading *the bread of knowledge with tears and groans*[5]— but presenting things as they inwardly are, the narrative transmits the conviction that into the darkness an as yet indiscernible light is shining. The flame may only be seen when the individual or society has been reformed and remade within the fervour. So the times must be endured and can be because the night has meaning, though that is hard to believe. 'Fearful and suspicious as it is, the human mind yet yearns towards a greater belonging, a vaster identification,' wrote another writer-advocate of myth, Ursula K. Le Guin. 'Wilderness scares us because it is unknown, indifferent, dangerous, yet it is an absolute need to us; it is that animal otherness, that strangeness, older and greater than ourselves, that we join, or rejoin, if we want to stay sane and stay alive.'[6] Blake would have wholeheartedly agreed.

*The Modern World's Fall*

As good mythologists do, Blake borrowed a great myth from the past, refitting it for present troubles. He retold the stories of creation and fall from the book of Genesis. He perceived that what he was witnessing was a historic process doing nothing less than remoulding souls, the inner corollary of the revolution that had revised the older charged experience of the world around us. As with the original Biblical story, Blake's version reads overwhelmingly like a terrible tragedy—at least at first. The main characters long to do well for themselves and each other, only, their confusions, amplified by fears, drive them to despair and unintended destruction. They act and react in dire ways, creating muddle and mayhem that is seemingly fatal. A fall is not a setback; it is a disaster. Blake was far from alone in believing that this was the measure of the tumult in Europe. Comparable apocalypticism is similarly widespread now. And yet, where there is a felt sense of transcendence, there is hope. This is what Blake seeks to instil.

The new undertaking was to stretch over several poems, but he embarked upon it with a particularly nightmarish creation, *The First Book of Urizen*—a mix of dramatic pictures, some of Blake's strongest, and verse. The scene is set on the title page, reintroducing the scientific bind. An old man with an extravagant grey beard is seen: Urizen in his ultra-rational guise, squatting, eyes closed. His sight is limited to what ricochets

Fig. 28: *The First Book of Urizen*, title page.

within his closed mind; his imagination is hallucinatory because bound. But that does not stop him writing books, in fact it probably goads him to do so: doomster-lit, peddling cures of bitter pills. Moreover, Urizen is penning not one but two tomes simultaneously, one with his right hand, the other with his left, the one not knowing what the other is doing: that is how confused he has become. His right foot can be seen as well, protruding from an extravagant white beard—the right foot, in Blake, probably represents certitude, as it is the foot that leads when a person steps forward with confidence. Urizen is a superhero, so he seeks to act, but he does so separated from his fellow Eternals—and, for us readers, Blake signals the fundamental problem with another detail: behind the old man are two stone slabs, akin to the tablets on which Moses received the Law. They look like the back of a throne. Urizen has become the sovereign of the materialistic mindset. Blake didn't live to see the unleashing of this imperious mentality to the extent that we have, but he described the temperament that underlies misenchantment and exploitation when he wrote of Urizen's misguided fantasies.

> *For he strove in battles dire,*
> *In unseen conflictions with shapes*
> *Bred from his forsaken wilderness*
> *Of beast, bird, fish, serpent & element,*
> *Combustion, blast, vapour and cloud.*[7]

A culture that can't see beast and bird, fish and serpent, or elemental dust breathing forth its joy, is one that readily abuses these lovely things.

The next page is dominated by a radically contrasting image. An innocent baby glides through a red-orange sky, guided by a woman, who gently flies alongside, her hand tenderly leading the child. Their eyes are both open and she is, presumably, the living spirit with which every person is born, a guardian angel which those whose eyes stay clear can learn to lean on. This requires trusting powers beyond those you yourself can control or understand, to the point of yielding to them, which Urizen will fail to do. The implication is that human beings need to know how to relate to energies that can be discerned only via feeling and intuition: nature as imagination itself.

Fig. 29: *The First Book of Urizen*, preludium.

The loss of this intelligence is highlighted in the prelude to the poem. In this myth he will speak *Of the primeval Priest's assum'd power*—priests being anyone in authority who passively serve self-interested power. Blake reckons that surfacing the foolishness is key and he makes a request to the Eternals for aid in his task: *Dictate swift winged words & fear not | To unfold your dark visions of torment.*[8] The spirit of myth is one of fearlessness. His verse will convey agony.

The poem itself opens with the injunction, 'Lo': look, behold, descry. That is not just an invitation but an announcement of a central theme: the fault of misperception. People must learn to look again, for we have ceased to know ourselves or the world in which we live. The nature of that ignorance is immediately stressed, as he continues: *a shadow of horror is risen | In Eternity!*[9] The nescience that characterises the times is falling from awareness of the All, the infinite—and knowing just what Eternity might be, and what state of mind the appreciation of it entails, is the crux of the problem. With the Fall comes forgetting; Urizen does not know what he does not know. He has wandered far into a desert of his own

155

making, Blake continues—*unknown, unprolific, self-clos'd, all-repelling*.[10] Any recovery of the lost realms open to the imagination will come about not primarily by argument or action, but renewed apprehension. A cave must be escaped, doors of perception cleansed. The issue is one of conversion, the re-emergence of a third thing. Myth can help with that, in ways that persuasion or effort alone cannot. It provides a container within which suffering can be borne, breakdown tolerated, and breakthrough awaited. Following wise adepts from Plato to Emanuel Swedenborg, Blake understood that the way down is the way up—which is another insight that cannot just be told. Even those who believe it, typically struggle to hold to it; the suffering can be immense. But the trial must be undergone, it has meaning, and myth can be an aid.

Urizen is the one doing the falling in the story and soon he starts to panic and become manic. He can't relate to the things around him, so as a proxy he launches into a frenzy of analysis, like a crazed billionaire convinced that the larger the datacentre the greater the power. *Times on times he divided & measur'd | Space by space in his ninefold darkness.*[11] What is doubly sad is that his goal is admirable, or seemingly so. *I have sought for a joy without pain, | For a solid without fluctuation*, he says: a secure foundation for a happy life.[12] What's wrong with that? Well, his error grows clearer when he continues by promising to realise his dream *of peace, of love, of unity, of pity, compassion, forgiveness* by diktat. The trouble is that decrees cannot deliver these things without becoming oppressive, as is revealed when Urizen next adds: *Let each chuse one habitation… One command, one joy, one desire, One curse, one weight, one measure, One King, one God, one Law.*[13] Ask not what your country can do for you, but how you must conform for your

Fig. 30: *The First Book of Urizen*, plate 11.

country. Further, he does not even rule the roost that he hopes to govern. Human beings are marvellously various, as are all living creatures, but we are also imperfect, subject to *the seven deadly sins of the soul*.[14] Such flaws cannot simply be legislated against, any more than peace, unity and forgiveness can be enforced; the fatuity of trying to impose tolerance and inclusion comes to mind. Inevitably, the moralising mood backfires. So, in spite of his mighty and anguished labours, Urizen soon finds himself broken, *In despair and the shadows of death*.[15] He cannot actually die, being immortal, but his life becomes a living hell.

*Beast Machines*

Urizen had left the community of the Eternals and stepped out alone; his strategy is quickly found wanting. But he is also being watched. In the next section of the poem, Los appears, the noble bearer of flickering hope, as if showing that humanity can never become wholly uncoupled from the light of transcendent imagination. *The eternal Prophet* attempts to halt the descent into the meaningless void towards which Urizen is tumbling and succeeds with a remarkable act of creation.[16] He makes time and space. These dimensions were created, Blake explains, to contain suffering: to limit pain. The innovation is striking. Time, for example, can feel like a curse, as the months and years whizz by, but Blake suggests there is another side to the flow. As he writes elsewhere: *Time is the mercy of Eternity; without Times swiftness | Which is the swiftest of all things: all were eternal torment*.[17] Suffering would go on forever but for space and time to cap it. The insight is not completely original. The ancient Epicureans taught it: 'What's terrible is easy to endure' is one summary. The logic is that the more harrowing something is, the less likely it is to last. Or, as the Buddhist adage on impermanence says: 'This too shall pass.'

The thought is not a bad one, though having worked in a psychiatric hospital, I'm not convinced that there is a reliably kind correlation between depth of suffering and brevity. But there is more to Los's attempt at damage limitation. He next makes Urizen a body. The hope here is that embodiment might help Urizen snap out of his heady reasoning—though there is a flaw to Los's plan. He acts with a purely biological perception of embodiment: our form as 'beast machines,' to use the comfortless phrase of bestselling author and neuroscientist, Anil Seth.[18] Sure enough, the account that Blake pens of the creation of Urizen's head, torso and limbs reads like a Georgian public dissection. The operation, which is ominously spread over seven ages like a miserable version of the seven days of the Biblical creation, includes these lines: *A vast Spine writh'd in torment; Ribs, like a bending cavern; His nervous brain shot branches; Like a red flame, a Tongue Of thirst & of hunger appear'd.*[19] All in all, embodiment sounds like a good idea but with a body experienced as a biological robot, Urizen's anguish increases all the more: he feels himself to be in *a state of dismal woe*—wired that way, someone might say today.[20] Further, whilst time and space limit things, they also fill a person with memories and introduce new fears, such as that of being nothing but a body subject to ageing and disease.

Blake has mythologically captured the ambivalences with which we must wrestle. Modernity produces better theories, possibly; advanced technology, for sure. But also a sidelining of the animate, of the spirit, of the transcendent. Urizen, in the poem, faces the trade-off between more knowledge and less meaning. *And now his eternal life | Like a dream was obliterated.*[21] Los, as well, becomes enmeshed in the tragedy: *Cut off from life & light, frozen.* He joined Urizen to save him and traps himself in the process. That is what happens when a civilisation forgets its source. No one escapes unscathed.

Fig. 31: *The First Book of Urizen*, plate 6.

The collapse does not stop there. It brings new moods, not known to human beings before. Strange as it may seem, the key one that Blake draws out is sympathy, which he saw simultaneously uniting and dividing people around him. In the poem, he uses the word 'pity' so as to highlight the aspect of separation, adding that *pity divides the soul | In pangs.*[22] But is he right to emphasise as a problem what many would assume to be a remedy to animosities and loneliness? Moreover, people in the ancient and medieval world clearly felt sympathy for friends and the converse, hostility towards enemies, so why has it become a special issue now?

Blake had realised something momentous. Our ancestors had experienced sympathy in a dramatically different way. For example, in Middle English, 'sympathy' refers to the occult influences that were felt to propagate between living bodies. Take the planets. They were experienced as radiating dispositions that were jovial, saturnine, mercurial or lunatic and a person was said to be in sympathy, or sympathetic, when absorbing these rays. Blake describes it in this way: *Man anciently contain'd in his mighty limbs all things in Heaven & Earth.*[23] Permeability was a characteristic of living in an enchanted cosmos—which is also to say that sympathy did not mean feeling favourably towards someone from within the confines of a 'buffered self,' to use the expression of the philosopher of secularism, Charles Taylor, nor being impelled as an ethical imperative to reach out to others.[24] Rather, sympathy was a natural consequence of being porous; there was no disconnection to overcome, but the opposite: a default experience of being involuntarily enterable. This vulnerability to possibly

Fig. 32: *The First Book of Urizen*, plate 14, showing figure tormented in flames.

malign spells and forces was why people sought ways of distancing themselves from others. Magical charms and astrological signs were valued because they could minimise exposure to unwanted sympathetic possession. But modern sympathy requires precisely the reverse effort: to overcome the feeling of being cut off. *But now the Starry Heavens are fled from the mighty limbs of Albion*, Blake laments.[25]

Adam Smith and David Hume were busy developing theories of sympathy that caught the reversed sensibility. When we feel sympathy for another, they said, we are projecting onto them a memory from the store of our own experiences, according to what we infer is going on for them. And that 'never did, and never can, carry us beyond our own person,' Smith explains.[26] A similar understanding is still expounded today. Anil Seth writes that our brains extrude a continual 'controlled hallucination.'[27] That forms the basis of our experience of the world. We navigate a lonesome path through life, finding periodic solace when discovering that other people's hallucinations coincide with ours.

*Sympathy Came forth*, Blake had written in his youth and he now saw this bad trip for what it is.[28] Isolation is the baseline, vividly captured by him as cascades of feeling washing over the insurmountable walls that Los feels separate him from Urizen: *Life in cataracts pour'd down his cliffs.*[29] The point is stressed when sympathy is personified by Blake as an atomised individual. In his myth, Pity is born from Los's labours in the form of his partner, Enitharmon, and Los pities her: he pities pity, believing that feeling for another ultimately cannot reach across the abyss of separation. *He embrac'd her; she wept, she refus'd; | In perverse and cruel delight | She fled from his arms, yet he follow'd.*[30] Within this worldview, love cannot bring genuine communion but merely respite from solitude, which is presumably why people seek intensity from experiences, not intimations of the sacred; the goal is a mutual anesthetising of the pain.

### *Life in a Flatland*

The nature of pity had been a longstanding theme in Blake's poetic inquiry. 'The Divine Image,' an early poem, expresses an apparently simple account of it.

> *To Mercy, Pity, Peace, and Love*
> *All pray in their distress;*

## SYMPATHY CAME FORTH

*And to these virtues of delight*
*Return their thankfulness.*[31]

The rendition, though, is more complex than may first appear. For one thing, pity has *a human face*, as well as being *God, our father dear*; this is pity known not in the abstract, but in particular contexts and moments. This is the only way it could be known, Blake would stress, though as a result it is rarely known straightforwardly or without taint. In another poem entitled 'A Divine Image,' Blake reminds us of the converse: jealousy can have a human face, too, the face itself being *a Furnace seal'd*.[32] In other words, who knows what feelings might lurk in another's apparently kindly presence? To that doubt can be added the conditions that prompt pity for, as Blake also notes, *Pity would be no more | If we did not make somebody poor*.[33] This is to say that pity can be a cover for a more widespread lack of practical care and, even if not that, it only exists because of isolation. There would be no pity if unity were our fundamental feeling.

If you reckon that Blake is overplaying his hand, then consider why social media appears to be exacerbating social fragmentation. Compassion fatigue is a factor, amplified by being continually presented with images of suffering or joy, shuffled by the flick of a thumb. In a culture so dominated by the torrent, that itself becomes a problem because the flood insists on instant responses, which turns interactions into a binary game: I want, I don't want; I like, I don't like; I approve, I don't approve. The connection that might be healing is actually a practice in splitting. Divisions are, thereby, deepened and sustained.

To this can be added another issue, suggested to me by the work of evolutionary psychologist, Robin Dunbar. He is famous for Dunbar's number—set at about 150—which is the number of people we can expect to know personally. Beyond that circle, we inevitably relate to others via social codes and fashionable norms. In an offline world, that is a marginal concern because our circles of direct acquaintance rarely reach beyond 150. But in an online world, we are flooded with the bitter confessions and heartfelt opinions of strangers whom we can never hope to know personally. The only way we can respond to the deluge is via assumptions and stereotypes; there are just too many messages to do other than pigeonhole the people behind them. Sometimes that prompts goodwill, sometimes hostility. But the upshot is that the technology that looked at first like it offered connection, actually feeds conflict. A further factor is being uncoupled from the infinite—the third thing. That

Fig. 33: *The First Book of Urizen*, plate 26.

dislocation means we have no higher frame, no wider perspective, within which to place ourselves and others, and so feel less embroiled and a bit freer. The result is fragmentation on stilts. In a flatland, sympathy overload does indeed divide the soul.

Much is at stake and, in *The First Book of Urizen*, the Eternals try to respond to the situation. They attempt to halt the uncontained outpouring of feeling by erecting a system of *Science*, meant in its old sense of a coherent network of understanding that can bring order to chaos.[34] Blake pictures their plan as a set of silos, giving everything a place, though that also, of course, perpetuates the sense of fracture. *They began to weave curtains of darkness, | They erected large pillars round the Void, | With golden hooks fasten'd in the pillars; | With infinite labour the Eternals | A woof wove, and called it Science.*[35]

The constructions don't help Los and Enitharmon, who long to be reunited, though something unexpected does happen. As a by-product of their attempted union, the couple conceive a child. Blake has offered another meaning for the significance of sex, that alongside love it can bring procreation, and Enitharmon's pregnancy comes to term. *In his hands [Los] seiz'd the infant, | He bathed him in springs of sorrow, | He gave him to Enitharmon.*[36]

The birth is an origin story for human existence, with Los and Enitharmon a bit like Adam and Eve. The implication is that we are, in our fallen state, the product of a connection that is a combination of yearning and pity, and must learn to contend with these forces if we are to look higher. Blake borrows a name with which we are familiar to identify the

# SYMPATHY CAME FORTH

child of this predicament: Orc. We know how easily he can lose control of himself.

The story continues with another twist. Los and Enitharmon grow jealous of Orc, presumably because every time they look at him they see a unity in his individuality that they long to have for themselves. Their envy prompts them to chain him to a mountaintop and his Promethean imprisonment has a knock-on effect. He calls out and his voice stirs Urizen, who takes the science of the Eternals and makes a garden of the created world: an effort to restore a lost Eden. But the only world that Urizen can imagine in his current state of mind is Hobbesian, red in tooth and claw,

Fig. 34: *The First Book of Urizen*, plate 19.

a product of his beast-machine biological understanding of life: *For he saw that life liv'd upon death* and he makes a world accordingly.[37] *The Ox in the slaughter house moans, | The Dog at the wintry door; | And he wept & he called it Pity, | And his tears flowed down on the winds.*[38] His efforts are threatened by a tangle of emotions, which he can't unscramble, but must try to manage: *None could break the Web, no wings of fire, | So twisted the cords, & so knotted | The meshes, twisted like to the human brain. | And he call'd it The Net of Religion.* This is a Blakean origin story for religion: a system of control that binds with briars and enslaves those it promises to release.[39]

## *A Sentimental Education*

Blake has arrived at an etiological myth to account for the world manifesting around him, forged by inhuman laws, splintering sympathies, caged imaginations and a distant, half-forgotten God. He describes the quality of life people experience within it: *They lived a period of years; | Then left a noisom body | To the jaws of devouring darkness. | And their children wept, & built | Tombs in the desolate places, | And form'd laws of prudence, and* *call'd them | The eternal laws of God.*⁴⁰ The laws are not really prudent or of God, but that is how they seem and are taken to be. Result? The hedonic treadmill, lives at the grindstone and, inwardly, quiet desperation.

*The First Book of Urizen* draws to a close as one of the children of Urizen, Fuzon, leads a group who attempt to flee *the pendulous earth*, like the Israelites escaping bondage in Egypt.⁴¹ In a subsequent, shorter poem, *The Book of Ahania*, Urizen catches up with Fuzon and nails him to a tree. The allusion is to the widespread Christian belief that God the Father required a sacrifice for sin and so sent his son, Jesus, to die on the cross. Blake is signalling that whatever conclusions he will come to about Christianity, the proposal that Jesus bore a punishment due to us will not be part of it.

He clearly thought by composing verse, trusting the spirit of poetry as his guide. Take the character Ahania. The name is a reference to the Greek for pleasure, as in 'hedonic,' which, with the prefix 'a,' negates the word: in psychology, someone who is anhedonic is unable to experience pleasure. In the poem, Ahania is identified as Urizen's *parted soul*, or *emanation* as Blake will come to call the spirited aspect of ourselves that we need to embrace if we are to know our true unity with others.⁴² Divided from Ahania, Urizen's capacity for reasoning narrows and so Ahania tries to show him that *Experience & not Abstinence is the food of Intellect;* the richness of life can be the basis for reason.⁴³ She approaches him with this good news, but he grows confused and seizes her, *kissing her and weeping over her*, whilst, guilt-ridden, simultaneously blaming her and calling her *sin*.⁴⁴ We met the same sexual confusion in *Europe a Prophecy* when Enitharmon instructs her children to declare, *Go! tell the Human race that Woman's love is Sin.*⁴⁵

I think Blake is stressing that whilst sympathy divides as much as it unites, particularly when preached as a solution to a fractured society, this does not mean he is suspicious of mutual understanding and warmth per se. Rather, as before, the point is that love should not be a sticking-plaster for the trauma of life in an otherwise bleak cosmos, but rather a sacrament, an outward sign of an inner truth: the presence of Eternity awakened by the experience of love as it expands. *Where is my golden palace?* Ahania laments. *Where my ivory bed? | Where the joy of my morning hour? | Where the sons of eternity singing?*⁴⁶ She seeks the kind of sex that can awaken her to a larger, infinite, divine love.

The Urizen myth offers an advance, therefore, in terms of understanding. Ever since *The Marriage of Heaven and Hell*, Blake had been insisting that everything that lives is holy. Now, though, he has a deeper insight. He has understood why people don't see that fact: the sacred has been replaced with mere sentiment, and sentiment, no matter how keenly felt, isn't enough. Empathy, altruism, tolerance, inclusion—love is all you need, would be another way of putting it, though clearly it isn't. Blake summarises the situation: *And their thirsty cities divided | In form of a human heart. No more could they rise at will | In the infinite void, but bound down | To earth by their narrowing perceptions.*[47] What the myth has shown is that we should not focus on sympathy as a remedy, any more than morality, reason or law, but instead seek illumination. Enlightenment comes from Eternity and though that awakening may feel beyond reach, and some would say is an outdated superstition, Blake holds out for it. His telling of the claustrophobia and consequences of closed horizons, of life in Babylon not Golgonooza, might stir an imaginative re-opening, not by resorting to social revolution—the *thought-creating fires of Orc*, howling and *raging in European darkness*—but imaginative transformation: *Mental Fight*, not corporeal war; wise innocence, not emotionalism.[48] The depths of despair are like one pole of a contrary. The question is whether human beings can relocate the other transcendent pole. Blake had intimated it at the beginning of the poem, when he depicted a child being led by a guiding spirit.

The assessment is crucial today, I reckon, in part because sympathy is again in vogue. The proposal that we are, at root, narrowly Urizenic individuals making insular decisions based on calculations of self-interest has been tested and found wanting. *Homo economicus* is out, *Homo socialis* is back, yes, suggesting that relationality is the fundamental we now need. That has even become a metaphysical principle for some. Take the work of Iain McGilchrist. The philosopher and psychiatrist is becoming increasingly known for his exploration of brain lateralisation, which is the thesis that the left and right hemispheres perceive the world in radically different ways: the left makes maps and loves focus; the right is porous to others and aware of its blind spots, which makes it the seat of communion. McGilchrist develops the thesis by arguing that reality itself is fundamentally mutual. Connection exists prior to the things that are connected, because all things are first dependent upon affiliation for their existence. As McGilchrist puts it: 'relationships are primary, more foundational than the things related.'[49] So, here Blake's myth and its warning becomes highly relevant.

What the poet is saying to us is that in relationships, we shouldn't just look for sympathy and consolation, lovely though those things are. We should attend to the transcendent dimension from which that experience of our shared humanity flows. The full truth is that we strive to be known not just because we long for love; more deeply, too, when we love we can come to appreciate the shared ground of being that all beings share. When people enjoy each other's presence, they can consciously perceive Eternity, the All, which is the living fount of being. The promise, then, is not to know another as other and hope to bridge the divide, as sympathy implies. It is to know another as one more manifestation of the glorious whole, which with imagination we can see. Love, then, becomes a gateway to the infinite, a way of seeing that everything which lives is holy. Communicating this will become a key task for Blake in the final decades of his life, and typically for him, the quest will turn first to the immanent, wonderful world of nature, the reality that is closest to us. For transcendence hides in plain sight and Eternity can be held in an hour.

# 10

## NATURE, MOTHER OF ALL

William Hayley, to whom Blake wrote the moving letter of consolation when his son died, was a good person. He was no fool either but, being a landed squire, his patrician means could both aid and frustrate the socially inferior mortals on whom he turned his beneficent eye, as Blake was to discover.

In the summer of 1800, he visited Hayley in the Sussex village of Felpham, an attractive spot south of London on the floodplain between the South Downs and the English Channel. It was a slice of *England's green & pleasant Land*, a line Blake was to write whilst there; he was not immune to the charms of the coast and instantly fell in love with the wide skies and distant horizon.[1]

A few months later, he and Catherine moved to Felpham, into a three-bedroomed thatched cottage, one of only two of their houses that remain standing today. From it, across a cornfield of common land, they could walk to the pebbly beach. *It is certainly the sweetest country upon the face of the Earth*, he enthused,[2] and Catherine adored it too, at first, writing to her friend, Nancy Flaxman: 'O how we delight in talking of the pleasure we shall have in preparing you a summer bower at Felpham.'[3] The place was a change for them both.

With Hayley as patron, Blake could be sure of work, and a move from the capital promised a reduction in the cost of living, as well. The latter proved right enough—*Meat is cheaper than in London*, he reported to his friend Thomas Butts.[4] But, like other town-dwellers who flee for a seeming Eden, the Blakes underestimated the trials of the fresh air, especially when the skies clouded in autumn and winter. Fairly soon, Catherine became ill because the cottage was damp; the rheumatism she contracted plagued her for the rest of her life. Then William developed

# AWAKE!

Fig. 35: The Blakes's cottage in Felpham.

intermittent fevers, within a year of their arrival penning: *We eat little, we drink less | This Earth breeds not our happiness.*[5]

Life in the countryside had its ups and downs, though in spite of being worried about Catherine and suffering from his own *Nervous Fear*, Blake remained resilient.[6] He was more sure than ever that nothing could permanently injure him because everything that happens has meaning and, ultimately, that is for the good: *every Natural Effect has a Spiritual Cause, and Not A Natural: for a Natural Cause only seems, it is a Delusion of Ulro: & a ratio of the perishing Vegetable Memory.*[7]

The phrase takes a little unpacking but follows from the universality of the imagination. Ulro is the fallen perceptual domain within which the wilful Urizen dwells, the zone of *Bacon, Newton, Locke* in which people's minds narrow. In particular, they forget about spiritual, non-mechanistic causes, including impulses, relationships and inherent purposes. These causes possess the fundamental efficacy, Blake is saying—more so than secondary natural causes, meant here as the push and pull focused on by mechanism-based science. To put it the other way round, the push and pull is just a means by which deeper patterns and purposes express themselves.[8] Plants have purposes such as reaching for the light, which involves, say, tracking the Sun, a purpose fulfilled by phototropic cells. Animals have numerous purposes, too. Even rocks act meaningfully according to the logic of rocks: drop a stone and it falls—and it will do so with an almost perfect regularity compared with, say, dropping a cat, which will likely claw you—or elegantly bound to the ground. What Blake is stressing again is the variety of nature. Its minute particulars do not adhere to laws, though in many cases laws offer good approximations for what happens (stone behaviour is relatively easy to model this way, whereas cat behaviour is not). Instead, the many entities in the world around us follow what might be called intelligent imperatives. Blind chaos does not rule, nor invariant order, because the world lives and moves and has its being in between the two extremes; it is more like a great sea of thoughts than a welter of random thrusts. Scientists and artists alike love the brilliance of these myriad manifestations and a visionary can reveal that the meaningfulness within them is basically for the good. That is what *the perishing Vegetable Memory* forgets and the alive imagination can see.

Blake knew as much from daily experience in his workshop, where the materials and items scattered on the benches around him exhibited character, habits and preferences. His work proceeded more effectively, more efficiently and with a whole lot more reward, when treating copper, paints and burins as persons to befriend, not tools forcibly to wield. He had a direct experience of this buzzing clamour in the outdoors, too, which, in the early weeks following their move to the sea, led him to

Fig. 36: *Milton*, plate 36, showing the Blakes' cottage in Felpham.

write one of his most effortlessly dazzling poems. The lines describe him watching a sunrise creep across the waters and being awed by the glowing seascape.

> *My first Vision of Light*
> *On the yellow sands sitting:*
> *The Sun was Emitting*
> *His Glorious beams*
> *From Heavens high Streams*
> *Over Sea over Land.*

The light show then lifts him out of himself and into the warming atmosphere.

> *My Eyes did Expand*
> *Into regions of air*
> *Away from all Care,*
> *Into regions of fire*
> *Remote from Desire.*

And next, in a shift of awareness, he detects the very soul of the spectacle.

> *The Light of the Morning,*
> *Heavens Mountains adorning,*
> *In particles bright*
> *The jewels of Light*
> *Distinct shone & clear.*
> *Amaz'd & in fear*
> *I each particle gazed*
> *Astonish'd, Amazed:*
> *For each was a Man*
> *Human form'd.*[9]

### Natural Intelligence

There is more of this wonderful ecstasy which we will return to shortly, but before that pause, because the last two lines, *For each was a Man | Human form'd*, express an important feature of Blake's understanding of nature. For him, as a youngster, fields and trees had been *learning's bower*.[10] Flowers and birds had taught him about innocence and experience, and he had subsequently turned to the lifecycle of insects like butterflies and moths to figure out more of the relationship between life and death: what he called regeneration. But in this poem, he pinpoints the fundamental reason for this longstanding love of nature. His devotion reaches beyond the inspiration the living world can provide for the human observer into the extra-human *Arts of Imagination* embodied in landscapes and ecologies.[11] The crux of Blake's belief is that everything which exists has its own power and presence, speaking of the *real & eternal World of which this Vegetable Universe is but a faint shadow*.[12] This depth is what he was amazed at by his *first Vision of Light* in Felpham. Each particle bright and jewel of light *was a Man*—meant in the generic sense of 'thinking being,' from the root 'men-,' like 'mental,' meaning one who has intelligence. He saw that *On the yellow sands sitting*: nature revealed as countless independent though thoroughly interrelated creatures. The verse continues:

> *Swift I ran*
> *For they beckon'd to me*
> *Remote by the Sea*
> *Saying, Each grain of Sand,*
> *Every Stone on the Land,*
> *Each rock & each hill,*
> *Each fountain & rill,*
> *Each herb & each tree,*
> *Mountain, hill, Earth & Sea,*
> *Cloud, Meteor & Star*
> *Are Men Seen Afar.*

Nothing on earth or in the skies is merely an object and Blake is not just being hand-wavy here, or making the mistake of universalising a trippy experience triggered by sunbeams glancing from dancing waves. He is directly perceiving what the logical mind might infer from the self-evident fact that we human beings are natural beings. First premise: we are conscious. Second premise: something cannot come out of nothing. Conclusion: our consciousness cannot be *sui generis*, with nothing else like it in the cosmos; that would make our awareness into an unaccountable miracle. So the natural conclusion, for someone not constrained by the delusions of Ulro, is that we are conscious because a wider consciousness bore us, along with all that is, and further that all things in some way partake of that intelligence.

If that seems too much to stomach, Blake offers advice, spiced with a bit of a dig: try following what your imagination tells you and put aside any scepticism. The world will wake up for you. Give it a try!

# AWAKE!

*You don't believe? I won't attempt to make ye.*
*You are asleep? I won't attempt to wake ye.*
*Sleep on, Sleep on, while in your pleasant dreams*
*Of Reason, you may drink of Life's clear streams.*
*Reason and Newton, they are quite two things,*
*For so the Swallow & the Sparrow sings:*
*Reason says Miracle. Newton says Doubt.*
*Aye, that's the way to make all Nature out:*
*Doubt, Doubt, & don't believe without experiment.*
*That is the very thing that Jesus meant*
*When he said, Only Believe, Believe & Try;*
*Try, Try & never mind the Reason why.*[13]

We are inclined to forget that this world is a home, not only physically, in the sense that we depend upon planet Earth and its intricate chains of living interaction, but psychologically. We are a part of a totality and creation is a part of our whole. 'Just as our bodies are continuous with the elements, so is all that is visible, audible, tangible to us continuous with our total field of knowledge, our total consciousness,' said the poet and Blake scholar, Kathleen Raine.[14] There is no neat division between me and not-me, the animate and inanimate, inner cognition and outer behaviour, which is why Blake writes of dwelling amidst myriad subjectivities.

He rejects the idea that we merely project our feelings onto trees and mountains, animals and stars, and thereby give them a faux vitality; that is the lie of misenchantment. We do project for sure, but we can also realise that everything speaks back to us, if we listen. A discourse and exchange is possible. Our imagination connects with the imagination that is expressed in rocks and plants, thereby discovering a mutual ground and shared energy. The alert face of the world looks back at us when we look at its offspring. Sometimes they smile, sometimes grimace, sometimes weep, often they express a mood beyond comprehension. Interactions with unexpected powers and alien personalities offer opportunities for discovery, much as we get to know ourselves and others in relationships with those who are both similar and strange.

Blake's poetry is animated by this kind of encounter. In 'The Sick Rose' notice the sense of sickness stirred in you as the infestation is described. The poem is not just an extended metaphor but the surfacing of a shared, tragic predicament.

## NATURE, MOTHER OF ALL

> *O Rose thou art sick,*
> *The invisible worm,*
> *That flies in the night*
> *In the howling storm:*
>
> *Has found out thy bed*
> *Of crimson joy:*
> *And his dark secret love*
> *Does thy life destroy.*[15]

Or there is 'The Clod & The Pebble,' which asks: who do you want to be, a malleable clod of clay or a rigid pebble? They have personalities by necessity, but you have a choice.

> *'Love seeketh not Itself to please,*
> *Nor for itself hath any care;*
> *But for another gives its ease,*
> *And builds a Heaven in Hell's despair.'*
>
> *So sung a little Clod of Clay,*
> *Trodden with the cattle's feet;*
> *But a Pebble of the brook*
> *Warbled out these metres meet:*
>
> *'Love seeketh only Self to please,*
> *To bind another to Its delight;*
> *Joys in another's loss of ease*
> *And builds a Hell in Heaven's despite.'*[16]

A further poem, 'The Fly,' makes the interspecies link explicit, a buzzing fly having something profound to teach the alert human.

> *Little Fly*
> *Thy summer's play,*
> *My thoughtless hand*
> *Has brush'd away.*
>
> *Am not I*
> *A fly like thee?*
> *Or art not thou*
> *A man like me?*

# AWAKE!

*For I dance*
*And drink & sing*
*Till some blind hand*
*Shall brush my wing.*

*If thought is life*
*And strength & breadth;*
*And the want*
*Of thought is death;*

*Then am I*
*A happy fly,*
*If I live,*
*Or if I die.*[17]

The languages of nature are explored in parts of Blake's epic poem, *Milton,* including the celebrations of the dawn chorus I cited earlier. His poetic predecessor, the English radical and republican, was a huge presence in his mind, for all that Blake voiced the objection that has dogged Milton's famous *Paradise Lost* almost since its publication: Satan is the most engaging character in the poem and that can't be right. Blake enjoyed toying with this flaw when he wrote about Milton in *The Marriage of Heaven and Hell.* He joshed that Milton's writing on angels and God was fettered, whereas his lines on devils and hell broke free for the reason that Milton was *of the Devil's Party without knowing it.*[18] He felt that Milton had been too wary of that great power which floods

Fig. 37: *Songs of Innocence and Experience*, "The Sick Rose," detail showing the bloom and the worm and a human figure emerging.

all souls: desire. So, when the earlier poet wrote that Satan sought to express his longing by reigning in hell rather than being ruled in heaven, he had inadvertently exposed one of the failures of Puritan religiosity: turning Christianity from a loving creed into a moral one that would more quickly condemn than liberate us.[19] Blake began working on his rectification of Milton's misperception whilst in Felpham, with his own poem *Milton* having the telling subtitle, *To Justify the Ways of God to Men*. No small part of that justification came with reassessing the way in which nature speaks the divine language of love and desire, so that plants and animals can be known not only as possessing their own wisdom, but a wisdom that collaborates with our deliverance.

There are more lines from *Milton* below. As you read them, remember how a person with an unsteady temperament can be aided by an unwavering mountain; how a troubled spirit will find a friend in a turbulent wind; that a person who seeks illumination might contemplate the ever-illuminating sun; and a clear-sighted mind will shine before you like a star. The poetry invokes what prose can only point to, and Blake is good at capturing the insights that can free the mind from its caverns.

> *Thou seest the Trees on mountains.*
> *The wind blows heavy, loud they thunder thro' the darksom sky,*
> *Uttering prophecies & speaking instructive words to the sons*
> *Of men.*
>
> *Thou seest the gorgeous clothed Flies that dance & sport in summer*
> *Upon the sunny brooks & meadows: every one the dance*
> *Knows in its intricate mazes of delight artful to weave:*
> *Each one to sound his instruments of music in the dance,*
> *To touch each other & recede; to cross & change & return.*
>
> *Thou seest the Constellations in the deep & wondrous Night.*
> *They rise in order and continue their immortal courses,*
> *Upon the mountains & in vales, with harp & heavenly song,*
> *With flute & clarion, with cups & measures fill'd with foaming wine.*
> *Glitt'ring the streams reflect the Vision of beatitude,*
> *And the calm Ocean joys beneath & smooths his awful waves!*[20]

This terrestrial and celestial mix, uttering both gossip and praise, is why being out in nature is so restorative. Even to go for a modest walk in a city park can be, with the right attention, a discovery of spirits that are at once familiar and curious. 'The discourse of life itself [appears] in and through the myriad forms of the natural world,' Raine continues, and that revelation is tremendously liberating.[21]

### Countering Misanthropy

The conviction that *Cloud, Meteor & Star | Are Men Seen Afar* raises a particular issue, pressing now, of the place of humanity in nature.[22] The insight implies that we are at once part of the natural world and unique within it, as in fact Blake perceived all creatures to be—distinctiveness and commonality being the contraries that make a dynamic, mobile whole. But we do no less have a particularity as the animal who laughs and cries, speaks and plans with striking acuity; we seem to hold something, no doubt shared in part by other creatures, with a particular intensity. Blake suggests that this human exceptionalism, as it is called today, need not be shirked or disdained. Rather, because we are not parts but participants with a vocation to fulfil, a purpose for humanity can be discerned. Blake reckoned it was for the enlarging of consciousness, a necessity for us and all creatures to live well.

We can be aware that all creatures speak; science might, in fact, be described as the effort to encourage even stones to talk.[23] Certainly, if we don't take the task seriously, calamity looms. At one point in the unfinished poem *VALA or The Death and Judgement of the Eternal Man*, Blake writes about fallen Urizen, whose self-referential reasoning has lost this capacity. Echoes of contemporary environmental concerns are clear when he suggests how Urizen's detached voice sounded to the creatures around him. Might this be how the natural world hears humanity now?

> *His voice to them was but an inarticulate thunder, for their Ears*
> *Were heavy & dull & their eyes & nostrils closed up.*
> *Oft he stood by, a howling victim Questioning in words*
> *Soothing or Furious; no one answer'd; every one wrap'd up*
> *In his own sorrow howl'd regardless of his words, nor voice*
> *Of sweet response could he obtain tho' oft assay'd with tears.*
> *He knew they were his Children ruin'd in his ruin'd world.*
> *Oft would he stand & question a fierce scorpion glowing with gold*
> *In vain; the terror heard not. Then a lion he would Sieze*
> *By the fierce mane, staying his howling course. In vain the voice*
> *Of Urizen; vain the Eloquent tongue. A Rock, a Cloud, a Mountain*
> *Were now not Vocal as in Climes of happy Eternity*
> *Where the lamb replies to the infant voice & the lion to the man of years*

# NATURE, MOTHER OF ALL

*Giving them sweet instructions; where the Cloud, the River, & the Field*
*Talk with the husbandman & shepherd. But these attack'd him sore,*
*Siezing upon his feet & rending the Sinews that in Caves*
*He hid to recure his obstructed powers with rest & oblivion.* 24

The field that attacks rather than converses with the husbandman and shepherd echoes a predicament with which we have now become familiar: the denudation of soils and leaching of nitrates into lakes and rivers. But Blake's aim is not only negative but practical: to restore the conversation and our contribution to it.

I was reminded of this possibility when speaking with Andrew Whitley, a maker, researcher and campaigner for real bread. His concern is partly about the health of the environment but also of human beings; there has been a steady decline in the nutritional value of this basic foodstuff, Whitley has discovered, because milling by machine rips grains and reduces the elasticity of wheat proteins, reducing the quality of flour and necessitating the use of additives. (Blake almost foresaw this systemic damage when he wrote of *the wither'd field where the farmer plows for bread in vain*.[25]) Whitley is, therefore, worried about the survival of what might be called bread's intelligence preserved in cultures of bread-making. 'In the age of 'no-time dough' and 'instant yeast' we forget that for most of our bread-eating history, it was a given that the mysterious force which brought flour and water to life and made bread rise was passed on from one batch to the next,' he writes.[26] The point is that bread-making is not primarily a mechanical process but a skill requiring training and know-how; all manner of agents of transformation are involved—some seen, some unseen; some human, some other-than-human.

The science of yeast and the discovery of the numerous bacteria that contribute to the best conditions for bread-making casts a light on this complexity, Whitley continues, highlighting what is not yet well understood as well as what is. For this reason, he believes it is vital to respect the peculiarities of the ancient relationship between people and bread: knowledge is held in the associated rituals and myths. The culture reaches back at least to the so-called agricultural revolution when wheat, barley and rye began to be domesticated—though Whitley is wary of describing the history in that way because grasses and humans have co-evolved; to talk of humanity domesticating grasses, or grasses domesticating humanity for that matter, is to make the mistake of treating active participants as passive parts. Better to think of cultivation as a loving union, which the philosopher, Mary Midgley, argued is a good definition of wisdom: the intelligence that springs from communion and dialogue.[27] This wisdom dwells in the imaginative, in-between zone.

*Waste Lands*

A different example of this mutuality is found in the idea of a wilderness, much discussed in Blake's time because in the seventeenth century, there grew a widespread assumption that places untouched by human hands were sterile. John Locke, Blake's familiar foe, argued that God gave the natural world to humanity for humanity's benefit, a gain only realised when people 'subdue the Earth.' In other words, human beings bring the value-add: 'nature and the earth furnished only the almost worthless materials,' he wrote.[28] For instance, when Locke looked across the Atlantic towards remote tracts of apparently feral American forest, he saw what he called 'waste land,' coining the phrase.[29] The continent was mostly a barren wilderness to him because it had no utility or economic value.

However, the contrary view that the wilds are precious because they are untouched was in the air, too—surprisingly enough, the alternative being articulated by an erstwhile student of Locke. Anthony Shaftesbury experienced communing with nature. The philosopher and English peer saw within his soul that 'the Wildness pleases' and wrote about nature's 'masterpieces' and the pleasure they provide.[30] He was drawn to wildernesses because he detected in them a beauty beyond human contrivance, though which the imagination can appreciate. In contrast to the beauty of a garden, say, made by human hands, a desolate mountain or plunging gorge draws us because its allure originates elsewhere; our reactions to the sublime, as this wild beauty is called, speak of an imaginative order that we can both appreciate and never wholly understand—which is where its value lies: not in economics but in an aesthetics inherent in it. The untamed landscape is not barren but, marvellously, speaks of the supreme, which exceeds us, too: that is its wisdom. In time, Shaftesbury's view prevailed and Blake was influenced by it. 'Shaftesbury argued that all aspects of nature unaltered by human activity are part of a singular beautiful system,' explains Michael Gill. 'It subsequently became increasingly common to cherish wild nature as the pinnacle of beauty.'[31]

Blake sensed another aspect of the intelligence of the wilderness. Deserts and rough places not only take us out of ourselves but invite us to be remade by them; they are revered because they might change us. He was thinking of the Biblical accounts of Jesus going into the wilderness, there to be tempted by the Devil and, having wrestled with himself, emerge clearer about his task. The wilderness can be encountered as a place of challenge, as many today who visit desolate places seek to discover. *I will lead thee thro' the Wilderness in shadow of my cloud | And in my love I will lead thee*, Blake writes, recalling another famous encounter with the wilderness, that of the ancient Israelites en route to the Promised Land.[32]

For myself, I have struggled with Blake's insistence on the subjectivity of all things, unsure how to move beyond a vague, romantic sense that the Moon might calm or a horizon inspire. But then I travelled to the ashram of Ramana Maharshi in south India. This saint of Tamil Nadu, who died in 1950, often spoke of the sacred mountain that stands over the town where he taught, describing Arunachala as his guru. He would regularly circumambulate the tree-lined peak so as to stay in touch with his wise friend. I presumed the description was a colourful elaboration, excusable from a saint, until I arrived there. For it is true: the mountain's presence speaks of the inner quality that lies at the heart of Ramana Maharshi's teaching, which stresses the value of imperturbability. Moreover, there is a link between the way these perceptions are valued in the traditions of India and Blake's own development. He was an early reader of the Indian sacred text, *The Bhagavad Gita*, and learnt much from it about the way nature's intelligences can be masked.

## *Insight from India*

The *Gita* had been translated into English in the mid-1780s by an acquaintance of Blake, Charles Wilkins, a founding member of the Asiatic Society. This research body was created to further British understanding of India in one of the more constructive acts of the East India Company. Around 1809, celebrating his engagement with the *Gita*, Blake drew a picture of Wilkins consulting Brahmins, though the work is now lost. The likelihood is that for a decade or more prior to this drawing, he had been reading the *Gita* and it had become seminal in helping him to work out how to write about his prodigious perceptions. In fact, the impact of the *Hindoo* scripture can be detected all over later Blake's work.[33] The name of the holy book itself is a sign, translatable as 'the Lord's Song.' That would have resonated with Blake's appreciation of the power of combining music and words.

## AWAKE!

The rich pantheon of Blakean mythological superheroes are likely indebted to the text, and one, in particular, whom we have not yet met directly: Vala. Her name is in the title of Blake's unfinished epic, *VALA or The Death and Judgement of the Eternal Man*, and she features extensively in the finished work that came after it: *Jerusalem: The Emanation of the Giant Albion*. One of the things Blake worked out in these poems is how to capture what nature feels like when known only through the filters of Ulro. How might the enclosed mind understand the natural world and relations with it? Thinking through Vala provided an answer.

*Art thou Nature, Mother of all?* Blake muses, for Vala is his name for Mother Nature.[34] She is an expression of the tradition that personifies nature, largely because of the responses nature provokes in human beings; Mother Nature is said to be both nurturing and destructive, beautiful and wild, generous and deadly, and therefore best treated with respect and wariness.[35] Comparing that with the different attitudes fostered by Newtonian assumptions is illuminating, the biologist and author, Rupert Sheldrake, suggested to me. He argues that the mechanical turn in modern science has no place for Mother Nature, and in some ways that is a relief. A technologically-driven culture consigns her to the category of myth, meant in the pejorative sense, and assumes her power for itself, insofar as science and technology allow. Though, as is clear today, this assumption is at least partly deluded and has widespread unintended consequences.

Think of the word 'nature' itself, another one with an evolving meaning in the eighteenth century. In Latin, *natura* means birth and implies a divinely endowed wisdom of regeneration and restoration. Mother Nature, therefore, referred to the active power that births the natural world. However, in Blake's time, nature was on the way to being redescribed in impersonal terms as 'materialized logical process,' to cite T.H. Huxley, also known as Darwin's bulldog.[36] That invokes a very different set of descriptive metaphors—as if nature adheres to laws rather than manifests purposes, is driven by reproduction rather than regeneration, acts automatically rather than with responsive powers. That said, the applicability this reductive worldview is being much debated. Charles Darwin himself recognised the aptness of talking about Mother Nature when referring to evolutionary phenomena such as fertility and adaptation, though he simultaneously insisted that natural selection is not an intelligence and warned against taking his references to Mother Nature literally.[37] The upshot was that she was forced underground; people forgot how to relate to her and sought all the more to manipulate

## NATURE, MOTHER OF ALL

a world deemed purely material—though notice how she dwells even in that description: the word 'matter' is, in part, derived from *mater* or mother.

Blake saw that people were becoming less conscious of Mother Nature and, as can happen when things are repressed, that meant she was becoming frightening and shadowy. In his poems, Vala usually represents nature according to this fallen state of mind. She is experienced as having a dangerous character and isolated from her spiritual aspect, whom Blake names Jerusalem, and that diminishment explains her name: Vala is probably a pun on the Indian word *maya*, or illusion. That concept describes the ways in which human beings become ignorant of the true character of reality because *maya* veils it; Blake probably substituted the 'm' for a 'v' and derived 'Vala.'[38] The veiling makes matter seem like inert stuff and nature rule-bound, with life typically capricious. Blake describes the veil as a net of *Cruel Laws,* ensnaring *the Souls of the Dead*: nature red in tooth and claw—alien, not a friend, a presence to tame not know.[39] A

Fig. 38: *Jerusalem: The Emanation of the Giant Albion*, plate 32, Vala with her veil tempts Jerusalem, as her daughters of inspiration urge her to think again.

sense of uneasiness pervades this mindset, to which Urizen gives voice in a lamentation: *The Forests fled, | The Corn-fields & the breathing Gardens outside separated, | The Sea, the Stars, the Sun, the Moon, driv'n forth by my disease*—his disease being the failure to converse with the sea, stars, sun and moon.[40]

Conversely, when Vala is united to Jerusalem, and therefore to her visionary as well as material powers, her veil is transformed. It becomes a holy garment—*a beautiful net of gold and silver twine*.[41] Dressed by it, nature's sacred intelligence is made present.

Human beings play the major part in uncoupling Vala from Jerusalem, Blake insists, because science can raise a wall of laws and fog of maths between us and her palpable presence. Again, he is stressing that the generalising character of the scientific study of nature needs correcting, for the truth is that when well-conceived, science can enhance not hinder the relationship. This augmentation is the gift of the exceptional capacities of the human mind: listening to and loving creatures in their own languages.

Further, Mother Nature has things to say to us directly herself, not only through the creatures that she sustains. The traditional way of drawing that distinction is to speak of two aspects of nature. There is *natura naturata*, or 'nature natured,' which is the manifest world of phenomena—sea, stars, sun, moon and so on. And there is *natura naturans*, or 'nature naturing,' which is the creative power of Mother Nature herself: nature as imagination itself. Blake's work urges us to grow interested again in nature naturing, so as to complement the remarkable success that science has had with the investigation of nature natured. The extension is vital because the power gained by documenting the many things that make up the manifest world tends to go to human heads. The knowledge is exploited to develop technologies from nuclear weaponry to intensive farming. Excesses inevitably result, with the usual way of trying to constrain them being regulations and ethics: setting limits on how the technologies are deployed. But a culture in love with progress readily objects to limits and turns them into targets to exceed. The key missing move, Blake explains, is to redirect that desire for more so as to fall back in love with Nature herself, known once again as an imaginative, responsive presence to respect and collaborate with. Human beings are uniquely positioned to do that because of the capacity consciously to perceive nature naturing. In that, we might establish a relationship that can provide what ethical principles alone cannot: a wisdom of mutuality.

## NATURE, MOTHER OF ALL

I think that sensing the importance of this possibility lies behind much of the growing appeal of Indigenous ways of knowing. 'Indigenous peoples live in relational worldviews,' Melissa Nelson told me. A professor at Arizona State University, whose heritage includes Anishinaabe, Cree, Métis and Norwegian, she researches and preserves the rituals and myths around which Indigenous ways of life are structured. These patterns of organisation are partly practical but hold intelligence, too, joining skills with a lived awareness of the more-than-human. 'There is a nurturing quality to the universe that is for us like a natural law, a universal principle that we can tap into: this field of love that is the matrix of the universe,' Nelson continues. Indigenous knowledge invites us to consider the possibility of participating in the world not from assumptions of difference and isolation, but difference and communion. Blake's mythology can help in that imaginative task.

*Eternity's Sunrise*

He also takes the insight a step further. When learning to discourse with Nature's powers, another revelation becomes clear. The sacred aspect not only re-enchants the world but, when conversing with the subjectivities of *Each rock & each hill, Each fountain & rill, Each herb & each tree, Mountain, hill, Earth & Sea*, there can be detected something else. Speaking too is the eternal source of all transient things: the third, divine dimension.

As with human relationships, so with Mother Nature: we can be alerted not just to other presences but a shared ground of being and source of all vitality. This is why, when the doors of perception are cleansed, everything appears not myriad but infinite—the infinite being the one fount of *Each grain of Sand, Every Stone on the Land, Cloud, Meteor & Star*. Heaven is indeed in a wildflower, eternity is indeed in love with the productions of time, because heaven is in the flower, eternity is in the events of time. Blake advises us to enter the transcendent dimension within the immanent world via our imaginations, with words, through the arts, in the sciences. He shows how to make these disciplines a *Fiery Chariot* of *Contemplative Thought* that can enable us to make *a Friend & Companion of one of these Images of wonder, which always intreats* [us] *to leave mortal things* and thereby learn to commune with the immortal.[42] Inspiration and intuitions of Eternity will follow as a reminder of Blake's stress on the primacy of what is immediate: *It is in Particulars that Wisdom consists & Happiness too, Both in Art & in Life.*[43] *So he who wishes to see a Vision, a perfect Whole Must see it in its Minute Particulars, Organised.*[44]

In short, Mother Nature does not treat the natural world as her personal fiefdom because what she tends exists at a threshold to the All. *The Vegetable Universe*, Blake explains, meaning the world as seen biologically, *opens like a flower from the Earth's center: In which is Eternity. It expands in Stars to the Mundane Shell* [the sky's dome]; *And there it meets Eternity again, both within and without.*[45] Any finite thing reflects, in some manner or mode, an aspect of the infinite and Blake invites us to consider how Nature always displays more than a kaleidoscope of colour and tumble of activity. When imaginatively speaking with *Rock, Cloud, Mountain,* there can also be felt moving *the Spirit which Lives Eternally.*[46] This divine aspect, implicit in every exchange or encounter, helps foster the shift from possessing to participating, from grasping to loving, as with that larger awareness we are freed from feeling self-concerned, knowing that our life too is held. That awakening might be said to happen in two stages. First, our reception of the world around us is transformed from self-centredness to other-centredness. An example might be what happens when, say, at dusk, a shadowy shape on the roadside turns out to be not a threat but a shrub. In that moment, there is release from self-concerned fear, enabled by self-forgetting attention. That relief might prompt a second stage: a realisation. The shrub shares my path literally and metaphorically, having embarked on a life course, too, and shares a common wellspring. The awakening is one reason Blake remarked, *A fool sees not the same tree that a wise man sees.*[47]

The unfolding liberty might inspire a totally changed attitude to transient life, as expressed in the beautiful quatrain entitled *Eternity*.

> *He who binds to himself a joy*
> *Does the winged life destroy;*
> *He who kisses the joy as it flies*
> *Lives in eternity's sun rise.*[48]

*Kissing the joy as it flies* is the selfless stance of attention, taking delight in what passes because it participates with us in the timelessness of all things; when enjoyed without possessiveness, the All becomes present.

The possibility of living in such a transformed way is to press the next issue to consider head-on: Blake's religious convictions. They matter because God is crucial for Blake's hope that we can be changed. He came to believe that human beings can recover from the distress and destruction of the modern fall only through a revived awareness of this dimension—not as the deists traduced it, but in the form of the living deity who cries, *I am in you and you in me, mutual in love divine*.[49] The time in Felpham seemed to sharpened this emphasis for him, particularly when after almost three years, the time by the sea became marred—irretrievably so, Blake felt.

We know of two things in particular that spoilt the sojourn. First, Blake admitted to himself what had really been evident from the start, that proximity to William Hayley was stifling. The squire was devoted to the poet he regarded as his prodigy, but didn't understand the extent of Blake's aspirations. For instance, he hoped that his kind largesse would enable Blake to become his artist-companion—content, say, to execute illustrations for his own mediocre verse. But Blake needed patrons who could secure him the freedom and imaginative space required to converse with the infinite. The result was that Hayley's financial support increasingly felt to Blake like a constraint. *Mark well my words*, Blake concluded: *Corporeal Friends are Spiritual Enemies*.[50] Someone may provide for you materially, and generously to boot, and still simultaneously demoralise you.

Second, there was an unfortunate incident. Blake had an altercation with a soldier, one of many billeted in Felpham because of the clear and present danger of invasion from France. The private had paused in the Blakes' front garden, presumably to relieve himself. William took exception, manhandling the uniformed man to his lodgings, a public house that was a few yards down the road. The soldier filed a complaint, including an accusation that Blake had cursed the King. That was a treasonous hangable offence, and led to an investigation and a court case. A few months later, the trial took place. Blake was not convicted, in part due to Hayley's testimony, but the episode as a whole was unnerving for William and terrifying for Catherine, as is evident from these anxious lines that he wrote to Thomas Butts:

> O why was I born with a different face?
> Why was I not born like the rest of my race?
> When I look, each one starts! when I speak, I offend;
> Then I'm silent & passive & lose every Friend.
> Then my verse I dishonour, My pictures despise,
> My person degrade & my temper chastise;
> And the pen is my terror, the pencil my shame;
> All my Talents I bury, and dead is my Fame.[51]

Peter Ackroyd, one of Blake's recent biographers, notes that these misfortunes provoked both fresh angst and renewed resolve in Blake, leading him to become 'more assertive and determined than ever.'[52] The time had come. He and Catherine decided to move back to London and he took a replenished concern for the divine with him.

## 11

## NO OTHER CHRISTIANITY

The apartment that William and Catherine moved into upon their return to London was cramped. For the next eighteen years, 17 South Molton Street was their workshop and home. Back then it was on the far edge of London: the West End. Now the building is a smart Mayfair location for the 'Ministry of Waxing.'

In two rooms on the first floor they squeezed a bed and their possessions, plus a printing press and all the gear needed for engraving and colouring. The sea was gone, but so was the damp, and although the urban sprawl was growing, the countryside was little more than a brisk walk away. And Blake still clearly loved his hometown. *Everyone complains, yet all go on cheerfully and with spirit*, he wrote to Hayley from their modest abode in October 1803. *The shops in London improve; everything is elegant, clean, and neat; the streets are widened where they were narrow.*[1] Progress brings gains and, ever alert to the spirit around him, his letters from the period are scattered with intriguing details about the cares of everyday life. He expresses concern for King George, suffering episodes of madness, *poor man*.[2] He reports on Catherine trying the new cure of electricity for her rheumatism; apparently the treatment brought the promised relief.[3]

As to finding paid work, Blake's few loyal friends and patrons—Hayley, the Flaxmans, Fuseli, Butts—did not shirk from trying to keep him connected. But they faced a difficulty because a narrative about Blake had become fixed: he was peculiar or mad. People wanted to meet him but not part with their cash to employ him. As a commercial artist, he was therefore frequently unemployed and, to earn a living, he spent much of his time running errands for Hayley in London; the physical distance between them made the work bearable. On occasion commissions arrived, but the reviews Blake received expressed ambivalence. Connoisseurs would acknowledge his skill and talent, but simultaneously judge the designs wild and eccentric.

Finally, in 1809, Blake made what was to be his final attempt to gain recognition. He staged his only solo exhibition in his brother's haberdashery shop, and wrote an accompanying *Descriptive Catalogue*. Staging shows in such venues was working well for some artists; a year before, J.M.W. Turner had mounted one in his Harley Street townhouse that was celebrated, bringing sales and high-profile buyers. A show was worth a try.

The effort was a disaster. Blake failed to shift any of the pictures, few people came, and the catalogue tended to confirm the view amongst those who read it that he was either outlandish or insane. To be fair, this is not wholly surprising: Blake was not backward at declaring his genius and did not withhold from lampooning the *narrow blinking eyes* of the critics upon whom commercial success depended.[4] The result was that, from this point onwards, he stopped seeking publicity. He realised that he had to become reconciled to the fact that *The Cunning sures & the aim at yours*, as he called his attackers, were not going to understand him.[5] And yet, hidden in their flat, he did not relent from working on his creations: spirits and angels demanded industry. With Catherine, he carried on, producing some of his greatest work, including the beautiful *Illustrations of the Book of Job* and printings of the poems *Milton* and *Jerusalem: The Emanation of The Giant Albion*.

He complained from time to time, though typically in statements softened by wit. *Money flies from me,* he observed in another letter to Hayley. *Profit never ventures upon my Threshold, tho' every other man's doorstone is worn down into the very Earth by the footsteps of the fiends of commerce.*[6] Hope was never far from his thoughts either, though, as a man now in his fifties, this was not hope that his material fortunes might change, but that his efforts were still blessed and carried gravity. The awareness brought comfort and was testament to a settled philosophy of life, which he had found confirmed in the *Gita*, and knew as well from the lives of Socrates and Jesus: rejection comes to those who are not understood; but the task, then, is to stay true and not be affected by the ridicule. Blake summed up the attitude and the faith that sustains it with a few short lines that could be contemplated for a lifetime.

> *It is right it should be so:*
> *Man was made for Joy & Woe,*
> *And when this we rightly know*
> *Thro' the World we safely go.*

Fig. 39: *Chaucer's Canterbury Pilgrims*, 1810, similar to a picture Blake showed at his 1809 exhibition.

## AWAKE!

*Joy & Woe are woven fine,*
*A Clothing for the Soul divine;*
*Under every grief & pine*
*Runs a joy with silken twine.*[7]

He lived with demons and a wearing sense of anxiety, but also a direct experience of the Kingdom of Heaven that can be known on Earth. Joy and woe had become familiar contraries to him, often intertwined, though the light rarely left him for long. As Catherine told one confused admirer who paid them attention after they returned from Felpham: 'I have very little of Mr. Blake's company; he is always in Paradise.'[8] So what did Blake find there? What convictions restored his equanimity and, moreover, inspired him to keep speaking with unfailing tenacity to an indifferent public, sure that his work might yet redeem the times? This was his Christianity.

Blake's struggles in Felpham and back again in London renewed his sense that the faith was key. He had felt the threat of breakdown and what saved him was a deep-rooted sense of trust: he was not an isolated individual fated to bear the burdens of life alone; he was a person who could draw on a vitality that was closer to him than he was to himself and also reached way beyond him. To put it more generally: yes, human beings suffer existential crises but the dread can come to be known as an invitation to be aware of that which we do not possess but which possesses us. *Under every grief & pine | Runs a joy with silken twine.* This divine thread Blake recognised through the figure of Jesus. The man from Nazareth accepted life and death, joy and agony, hope and despair without that compromising his awareness of God. He is a type for all people, manifesting the intimacy of divinity and humanity, *mutual in love divine.*[9]

Jesus features regularly in Blake's compositions before the crises of his midlife, if with less frequency than was to come and less of a sense of urgency. For the younger Blake, Jesus was a model revolutionary, standing not for the ideals of revolt and reform, but mercy and fellowship. Blake spotted that Jesus's greatest innovation was advocating an almost reckless belief in the forgiveness of sins, a virtue which is not found in pre-Christian philosophy. In an unpublished late work, *The Everlasting Gospel*, Blake imagines a conversation. '*There is not one Moral virtue that Jesus Inculcated but Plato & Cicero did Inculcate before him.*' '*What then did Christ Inculcate?*' '*Forgiveness of Sins. This alone is the Gospel, & this is the Life & Immortality brought to light by Jesus.*'[10] Everyone will be saved.

# NO OTHER CHRISTIANITY

Forgiveness is central because to forgive and be forgiven frees us from guilt and the quest for revenge, thereby opening the transnomian path, which neither obeys for obedience's sake, nor disobeys in empty, libertarian protest. *All deities reside in the human breast*, Blake had insisted, which means that conscience can be attuned to and followed.[11] That is the dissenter's way.

Now, though, in his later life, Blake elaborated his understanding of Christianity further. He marvellously re-expressed it in a form that was known amongst the mystics familiar to him, like Teresa of Ávila and Jakob Böhme, though is largely lost to conventional religiosity. Moreover, in this interior form it might appeal today. Blake insisted that the vision he received can counter not just the strong presumption that real transcendence is a delusion; it can also usurp the pernicious implication of that nihilism, namely that human minds are lonely originators of meaning. Subdue that dark Spectre, he would cry! Refuse its cruel whispering!

He did risk the charge of impiety on one or two counts; no interesting writer on Christianity hasn't. But that is only because this kind of heterodoxy follows not the letter of the law, but the *Spirit of Prophecy*.[12]

## *The Power of Now*

What the mystics identify is that Christianity and other wisdom traditions stand or fall to the extent that they address the individual now: in this moment. The instant of divine revelation is not historical—2,000 years ago, in the case of Christianity. Conversion comes with turning to the seemingly finite present and there finding the infinite. That is where a continuous eternal presence is located; a heartbeat is where and when the divine breaks through—or, as Blake puts it, *A pulsation of the artery... For in this Period the Poet's Work is Done*.[13] The attitude which dismisses these intuitions as fantasies or delusions will never know the light, Blake explains: *all the Great | Events of Time start forth & are conceived in such a Period | Within a Moment: a Pulsation of the Artery*.[14] This juncture, which stands between the lost past and the yet-to-be future, has been called the specious present. It ceaselessly presents fresh opportunities as a portal to Eternity, which itself keeps arriving in time in the present moment. The alert person attends to the *beam and twinkle* and reorientates themselves to it, loving the unfolding, absorbing the energy, not so as to possess it, but greet it.[15] That is true industry: the work required to cultivate the awareness of the mystic and receive the inspiration sought by the imaginative artist and scientist. Blake offers an enticing summary of the stance, also referencing his understanding of the Satanic as a form of ignorance because mentally curbed:

> *There is a Moment in each Day that Satan cannot find,*
> *Nor can his Watch Fiends find it; but the Industrious find*
> *This Moment & it multiply, & when it once is found*
> *It renovates every Moment of the Day if rightly placed.*[16]

The moment that comes not to order, but to those who actively pause, will be familiar to those who practise meditation. Others may discover it having been on a pilgrimage, say, when after hours of walking comes a flash of inspiration; the walking does not bring the moment but prepares the pilgrim's attention for the moment that arrives. I suspect that consumerism is so compelling because it distorts the promise of an instant that can renovate the whole of life; it slyly mutates the momentary halt into impulses to buy. Purchases promise satisfaction but really deceptively feed the urge for more—deceiving because *More! More! is the cry of a mistaken soul; less than All cannot satisfy Man.*[17]

I discovered a lot about the moment in each day that blind Satan cannot find from a friend who is an improvisor. At the end of a show, during which people have first laughed and then been so moved as to cry, Pippa Evans is often asked for the secret. How did she make up that song? Where did that link come from? What was the source of that witty retort? The assumption is that improvisors must have codes, or stock segments, or astonishingly voluminous memories. However, the remarkable truth is that if they tried to rely upon predetermined plans, the performance would fall flat. Calculation would kill the moment. Instead, Evans explains, an improvisor becomes adept at looking, listening and responding: kissing the joy as it flies. Moreover, they are also adept at giving themselves to the moment, letting that moment go, and then turning to the next one, without insisting that what follows be like the last or what they might want. You must have much to give and, by giving what you have, picked up by your fellow players, the performance emerges—springing from the in-between zone that is fostered. Evans writes: 'When you are fully present with someone—looking at everything in front of you and listening to everything that is being said—you have so much information, that what you want to do next—what you need to do next—becomes so clear. So intuitive. Because you are simply responding to what you have seen and heard.'[18] *The Industrious find This Moment & it multiply.*

# NO OTHER CHRISTIANITY

The truth that changes everything can only be apprehended in the here and now, the mystics say. Blake seeks to show it to us through his work, his poetry becoming a consciousness-shifting incantation, carrying us to the imaginative cleft through which the infinite bursts. The asymmetric power of resonating contraries is his method and to have a taste of it particularly in relation to his understanding of Christianity, take two of his best-known poems, *The Lamb* and *The Tyger*.[19]

*What's in a Name*

*The Lamb* is two stanzas long. The first is an apparently conventional celebration of these delightful creatures, though it is framed by a mantra-like question, pressed by repetition. The beat prepares the reader for a revelation, which will come in the second verse. And so the first begins:

> *Little Lamb, who made thee?*
> *Dost thou know who made thee?*
> *Gave thee life, & bid thee feed*
> *By the stream and o'er the mead;*
> *Gave thee clothing of delight,*
> *Softest clothing, wooly, bright;*
> *Gave thee such a tender voice,*
> *Making all the hills rejoice?*
> *Little Lamb, who made thee?*
> *Dost thou know who made thee?*

The reiterated inquiry about the lamb's maker stresses that Blake is not asking in a sentimental fashion, as if deploying a rhetorical gambit to excuse an indulgent love of cuddly creatures. By the end of the first stanza, we are awaiting a decent answer—a wait that will be intensified by two twists delivered in the second verse. Its opening four lines reference a Christian title for Jesus, the Lamb of God; he was both the incarnation of the timeless, creative principle—the divine Logos or Word—and someone whose lamb-like vulnerability led to his brutal slaughter. So the second part of the poem begins:

> *Little Lamb, I'll tell thee,*
> *Little Lamb, I'll tell thee:*
> *He is called by thy name,*
> *For he calls himself a Lamb.*

## AWAKE!

Jesus, the Lamb of God, is the immediate answer to the question of who made the little creature, because, according to Christian belief, all things are born not only of generative processes, but more fundamentally, of the living power of the creative principle—Blake's understanding of the imagination that he also calls *the Divine Body of the Lord Jesus*.[20] Though notice something else. Blake has provided an answer to the question with a twist. There is an intimacy between this creature and its creator because they share a name. *He is called by thy name, | For he calls himself a Lamb*. There is a connection between them. The apparently utterly different share something radical in common. And then there's a second twist, as Blake reflects further on the meaning of the name, Lamb, and the person, Jesus. What emerges is that the poet, too, is implicated in this connection. After all, if Jesus was a lamb, Blake was an infant. Jesus, lamb, poet. All three are linked. Referring to Jesus when born, the poem continues:

> *He is meek, & he is mild;*
> *He became a little child.*
> *I a child, & thou a lamb,*
> *We are called by his name.*

A far-reaching inference is drawn. The lamb is called by one of God's names and the poet is, too. Both share the Creator's gift of being; at the core of their existence is the divine wellspring of all existence, present in each moment. If that is true of the poet, it is true of us, too, who can also say, *I a child*. This is a dazzling inference—the third dimension made present once more—and the poem concludes with two exultant lines. Blake can put words to the praise that the lamb might inarticulately feel as it frolics and the hills rejoice in its tender voice, articulating praise being part of the human vocation to extend consciousness.

> *Little Lamb, God bless thee!*
> *Little Lamb, God bless thee!*

A vast distance has been travelled, from a question about who made the lamb to a revelation of the divinity of our nature and the whole of nature. When we attend to who we are, we discover more than we possibly expected. As Blake had put it in his vision by the seaside in Felpham, everything is *human form'd*—sharing the divine intelligence of which our intelligence can speak.

But what of *The Tyger*? This poem, from the later collection, *Songs of Innocence and Experience*, raises the revelation to another level by increasing the tension of the contrary between creature and Creator, adding a note of shock and awe to the intimacy of the earlier verse. Blake makes the link between this new poem and *The Lamb* indirectly at first, raising the same question as to who or what made the tiger, only this time, not by asking the creature itself, but by speculating on the matter from afar, contemplating the tiger's *fearful symmetry*. He dwells and lingers on the ferociously, fearsomely made big cat, which given half a chance would unthinkingly bloody the lamb's lovely body; this beast would kill the lamb.

> *Tyger! Tyger! burning bright*
> *In the forest of the night,*
> *What immortal hand or eye*
> *Could frame thy fearful symmetry?*
>
> *In what distant deeps or skies*
> *Burnt the fire of thine eyes?*
> *On what wings dare he aspire?*
> *What the hand dare seize the fire?*
>
> *And what shoulder, & what art,*
> *Could twist the sinews of thy heart?*
> *And when the heart began to beat,*
> *What dread hand? & what dread feet?*
>
> *What the hammer? what the chain?*
> *In what furnace was thy brain?*
> *What the anvil? what dread grasp*
> *Dare its deadly terrors clasp?*[21]

The lamb had been addressed close up. The tiger is contemplated at a safe distance, raising the stakes: can the divine intimacy that was experienced with the lamb possibly be known with the tiger? I once heard the account of a man who had seen a tiger in the wild, in the hills of south India— likely near where a tiger was captured and brought to one of London's Georgian menageries for Blake and other sightseers to behold. The man told me that he and a companion were walking up the mountainside with the wind in their faces, which meant that their scent was carried away from the tiger that, unbeknownst to them, was sleeping up ahead. Suddenly, the massive animal leapt up. The enormity of its presence struck them more than any detail. He and the friend pivoted in an instant

Figs 40 and 41: *Songs of Innocence and Experience*, plates showing "The Lamb" and "The Tyger."

and fled. By the time they had stopped running, the stress of the moment had become visible on their faces. Blood had seeped from their eyes.

Blake dwells on this terror for four stanzas, transmitting the fire, conveying the dread. And then he pauses. He offers us a transitional verse that shifts our gaze from the bright burning creature to the Creator, whilst simultaneously also recollecting the lamb; the fifth verse opens with an allusion to celestial comets and then presses home the central question.

> *When the stars threw down their spears,*
> *And water'd heaven with their tears,*
> *Did he smile his work to see?*
> *Did he who made the Lamb make thee?*[22]

A Creator who makes a woolly clothed, bleating lamb is one thing. But that very same God also made an animal that can rage and rip the lamb apart. Two seemingly irreconcilable acts of making are held in the mind's eye. *Did he who made the Lamb make thee?* The answer is yes, but that emphasises another question: why? I think we are not supposed to answer and are maybe not supposed to know. For in the moment of uncertainty can come a tangible awareness of an eternal hand that is active in every particular of the natural world, and is their source. *Did he who made the Lamb make thee?* The silence the question prompts speaks without words from the edge of the words that the poet has dared venture. An encounter with transcendence has been evoked by drawing attention to the bewilderment of being alive. The poem leads us to a door of perception and in that moment we might sense the All. The final stanza, which returns us to the first, releases us from the tension but invites us to integrate the wonder.

> *Tyger! Tyger! burning bright*
> *In the forest of the night,*
> *What immortal hand or eye*
> *Could frame thy fearful symmetry?*

### Salvific Turmoil

Lamb, tiger, human person, divine maker. Drawing together these elements to precipitate a glimpse of Eternity in time is not just Blake's idea; he felt that was the heart of the Christian message. In his opinion, the way in which the Biblical authors wrote about Jesus was clearly designed to transmit a revelatory spirit, much as his poems do. For Blake, the best bits of the Bible are made up of precipitous incidents that give pause. The Good Book is not a compendium of what he called *Fable* and *Allegory*—doubtful legends best read as moral instruction; the Bible is an agitator for *Eternal Vision or Imagination of All that Exists*.[23] It catalyses and goads, reveals and shows; like good myths, its many stories educate when inhabited rather than dismantled. To read the Bible's pages as if they were really records, from which might be extracted historical clues though few reliable facts, is to make a fundamental mistake: the scrutinising eye neutralising the metamorphic magic. To my mind, that blunder runs through much contemporary Christian apologetics, which attempt to mobilise scant evidence to prove, say, the resurrection or the virgin birth, overlooking that the passage from death to life or the birth of something marvellous could be happening right now.

People are put off by the apologist's manipulative charm; it has designs on you. And Blake would have understood why: being cornered is not the same as being converted—the latter being an awakening of the imagination. Moreover, the misstep starts with misunderstanding the intentions of the Biblical authors themselves because, for them, the modern notion of history as facts did not yet exist. In the Hellenistic age, the early Christian period and through much of the Middle Ages, the word 'history' meant knowledge gained by inquiry. For the enchanted mind that quest would naturally incorporate aspects of mythology and reports of portents, oracles and miracles. Anglo-Saxon histories, for example, are famous for their sightings of dragons, soaring across northern skies.

Only at the end of the fifteen century did 'history' begin to take on the modern meaning of an empirically reliable record of events. Before then, history was told primarily to discern the significance of events, not settle their veracity and order. Even manifest contradictions did not matter when meaning mattered more, which is why the Bible is packed with so-called errors—inconsistencies that, when understood and accepted, become a spur for piercing the literal in search of an epiphany. The invitation is to consider the contrary of both/and, awaiting what the tension precipitates, rather than losing the meaning in a moment of historicising pique.

On occasion, Blake mocks those who try to read the Bible as if it were a book of evidence. In a letter to a clergyman, Dr Trusler, he remarks: *Why is the Bible more Entertaining & Instructive than any other book? Is it not because they* [he has all inspired texts in mind] *are addressed to the Imagination, which is Spiritual Sensation, & but mediately to the Understanding or Reason?*[24] Imagination converts us, with reason and understanding offering back-up. No one would dismiss a painting or novel for playing fast and loose with the facts if they discerned an inner message: so, too, the Bible. If that were not so, it would not have remained a source of inspiration for millennia. A telephone directory is packed with accurate data but who consults one to dream dreams?

The Blakean stance towards the Good Book has far-reaching ramifications. Consider the incident in the gospel of John featuring a women who has been caught *in flagrante delicto* committing adultery. She is dragged by the Pharisees before Jesus, who ask him what should happen to her. The question is a trick because the law is clear: she should be stoned. But Jesus pauses writing in the sand, holding the moment, awaiting inspiration, and a new possibility presents itself. 'Let anyone among you who is without sin be the first to throw a stone,' he says.[25] They had not expected that and, caught out, drift away one by one.

Fig. 42: *The Woman Taken in Adultery*, c. 1805

# NO OTHER CHRISTIANITY

Blake knew the story and painted a picture of the confrontation for Thomas Butts, in about 1805. The image shows Jesus leaning over the sand with the woman's accusers in retreat. And, Biblical stories being spurs to the imagination, Blake takes the opportunity to draw out what he takes to be the core meaning of the incident. That emerges particularly in the way he paints the woman. Her clothes are dishevelled and her wrists are bound behind her back. The critic, Christopher Heppner, notes that he knows of no other painter to add these details to the scene.[26] Her breast is also showing, a probable allusion to the figure of Marianne, the allegory of Liberty that became popular during the French Revolution. What liberty might the woman caught in adultery stand for here? She appears to be shamed and trapped. Indeed, whilst Blake shows her accusers departing, the implication is that she is not yet free: might Jesus cast the first stone as, according to the gospels, he is without sin? 'The woman is thus in a state which combines bondage and helplessness with freedom and defiance. She is in a no-man's land between life and death,' Heppner writes.[27]

The observation is telling. The woman is held in an unresolved state: in between life and death. She is therefore like Jesus, who by this stage in his life had fallen foul of enemies who were plotting his death. For her, the tension will ease, when Jesus doesn't condemn her either. He, though, must continue to live in the no-man's land and I think this is Blake's point: Jesus is the person who inhabits contraries to the full, unrelentingly. He is human and divine, finite and from the infinite, a mortal revealing immortality—fully conscious of both poles of existence. Then, before the woman, Jesus indicates something remarkable, as Blake portrays the moment. He reaches for the sand and bows before the woman: he venerates her. Blake has Jesus imply that she is not dissimilar; she is destined to realise her divinity through participation in God's life, too. Hence when he tells her, 'Go your way, and from now on do not sin again' he judges her not so as to condemn her, but to liberate her.[28] Her liberty comes not after a revolution but with a realisation of what is already the case.

A section in *The Everlasting Gospel* has the woman telling the story of her crisis in her own words, confirming the point. First, she summarises the tragedy of her predicament: *Love too long from Me has fled;* | *'Twas dark deceit, to Earn my bread…* | *That they may call a shame & Sin* | *Love's temple that God dwelleth in.*[29] She knows that her real problem is abusing the *human form divine*, namely herself.[30] That is tantamount to *Blaspheming Love, blaspheming thee*—Jesus, the Logos, to whom she is speaking.[31]

201

# AWAKE!

Only that's not the last word. The recognition allows her to receive the forgiveness which *alone is the Gospel*. The contraries that shape him, shape her and all beings: finitude and infinitude. *This is the Life & Immortality brought to light by Jesus.*[32]

## Ego Trip

But does that beg a question—the big one when it comes to religious faith? If there is a divine spark within us, why do we need to experience mortality and finitude, and often feel stuck suffering in those vulnerable states? Couldn't God have made a world in which Eternity unequivocally blazed, one of ready fulfilment and ease?

In his poem, *Milton*, Blake strives to address this matter, suggesting that there is something crucial and distinctive in the human experience. In the poem, Blake imagines John Milton's spirit coming back to live again on Earth; Blake's conceit is that he returns to correct the misunderstanding he previously made about desire. The link with suffering is that desire is the sense of longing based upon lack and so penetrates our souls deeply; this is why the human psyche is such a powerful force, why we feel the tugs of opposites, the anxiety of living with perplexity, and also the terror of death. We long for things to be otherwise. In Blake's imagining, Milton recognises this struggle and sees that he must live again and, this time, fully embrace the human lot: he will not opt for reigning in the hell of a Satanic half-life, but will choose the possibility and uncertainty of reaching out to heaven. In a word, he must emphatically embrace mortality. *'I go to Eternal Death!'* he cries as he is reborn—the 'eternal' indicating that to truly embrace death is to face its adamantine finality: the phase-shift that Blake knew so directly.[33]

Blake is partly saying that freedom is a by-product of awareness because it is born not of fearful ignorance but brave clear-sightedness. But there is something else. As Milton falls he also calls: *'I will go down to self annihilation and eternal death, | Lest the Last Judgement come & find me unannihilated | And I be siez'd & giv'n into the hands of my own Selfhood.'*[34] He is onto something that is truly strange about our humanity, arising from the contraries of existence.

We are the creatures for whom our immediate life is too small for us, hence existential crises and the yearning for the All. That is because within each of us is an infinite core that is both of us and far beyond us—of which we are at least partially aware, whether religious or not, Blake would say. So, paradoxically, we only find ourselves fully by giving ourselves up. In that sense, dying to ourselves brings us the fullness of life; human beings must face their limits—their mortality, their cravings, their fears—to awake to the limitless. The path, then, is not to curb desires or feed them, but free them by being cured of *Selfhood*, as Blake describes *this dread disease*, in the grip of which *we are nothing, but fade away in mornings breath*.[35]

For finite creatures with a taste for the eternal, the delusion that we are separate selves becomes an *Incrustation over my Immortal Spirit*;[36] it feeds the *Spectrous* (meaning insubstantial) *Reasoning Power in Man*—the kind of intellect that insists on trusting its own logic alone.[37] Blake has Milton declare that he recognises '*a Selfhood which must be put off & annihilated away | To cleanse the Face of my Spirit by Self-examination, | To bathe in the Waters of life.*'[38] Blake is not saying that our humanity is sinful in the sense of abhorrent before God, which is the teaching of the kind of Christianity he despised. Rather, he is pointing to a subtler issue. Selfhood is the belief that we must protect ourselves because we are lost in the cosmos. Feeling that void, we react with fear, withdrawal, lies. Annihilating selfhood is, therefore, about *driving down the pyramids of pride* so as to *Open the hidden Heart in Wars of mutual Benevolence, Wars of Love*: striving for a realignment, engaging the *Mental Fight* to discover a life that, when shared not clung to, is abundant not scarce.[39] A small, guarded, deluded sense of self can open onto to an expansive, porous, undefended sense of personhood, located in our true identity, which is at once transcendent and immanent. The *Divine appearance* shines in the moment of that awakening,

Fig. 43: *Milton*, plate probably showing Blake before Los, or his divine self, stepping out of a flaming sun.

revealing Eternity.[40] To accept that we die can be simultaneously to discover the love that runs through the cosmos.

This is hard to do, which is where Jesus comes in. In the poem *Jerusalem: The Emanation of the Giant Albion*, Blake reframes the Christian understanding of Jesus's death from being a sacrifice demanded by a cruel god to a demonstration of putting off selfhood. Jesus did not die to blot out sins, Blake has Jesus tell the human superhero, Albion. Rather, he died to make possible the recognition of the *human form divine* in each and everyone.[41] The contraries of the human and the divine meet in continual self-giving, initiated by God. Jesus appears to Albion & *they conversed as Man with Man in Ages of Eternity* and Jesus says:

> 'Wouldst thou love one who never died
> For thee, or ever die for one who had not died for thee?
> And if God dieth not for Man & giveth not himself
> Eternally for Man, Man could not exist; for Man is Love
> As God is Love; every kindness to another is a little Death
> In the Divine Image.'[42]

The end of what impedes us can be known in acts as modest as kindness; transformation can be practiced by anyone. Great wisdom is like that; it is simultaneously the simplest advice. Every moment, every breath, every pulse of the artery is awash with possibilities of transcendence. This is Blake's Christianity. *For God himself enters Death's Door always with those that enter | And lays down in the Grave with them, in Visions of Eternity, | Till they awake & see Jesus & the Linen Clothes lying.*[43]

## Eternal Worlds Open

The natural world can help foster this continual resurrection, too. One of the most beautiful couplets in *The Marriage of Heaven and Hell* conveys the expansive awareness that, in moments of self-forgetfulness, contacts Heaven.

> *How do you know but ev'ry Bird that cuts the airy way,*
> *Is an immense world of delight, clos'd by your senses five?*[44]

It's a rich phrase, though the heart of its meaning is clear. The swooping bird lives its inner animation and the person who, momentarily stepping out of themselves, glimpses joy powering flight through the skies might feel that good news within themselves, too.

I suspect that Blake was aided in his recovery of this mystical understanding of Christianity by his reading of *The Bhagavad Gita*. The Indian text features a conversation between Arjuna, who is facing a dire crisis, and Krishna, who will be revealed as a manifestation of the supreme: as an incarnation of God. A central teaching which Krishna insists that Arjuna absorbs concerns acting without desire or concern for the results of his actions. 'For it is through acting without attachment that a man attains the highest,' Krishna says.[45] Self-sacrifice is being advocated, though of a certain sort, chiming with what Blake prayed for himself: *Annihilate the Selfhood in me, be thou all my life!*[46] What Arjuna learns is that all he does, moment by moment, can be offered to Krishna, which in turn reorientates his appreciation of reality away from what he himself might seek. A wilful life bolsters the sense of being an isolated self quite as effectively as a fearful life; in pitching his power against others, Arjuna cuts himself off from reality. Conversely, a liberated life grows into an awareness of the mutual source of all beings, namely God. Arjuna is being invited to annihilate his selfhood by offering his best, as the moment requires, trusting that his actions contribute to the divine work that he himself can only in part understand.

As the *Gita* continues, particular virtues are stressed that resonate with qualities Blake celebrates. The self-sacrificing individual will live 'beyond dualities,' which is to say towards the divine presence detected at the threshold the contraries reveal.[47] Relatedly, this person will become freer from possessiveness; they will be at liberty to follow the imagination continually beckoning in the activity around and within them. This is what Blake meant when he wrote: *I know of no other Christianity and of no other Gospel than the liberty both of body & mind to exercise the Divine Arts of Imagination.*[48]

In *Jerusalem*, Blake develops the meaning of the divine-human intimacy. *I am in you and you in me, mutual in love divine*, he records hearing Jesus cry in the opening section, before the divine voice continues: *I am not a God afar off, I am a brother and friend; | Within your bosoms I reside, and you reside in me.* Nothing should hinder this communion. Blake confesses: *He who waits to be righteous before he enters into the Saviours kingdom, the Divine Body, will never enter there. I am perhaps the most sinful of men; I pretend not to holiness; yet I pretend to love, to see, to converse with daily as man with man.*[49] Faith in divine intimacy and that God is the life within him drove his vocation. *I rest not*

# AWAKE!

*from my great task! | To open the Eternal Worlds, to open the immortal Eyes | Of Man inwards into the Worlds of Thought, into Eternity | Ever expanding in the Bosom of God, the Human Imagination.*[50]

The Christianity that Blake sought to revive is best felt, not dogmatically described. That said, from time to time, he confessed to confidants his belief in the unity of the One and the many. There was the occasion when he was talking with the confused journalist Henry Crabb Robinson, who asked him about the divinity of Christ, perhaps suspecting that Blake had interesting or unusual views. If so, Crabb Robinson was right because Blake replied: 'He is the only God,' before adding, 'And so am I and so are you.' Crabb Robinson was shocked, but Blake explained what he meant when, on another occasion, he affirmed that, 'We are all coexistent with God, members of the Divine body. We are all partakers in the divine nature.'[51] This is what Jesus the God-Man reveals. *Therefore God becomes as we are, that we may be as he is.*[52]

Fig. 44: *Milton*, plate 45, in which Blake shows the superhero Ololon in the form of Christ and ears of wheat with human heads, indicating that plant intelligence and human intelligence are unified in Christ.

## NO OTHER CHRISTIANITY

What makes the belief so hard to embrace is the settled sense that we are adrift from Eternity, to the extent of concluding it may not exist at all. The distant sky god of the deists, which has become a self-evidently false god to atheists, must be abandoned—as must the deity of those Christian believers for whom humanity is pitiful and lost. The cleansing of what obscures the infinite is so fundamental that, in *The Everlasting Gospel*, Blake imagines God telling Jesus not to belittle himself, given he is becoming human, because that would be to debase the presence of God in his humanity. Jesus must counter the idea of God as is a deity apart and so God tells Jesus: *If thou humblest thyself, thou humblest me; | Thou also dwell'st in Eternity. | Thou art a Man, God* [the Nobodaddy] *is no more, | Thy own humanity learn to adore.*[53] When a person is perceived correctly—or, for that matter, when a *Grain of Sand, Cloud, Meteor & Star* are—then the divine face is seen in that fullness.

The theme was brought to its greatest expression by Blake in his *Illustrations of The Book of Job*, which includes watercolours he painted after the return from Felpham as well as a set of twenty-two engravings that are masterpieces of the form. The pictures tell the story of Job from the Hebrew Bible—the drama of a self-contented man who, at the behest of Satan in the courts of Heaven, loses everything before having his life remade. Blake interprets the myth, of course, highlighting the dying and rising process of transformation by which an individual might come to know of their divinity. The series is full of details but his key insights stand out.

For instance, the first plate depicts Job as a pious man amongst his family, sure that he is doing right by his religion. But there is a warning below this opening image: *The Letter Killeth | But Spirit giveth Life,* Blake has inscribed. Job is unwittingly following the deadening *Wastes of Moral Law.*[54] Only after the annihilation of all that he presumed true will he understand the spirit that brings life.

Alternatively, God is shown according to the understanding of the mystics: in union with human beings. Blake makes that explicit by depicting God and Job as exact likenesses and also spelling out the nature of the identity in his inscriptions: *At that day ye shall know that I am in | my Father & you in me & I in you*, he writes on plate 17. Conversely, Job's fall is orchestrated by Satan who is the personification of erroneous, and therefore deadly, vision. Satan can also be said to be Job's shadow in that erratic state. The so-called patience of Job, as he undergoes his sufferings, therefore arises from a kind of ignorance, which means he

# AWAKE!

keeps faith with God but blindly. *We shall awake up in thy Likeness*, Blake writes on plate 2, signalling the nature of the transformation that Job must undergo: to perceive God not Satanically but as a mortal aware of immortality.

That comes only after pain. *Canst thou bind the sweet influences of Pleiades or loose the bans of Orion*, Job is asked on plate 14, which clearly he cannot. But he will acknowledge the one who can and thereby find his human vocation consciously to join creature and Creator in songs of praise. A related key insight is that suffering is not deserved as a punishment, as Job's accusers presume. No: the gospel is judgement that liberates. *When he hath tried me I shall come forth like gold*, says one of the verses on plate 10.

In the last period of his life I think that Blake not only endeavoured to express this awakened theology, he dwelt in it; he not only conjured the moment of discovery in his poetry, but did indeed expand. He attained this enlightenment first in South Molton Street and then knew it after a final move in 1821, into a two-roomed dwelling called Fountain Court, just off the Strand. He and Catherine squeezed all their belongings into

Fig. 45: *Illustrations of the Book of Job*, plate 17, in which Job and his wife see God because they have perceived their divine humanity, unlike Job's accusers who turn away in fear and shame.

another apartment, this time in a building on a slope that ran down to the Thames. From their first-floor bedroom window Blake enjoyed the river, 'looking like a bar of gold.'[55] For gold spoke to him. *I give you the end of a golden string, | Only wind it into a ball; | It will lead you in at Heaven's gate | Built in Jerusalem's wall,* he promised.[56] So what is it like to take Blake at his word and be guided by that thread? What arrives if we progress along the trail?

12

FOUNTAINS OF LIVING WATERS

From 1820 onwards, visitors to William and Catherine detected a newfound serenity in him.[1] The suspicion of madness began to fall away, replaced by an unmistakable 'air of inspiration.'[2] Relatedly, the stories of encounters with Blake from these final years often stress that, although poor, he felt immensely wealthy. One tale tells of him being introduced to a young lady who was elegantly and expensively dressed, in marked contrast to the unfashionable broad-brimmed hat and worn breeches he sported. He regarded her warmly for a time and then said, 'May God make this world to you, my child, as beautiful as it has been to me.' Later, as a rich woman, she recalled that she did not understand the remark, though it stayed with her, only releasing its meaning as she grew older: material affluence can detract from life's abundance because the greatest riches cannot be owned.[3] Blake had grown conscious of dwelling elsewhere than in a rented abode by the river, telling one visitor to the rooms that he had a palace 'of great beauty and magnificence.' The visitor cast a doubtful eye around the chipped panelled walls, prompting Blake to remark: 'You don't think I'm such a fool as to think this is it.'[4]

Most of the artistic output from what was to be his last decade evidences his unwavering absorption in these energies, found both within and without. Alongside the epic poems, *Milton* and *Jerusalem*, and the engravings on Job, he produced much else, including haunting woodcut illustrations to the Arcadian poems of Virgil and a tremendous set of over 100 illustrations to Dante's *Divine Comedy*, an undertaking for which he learnt medieval Italian so as to read the poem in the original.

He had been encouraged by meeting a new group of artists in the summer of 1818 who seemed to understand him. They were young, some still in their teens, and so called themselves 'The Ancients.'[5] The group included John Linnell, rival to John Constable, and Samuel Palmer, celebrated for his visionary landscapes. They styled Blake 'The Interpreter,' growing to love visiting what they called his 'enchanted rooms.'[6] They dined with him, accompanied him to soirées, took him to the theatre, asked for his opinion of their work and bought his work in turn. One day, Palmer took Blake and some others on an expedition to Shoreham, a scenic village south of London by the meandering River Darent. The place inspired many of Palmer's paintings and you can still see why, for all that the lush valley is now walled in by the M25, M20 and M26 motorways, rumbling in the distance. The party settled into a cottage that belonged to Palmer's grandfather and then decided to visit a nearby ruin that was said to be haunted. Nothing much came of their paranormal investigations and it must have been disappointing when, the next night, Palmer had to return alone to London. Only, an hour or so after his departure, Blake touched his head and murmured: 'Palmer is coming; he is walking up the road.' The others, chatting in the warm kitchen, dismissed the comment from the older man. But then, a few minutes later, Blake repeated: 'He is coming through the wicket... there!' Sure enough, the latched door opened and Palmer appeared. His coach to town had broken down a mile or two up the valley.[7]

Blake's alertness to approaching presences continued as well in his conversations with angels, spirits and the dead, which was doubly welcomed by another landscape painter whom he met through The Ancients. John Varley was an enthusiast for the occult and was soon encouraging Blake to draw what he saw clairvoyantly. The sketches became the series of portraits known as the 'Visionary Heads.' The most famous of them Blake developed into one of his now best-known paintings, 'The Ghost of a Flea.' A monstrous character—part-human, part-insect—creeps between curtains that look as thick as an animal's pelt. The fiend, tongue flicking, has a goblet in its scaley hand to hold blood. It is also stooped, echoing the bulbous body of a biting mite, for Blake detected a correspondence between sucking fleas and people who are 'by nature bloodthirsty to excess.'[8] The parallel is another clue as to how he saw so richly: receive the aura of people and things, don't just focus on their tangible features. Dwell in that atmosphere and see what semblance is called forth from the imagination. As he explained to Varley: many could see as he did, he only had the capacity to a more developed degree. The difference was that he treasured this visionary immersion more than practical ways of navigating a path through life, which most people invest their time in and cherish. They want to get on with things, which is entirely understandable, only busyness steamrolls subtleties.

So follow the golden string that the senses hand you, he invited, and become more active in acts of seeing and hearing. Track intuitions and contemplate what is present, not remaining passive as if eyes were merely cameras, ears microphones: image-snapping, sound-registering devices. You will be taught to filter out, Newton-like—that is the essence of a modern education—but don't lose the capacity to detect the whole, in the moment, welling up from Eternity. That ability can delight in the fractal nature of minute particulars and contemplate moments that reveal immensities, to *see Past, Present & Future existing all at once*.[9] Blake frequently evokes this fluidity, often as an ability of Los and Enitharmon in their roles as the superhero-guardians of time and space, respectively.

> *For Los & Enitharmon walk'd forth on the dewy Earth,*
> *Contracting or expanding their all flexible senses:*
> *At will to murmur in the flowers small as the honey bee;*
> *At will to stretch across the heavens & step from star to star;*
> *Or standing on the Earth erect, or on the stormy waves*
> *Driving the storms before them, or delighting in sunny beams,*
> *While round their heads the Elemental Gods kept harmony.*[10]

Language is another mode of transportation because it is not just a means of communication but of conveyance, carrying the mood of other times and the spirit of distant places to the immediate present. Blake thought that when rendered prophetic and poetic, words not only offer virtual trips but actual entry into facets of reality accessed through the imagination. Remember the *rural pen*. Reading his poetry can, therefore, become a training in attending. From that can develop a stance which, first, appreciates how the world is experienced in diverse ways and, second, realises that this is because the world discloses itself in diverse ways, in large part responding to the quality of attention paid to it. The widening of perspective is not merely about changing your opinion, as if persuaded by a good argument, but is an opening of the doors of perception, which in turn is really a form of conversion. Life changes altogether.

Blake's mature work can clarify the path of illumination because, in it, he explores the states of mind encountered on the way, presenting these dispositions as four broad categories of awareness. Further, his illustrations to *The Divine Comedy* can be used to elucidate the schema and how we switch from one manner of attending to another.[11]

# AWAKE!

First, a reminder of Dante's story. He tells of a soul, namely himself, who one morning wakes up terrified. He realises he is utterly lost, midway through the journey of life which, he says, is *nostra vita*: our life.[12] Dante the poet, who tells us about his midlife crisis, therefore wants his breakdown to initiate a lesson for us all. The ensuing odyssey to rediscover the right path is told in four parts, of which three are immediately clear: the dark trek down into Hell, the climb that ascends the mountain of Purgatory and the entry into the heavens of Paradise. There is an additional section, between Purgatory and Paradise, because, at the top of Mount Purgatory, Dante enters a mysterious forest which he calls the earthly Eden: a liminal space in which he readies himself for the final release. This is to say that as he journeys he moves between four states of mind. In fact, to enter each region of *The Divine Comedy* is to adopt a mode of attention characteristic to that region: first a hellish, trapped mentality; then a purgatorial attitude of self-scrutiny; next an Edenic phase of receptivity; and finally a state of illumination that stretches towards the infinite. I think that these four psychophysical terrains correspond to Blake's four imaginative dispositions, so Dante's journey can exemplify the awakening that Blake urges us all to pursue.[13]

## *Expanding Mentalities*

The first, hellish mode of attention is called Ulro by Blake; it is *Single vision and Newton's sleep*, haunted by nihilistic *shades of Death*.[14] Contraries become negations in this zone, collapsing in on themselves like black holes rather than expansively propelling souls out and up. The vastness of the universe is perceived as intimidating: *the space of the terrible starry wheels*.[15] In terms of human perceptions, 'that which can't be expressed quantitatively does not exist,' as the contemporary Blake scholar, Susanne Sklar, summarises Ulro's assumptions. Similarly, the imagination is constrained by scientific *cruelties of Demonstration*,[16] a phrase that is apt when one considers the conclusions reached by this mentality. Think of the remark of the atheist physicist Steven Weinberg. He wrote, 'The more the universe seems comprehensible, the more it also seems pointless,' adding a consolatory thought that understanding as much 'lifts human life a little above the level of farce, and gives it some of the grace of tragedy.'[17] Cold comfort. Ulro can't countenance that there might be other ways of seeing things and that is what keeps people trapped.

## FOUNTAINS OF LIVING WATERS

Many of the illustrations Blake made for *The Divine Comedy* capture aspects of this pinched view and one in particular gets to the heart of the perceptual issue. In a low circle of Hell, Dante encounters a character called Bertran de Born. He was a warring baron and bloodthirsty troubadour in life, whom Dante believed was a kind of fundamentalist. Dante depicts him, therefore, as carrying his decapitated head by the hair; it swings from his hand like a lantern. Bertran can literally see only by his own light, everything so far as he is concerned refracted through his angry, fundamentalist convictions. Such is single vision, an outlook that is hellish and haunting, for with it people can see no prospects other than twisted and traumatised ones. They become gripped by their preoccupations and fears, lost in tunnel vision. Violence may well accompany the paranoia, and conspiracies, from the sense of hopelessness. The imprisoned are isolated, indifferent to the grace of minute particulars and hence numb to the moment that offers change.

Hell seems eternal when you are in it: the *same dull round* that appears never-ending.[18] Only, nothing actually stands still and that movement, if only a perturbation, can seed a shift of consciousness to the second outlook Blake called *Generation*.

Fig. 46: *The Schismatics and Sowers of Discord: Mosca de' Lamberti and Bertran de Born*, from the illustrations to Dante's *Divine Comedy*, Inferno XXVIII.

215

## AWAKE!

Generation is deemed the basis of life when viewed organically: the cycles of *Vegetative Existence*.[19] The controlling narrative is the struggle to survive, which is not dull but seems possibly pointless and certainly worrisome—an existence subject to *the hungry ravenings of Destruction, | To be the sport of Accident, to waste in Wrath & Love a weary | Life, in brooding cares & anxious labours that prove but chaff*.[20] Individuals caught within this imaginative field are inclined to see competition wherever they look; empathy connects them to their tribe but the flipside of that feeling equally separates them from those deemed enemies or enviable because nudging ahead in the race called life. Division also manifests between the sexes: gender differences are deeply felt in Generation and what Blake called *the Female Will* is often taken to be at loggerheads with the male.[21] Men are from Mars and women from Venus, though the tension has a clear upside too: it can be exciting and generative, particularly in moments of love that bridge the differences, bringing unity and fostering children—though the relief is passing, psychologically complicated and accompanied by strife.

> *They revolve into the Furnaces Southward & are driven forth Northward,*
> *Divided into Male and Female forms time after time...*
> *The Male is a Furnace of beryll; the Female is a golden Loom;*
> *I behold them and their rushing fires overwhelm my Soul*
> *In London's darkness. And my tears fall day and night.*[22]

At a cultural level, Generation makes novelty an end in itself: production for production's sake. In conjunction with engrained habits of consumption, that creates a society devoted to growth for growth's sake. In this state, people forget the true goals of industriousness, readying for passage *to the Golden world*, and instead build *dark Satanic Mills* that spread over the face of the Earth.[23]

Generation is possibly how many people experience existence for much of the time in a society devoted to progressive economic systems: eat, drink, work, relax somewhat, repeat. A scene in *The Divine Comedy* that captures this effort is when, in Purgatory, Dante and Virgil meet souls who realise in the afterlife that there was more to mortal life than the hedonic treadmill, though they only grasped as much at the point of death. They wasted their allotted span and are akin to the proverbial individual who, looking back on their time, wishes they hadn't spent so much of it in the office or on a screen, but did so because they weren't

# FOUNTAINS OF LIVING WATERS

Fig. 47: *The souls of those who repented at the point of death*, Blake's illustration of the flying souls, from the illustrations to Dante's *Divine Comedy*, Purgatorio V.

quite sure what else to do. Dante depicts the souls as caught in great swirls of activity, driving them round and round in circles: running to stand still. In Purgatory, where it becomes possible to stand back and reflect on things, they will learn how they murdered their lives but can use these energies to lead them from rat race habits into wider and varied aspects of existence.

*Happy is he who can see and converse with them above the shadows of generation and death*, Blake remarked.[24] To see above the shadows of Generation is, then, to detect intimations of a mode of existence related to it but with a difference. Regeneration is the organic pattern of birth and death not simply on repeat, keeping things going, but instead begetting departures and imaginative opportunities. The passage of time takes on a different quality, too, from feeling sterile to pregnant with possibility. Regeneration can be found within Generation. It was discovered by Oothoon, who sang: *Arise, and drink your bliss, for every thing that lives is holy!*[25]

Blake's superhero of life, Los, is often depicted as trying to convert Generation into Regeneration, typically by working at things with imagination. He wields his hammer and fires his furnaces not passively, merely to manipulate like Newton, but actively to forge a different future: building Golgonooza. That is an important shift. When Generation is marked by Regeneration the third state of mind Blake envisaged might be glimpsed as well, as was discovered by Dante as he travelled out of Purgatory. This mood is as regular as the sunrise, too, though with a very different energy.

Blake called it *Beulah*—the word carrying a clue about the mental stance it denotes. As is noted by scholars, Beulah is Biblical in original, meaning 'promised to God.' It is, therefore, a state of mind in which a person trusts where they are headed, knowing it is ultimately good. The word is also used by the poet and preacher, John Bunyan. He deploys it in his best-known work, *The Pilgrim's Progress*, to name a garden in which souls wait to cross the River of Death. So to be in Beulah is to be in the condition of having suffered much, though now with an awareness of being well on the way to more: fulfilment is promised and can be felt.

The term may also be a corruption of 'beau-lieu,' or beautiful place, which is the name of a panoramic ridge in south London called Beulah Hill. William and Catherine knew the spot from their walks: *where Beulah lovely terminates in the hills and valleys of Albion*, Blake writes.[26] The location is striking even now, as an undulating suburb in Upper Norwood. The ridge runs roughly east-west so if you walk along Beulah Hill and look north, you see the plains of metropolitan London, whereas looking south, you see the rolling woodlands of the Surrey Hills and North Downs. Beulah Hill is an edgeland, a rest-place between urban activity and bucolic charm, and the physical location, when visited, inculcates a restorative mood; *the edge of Beulah*, as Blake calls it.[27] To be in Beulah is, therefore, to be on the cusp of a phase-shift in perception, temporarily regrouping. *There is a place where Contraries are equally True: This place is called Beulah,* he continues—the energic tension easing off here.[28] *There is from Great Eternity a mild & pleasant rest | Nam'd Beulah a Soft Moony Universe feminine lovely | Pure mild & Gentle in Mercy.*[29]

When in Beulah, therefore, time slows down; a strong sense of self eases. The mood can be called feminine in a certain sense: one feels held and, therefore, self-forgetful and receptive. The striving of life stills somewhat and the mind drifts, the imagination wanders. Blake talks of *the Couches of Beulah*, and I suspect that for many people this state of mind is experienced when they go to bed and, tucked up, relax: Beulah's *dark slumberous bliss.*[30] Good sleep is a great blessing, as those who don't have it know; without it, there seems no better tomorrow.

Dante describes experiencing this rejuvenation as he approaches the third realm in *The Divine Comedy*: the earthly Eden. In the story of his adventure, this begins during the third night that he spends on Mount Purgatory when he finds himself in a suggestive state of mind. Blake painted the moment in one of his most gentle illustrations, showing Dante stretching out on the steps up the hillside, alongside Virgil and another soul who had joined them. The Moon and the stars look preternaturally massive and cast a soothing light across the sea beneath. Dante rests and with slumber comes an enticing dream, which turns out to be a premonition and anticipation of Eternity.

Fig. 48: *Dante and Statius sleeping, Virgil watching*, from the illustrations to Dante's *Divine Comedy*, Purgatorio XXVII.

*Living Freedom*

Eternity itself is extensively explored in Paradise and the illustration in which I think Blake well captures its vigour and fulfilment features Dante and his new guide, Beatrice—the woman he had fallen for in his youth and who had, therefore, launched him on the great journey of adult life. Together they now dance in the high heavens with three saints, Peter, James and John, alongside other souls and angels. Enjoying communion with the All, Dante is invited to celebrate the virtues with which the three apostles of Christianity are associated: faith, hope and love. He must do so in a manner that shows he is not only ready for further revelations that still await him—the journey into the infinite never stops—but in such a way that he is able actively to contribute to what will be disclosed; the divine spark that is the heart of his personhood, and ours, has become a blaze that is both from him and a reflection of the luminescence of all that surrounds him.

In one way, Eternity is a step on from the previous three: a final developmental stage. But something previously unanticipated is realised with this disposition. Eternity reveals itself to be the source of all vision; it is the one true perspective, from which the previous three are fallen to varying degrees. So Eternity is marked by a sense of completeness rather than as if it were another phase; what might be called a fourth stage is really the discovery of the ever-present origin of all that had been previously experienced, fully and consciously known. I say this because it explains why Eternity brings complete satisfaction: in Eternity, desire is no longer driven by a nagging sense of lack but a delightful sense of continual outpouring. I think the nature of Eternity also explains why the infinite is detectable in finite things and eternity can be sensed in any hour. The grain of sand and the wild flower are manifestations of the One and fully convey the One, properly perceived, as the One is the *tertium quid* that springs from the contraries. Within Christianity, this epiphany is itself but a reflection of God who is understood to be the Trinity; the unity of God as three in one is a way of saying that the divine is not a monad but a productive source, eternally overflowing from within its very being.

Paradisal vision is depicted by Blake in the way he paints Peter, James and John, along with Dante and Beatrice; they are in overlapping, radiating circles, surrounded by stars and ribbons of rainbow light.

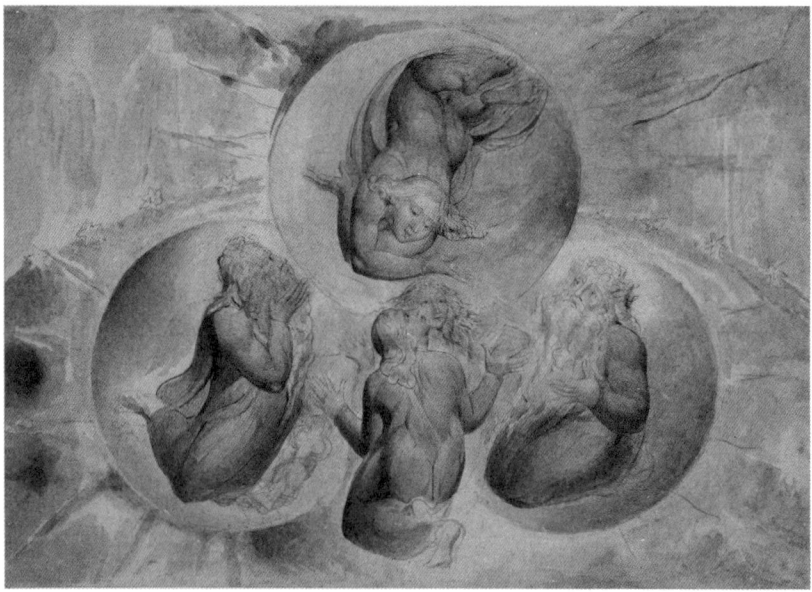

Fig. 49: *St Peter, St James, Dante and Beatrice with St John*, from the illustrations to Dante's *Divine Comedy*, Paradiso XXV.

## FOUNTAINS OF LIVING WATERS

Blake is good at describing Eternity's living freedom. Time, for instance, bursts into timelessness.

> *And every Minute has an azure Tent with silken Veils;*
> *And every Hour has a bright golden Gate carved with skill;*
> *And every Day & Night, has Walls of brass & Gates of adamant*
> *Shining like precious stones & ornamented with appropriate signs;*
> *And every Month, a silver paved Terrace builded high;*
> *And every Year, invulnerable Barriers with high Towers;*
> *And every Age is Moated deep with Bridges of silver & gold;*
> *And every Seven Ages is Incircled with a Flaming Fire.*[31]

Alternatively, from the perspective of eternal vision, the creatures of Earth are not stuck in a struggle for survival but are participating in Regeneration, which itself can be seen to presage the immortal and infinite. Blake refers to this process as being in *the Wine-presses of Luvah*—wine-presses being a Biblical way of referring to the unveiling called the apocalypse. For Blake, the apocalypse is not a calamity coming at some fearful moment in the future but is the moment-by-moment chance we have of discerning the path towards a fuller life: the judgement that frees not condemns. *Whenever any Individual Rejects Error & Embraces Truth, a Last Judgement passes upon that Individual,* he wrote.[32] Luvah is the superhero that facilitates this transformation. He gifts the desire needed to keep hope alive, which is probably why the name sounds like 'lover.' In a typical move, Blake dwells on bugs and worms to express the continual presence of the spiritually revolutionising apocalypse, when seen from the point of view Eternity. Read the following lines and you might never look in the same way at scrambling earwigs and scurrying woodlice.

> *The sportive Root, the Earth-worm, the gold Beetle, the wise Emmet*
> *Dance round the Wine-presses of Luvah: the Centipede is there;*
> *The ground Spider with many eyes; the Mole clothed in velvet;*
> *The ambitious Spider in his sullen web; the lucky golden Spinner;*
> *The Earwig arm'd; the tender Maggot emblem of immortality;*
> *The Flea, Louse, Bug, the Tape-Worm: all the Armies of Disease*
> *Visible or invisible to the slothful vegetating Man.*
> *The slow Slug; the Grasshopper that sings & laughs & drinks:*
> *Winter comes, he folds his slender bones without a murmur.*
> *The cruel Scorpion is there; the Gnat, Wasp, Hornet & the Honey Bee;*
> *The Toad & venomous Newt; the Serpent cloth'd in gems & gold:*

## AWAKE!

> *They throw off their gorgeous raiment: they rejoice with loud jubilee*
> *Around the Wine-presses of Luvah, naked & drunk with wine.*[33]

The so-called inanimate world takes on this vibrancy, too, and geographical places are equally translucent to Eternity, seen aright. We can imagine these perceptions striking Blake as, into the later years of his life, he continued to walk London's streets.

> *Lo!*
> *The stones are pity, and the bricks, well wrought affections,*
> *Enamel'd with love & kindness; & the tiles engraven gold*
> *Labour of merciful hands. The beams & rafters are forgiveness,*
> *The mortar & cement of the work, tears of honesty; the nails,*
> *And the screws & iron braces, are well wrought blandishments*
> *And well contrived words, firm fixing, never forgotten,*
> *Always comforting the remembrance; the floors, humility;*
> *The cielings, devotion; the hearths, thanksgiving.*[34]

The revisioning power of Eternity extends even to isolated Urizen, perhaps especially to Urizen, the one who had howled in *his soul-shudd'ring vacuum.*[35] The spectrous whispering that reason must rule with a rod of logical iron crumbles under the weight of its own demands: life is too big for it! And that brings Urizen's transformation: *at the clangor of the Arrows of Intellect*, which is the sound of true wisdom, *The innumerable Chariots of the Almighty appear'd in Heaven*—those *Chariots of fire* that belong to the cherubim, whose celestial intelligence is God's.[36] Then, in their midst is seen a great surprise, which is really a great relief: the human champions of science walk hand-in-hand with the human champions of the arts: *And Bacon & Newton & Locke, & Milton & Shakespear & Chaucer.*[37] In the light of Eternity, each knows how to contribute and give themselves to the whole. Ulro is no more.

Above all, human beings appear differently in the state of mind called Eternity. At one level, the smallest detail of an ordinary life will show distant reverberations of the divine wellspring; a smile, a gesture, a shadow of worry can intimate more than merely languishing in *the vegetative world*, because *the vegetative world* is replete with divine signs.[38] We are the sons and daughters of Los, according to Blake's mythology, and therefore bearers of transcendent light.

> *And Los beheld his Sons, and he beheld his Daughters:*
> *Every one a translucent Wonder, a Universe within,*

> *Increasing inwards, into length and breadth, and heighth,*
> *Starry & glorious. And they every one in their bright loins*
> *Have a beautiful golden gate which opens into the vegetative world;*
> *And every one a gate of rubies & all sorts of precious stones*
> *In their translucent hearts, which opens into the vegetative world;*
> *And every one a gate of iron dreadful and wonderful*
> *In their translucent heads, which opens into the vegetative world.*[39]

Another way in which people take on a different appearance in the light of Eternity concerns the nature of the sexes. Blake believed that from the fullest, unifying perspective, individuality shows itself to be androgynous—an androgyny represented in his images of men and women with Michelangelo-type bodies, physiologically having much in common. 'The androgynous is a consciousness that is neither masculine nor feminine; rather, it is a distinct third psychic possibility in which neither sex predominates,' writes the literary scholar, Diane Hoeveler, in a helpful discussion of this aspect of Blake.[40] The androgynous state has left the estrangement of the Fall and is anticipated in a longstanding Christian intuition arising from a comment of Jesus: 'When the dead rise, they will neither marry nor be given in marriage, they will be like angels in heaven.'[41]

A similar presentiment can be found in other traditions and might be explained in this way. As a person orientates towards the imagination, they become more porous to energies not previously active within them. They can then integrate within themselves characteristics often ascribed exclusively, either to the feminine or the masculine. The goal is not to become a kind male-female amalgam, which Blake terms *hermaphroditic*, but rather to embody a fuller humanity, a third thing. Blake describes a foretaste of this in Beulah, known when making love: *In Beulah the Female lets down her beautiful Tabernacle, | Which the Male enters magnificent between her Cherubim; | And becomes One with her Mingling condensing in Self-Love.*[42] However, in Eternity, sexual ecstasy is itself transcended. There comes a restoration, as the garments of gendered existence reveal themselves to be like a veil that has both concealed and signalled the *human form divine*.[43] 'Humanity is far above Sexual organisation & the Visions of the Night of Beulah,' Jerusalem tells her counterpart Vala.[44]

Blake's idea of androgyny is not, therefore, a reference to a person's biology but to their psychology. When embraced, a person becomes less defensive and rigid, less determined by the specifics of a narrow

# AWAKE!

Fig. 50: "Christ descending into the Grave," illustration for Blair's *The Grave*, in which the male Christ takes on androgynous form by being feminised.

personality. They still have a character but an expansive one. They are, thereby, capable of expressing what is universal through the particularities of who they are. Such people are hugely attractive because, whilst clearly being unique, they as clearly channel more than themselves. In a way, they have stepped aside so that the All can pour through them. *Annihilate the Selfhood in me, be though all my life!*[45]

Coleridge shared the intuition, writing 'a great mind must be androgynous'—by 'great' meaning a mind that has transcended being simply right or wrong because everything they say or do reflects aspects of truth.[46] The notion was taken up by Virginia Woolf, who wrote of it, too, in *A Room of One's Own*.[47] She explains that after the individual has grown weary of needing to voice their own suffering, troubles and difficulties, the mind can relax, becoming resonant and open, freer to range across wider circles of experience, impeded by less and less; 'naturally creative, incandescent and undivided.'[48] Such psychological reach is the creative's ideal, Woolf insists, manifest in the work of artists like Shakespeare; the bard not only had the imaginative power to bring a character to life, but also to make his characters timeless—a telling adjective given it means eternal. *In every bosom a Universe expands as wings*, Blake wrote: that imaginative potential is in us all.[49]

Human community is, similarly, not best based upon sentiment or solidarity, which are premised on an underlying isolation, but on who we are fully understood: as many reflections of the one life.

> *Mutual in one another's love and wrath all renewing*
> *We live as One Man; for contracting our infinite senses*

# FOUNTAINS OF LIVING WATERS

> *We behold multitude, or expanding, we behold as one,*
> *As One Man all the Universal Family, and that One Man*
> *We call Jesus the Christ; and he in us, and we in him*
> *Live in perfect harmony in Eden, the land of life,*
> *Giving, receiving, and forgiving each other's trespasses.*[50]

At heart, the invitation is to look, really look, moment by moment, and there find ourselves and others in the divine presence. Blake wants us to know what's real. Imaginatively peering through appearances, we can detect what surfaces are manifestations of. Asking what is stopping us from seeing that All—perhaps an ideology, perhaps fears, perhaps simple habit—we can put barriers aside. Becoming alert to what is passing and transient, which is only *a State*, we can enjoy a sharing in dynamic Eternity.

> *Judge then of thy Own Self: thy Eternal Lineaments explore*
> *What is Eternal & what Changeable? & what Annihilable!*
> *The Imagination is not a State: it is the Human Existence itself.*
> *Affection or Love becomes a State, when divided from Imagination*
> *The Memory is a State always, & the Reason is a State,*
> *Created to be Annihilated & a new Ratio Created.*
> *Whatever can be Created can be Annihilate; Forms cannot.*
> *The Oak is cut down by the Ax, the Lamb falls by the Knife,*
> *But their Forms Eternal Exist, For-ever. Amen. Hallelujah.*[51]

## Stronger and Stronger

One of the last impressions of William Blake is a recollection by the children of John Linnell. They remembered Blake visiting them in Hampstead, 'as a grave and sedate gentleman, with white hair, a lofty brow, and large lambent eyes... a kind and gentle manner.'[52] He was reluctant to travel to the high point outside of London. On the one hand, he enjoyed sitting with the youngsters, telling stories, helping them with drawings, but on the other hand, Hampstead caused him bouts of ill-health and for at least the last two years of his life, he was regularly afflicted with *abominable Ague*, serious stomach pains and shivering fits that he associated with the trips.[53]

He endured the sickness while it lasted, knowing that the *Furnaces of affliction*, when accepted, become *Fountains of Living Waters flowing from the Humanity Divine*.[54] He was gradually reduced *to only bones & sinews, All strings & bobbins like a Weaver's Loom*; his body wasted away but his wit did not and he continued working, particularly on the Dante illustrations.[55]

A few months before he died, Linnell suggested that he and Catherine move so as to be nearer to the assistance he could offer as a friend. (Linnell was to look after Catherine for the three years she lived after William was gone.) But Blake wanted to work: to *be Myself alone shut up in Myself*.[56] He knew that death was approaching and wrote in a letter: *I have been very near the Gates of Death & have returned very weak & an Old Man feeble & tottering, but not in Spirit & Life, not in The Real Man The Imagination which Liveth for Ever. In that I am stronger & stronger as this Foolish Body decays.*[57]

Towards the end, Catherine asked him where he would like to be buried and he replied in the dissenter's graveyard of Bunhill Fields, adding that he had no grief but in leaving her with whom he had lived happy and long. An hour or so before the moment came, he started to sing, his imagination active to the last. Then, on Sunday 12 August 1827, at about six in the evening, 'his spirit departed like the sighing of a gentle breeze.'[58]

The precise biological cause of his death is unclear, though it was likely exacerbated by *the infernal method, by corrosives* and long exposure to the vapours released when acids are poured on metals.[59] But also, Blake

Fig. 51: Blake's recently restored gravestone in Bunhill Fields.

knew that *a Natural Cause only seems*; it is the means to another end—the spiritual cause, which is that in losing life we find it.[60] As he had written in *Jerusalem* about the death of Albion: *the merciful Saviour in his arms | Receiv'd him.*[61]

He had first seen God at the age of four. He had known life in all its fullness with pain, loss, worry, rage and delight, satisfaction, friendship, love. He found himself out of sorts with his times, though paradoxically more consciously closer to the turbulent spirit of our age as a result of being able to be in the world but not of it. He had striven to revive the enchantment lost to others.

That is found by stepping into the infinity of each moment: awaking. Confined selfhood can yield to its eternal wellspring as a seemingly solitary subjectivity discovers that its active intelligence is, gloriously, not its own. For everything in time is timeless, finite beings springing from a shared divine source. Politics could change with this realisation to focus on a shared life orientated by the goal of enabling sight of Eternity; society could also be renewed by knowing that the human task is to seek communion with all that is, human and non-human. Materialistic philosophies might be undone, as well, by reflecting clearly on the wonder of experience. For the cosmos is an outpouring of the imagination that fills us, a celebration of creativity with which we can join. We will be transformed from within, as all beings and things becoming translucent to each other and God.

> *All Human Forms identified, even Tree, Metal, Earth & Stone: all*
> *Human Forms identified, living, going forth & returning wearied*
> *Into the Planetary lives of Years, Months, Days & Hours; reposing,*
> *And then Awakening into his Bosom in the Life of Immortality.*[62]

# NOTES

INTRODUCTION

1. K432.
2. K822.
3. K623.
4. K481.
5. K154.
6. K622.
7. K431.
8. K154.
9. K799.
10. K149.
11. K149.
12. K149.
13. See Weir, David, *Brahma in the West: William Blake and the Oriental Renaissance*, Albany, NY: State University of New York Press, 2003.
14. I am indebted to Owen Barfield for this formulation. See Barfield, Owen, *History, Guilt, and Habit*, Middletown, CT: Wesleyan University Press, 1979, 18.
15. K716.

1. SING YOUR INFANT JOY

1. Churchill, Winston, *A History of the English-Speaking Peoples, Vol III, The Age of Revolution*, New York: Bantam Books, 1963, 123.
2. Corfield, Penelope J., *The Georgians: The Deeds and Misdeeds of 18$^{th}$ Century Britain*, London: Yale University Press, 2023, 370ff.
3. Symons, Arthur, *William Blake*, New York: E.P. Dutton and Company, 1907, retrieved from https://en.wikisource.org/wiki/William_Blake_(Symons)/Blake%27s_Horoscope
4. Ackroyd, Peter, *Blake*, London: Minerva, 1996, 26.
5. K541.
6. K118.
7. K380.
8. K117–8.
9. K212.
10. Huxley, Aldous, *The Devils of Loudun*, London: Chatto & Windus, 1952, 237.

11. K701.
12. K125.
13. K100.
14. K127.
15. K128.
16. K128.
17. K128.
18. K129.
19. K129.
20. K130.
21. K380.
22. K217.
23. K216.
24. K213.
25. The Wikipedia entry for Negative Capability is informative: https://en.wikipedia.org/wiki/Negative_capability
26. Whitney, William Dwight, *The Century Dictionary and Cyclopedia: A Work of Universal Reference in All departments of Knowledge with a New Atlas of the World*, Volume VI, New York: The Century Co., 1904, 4990, retrieved https://archive.org/details/cu31924091890636/page/4990/mode/2up?view=theater&q=reason
27. K579.
28. K111.
29. K576.
30. Sklar, Susanne M., *Blake's Jerusalem as Visionary Theatre: Entering the Divine Body*, Oxford: Oxford University Press, 2011, 24.
31. Gilchrist, Alexander, *Gilchrist on Blake, The Life of William Blake Pictor Ignotus*, Richard Holmes (ed.), London: Harper Perennial, 2005, 53.
32. Retrieved from the British Library online at: https://www.bl.uk/collection-items/a-select-collection-of-english-songs
33. Bentley Jr, G.E., *The Stranger from Paradise: A Biography of William Blake*, London: Yale University Press, 2001, 133.
34. Ibid.
35. Coleridge, Samuel Taylor, Postscript of a Letter to The Rev. H.F. Cary, 6 February 1818, retrieved: https://en.wikisource.org/wiki/Postscript_of_Letter_to_The_Rev._H._F._Cary,_6_February_1818
36. Coleridge, Samuel Taylor, Fragment of a Letter to Charles Augustus Tulk, 12 February 1818, retrieved: https://en.wikisource.org/wiki/Letter_to_Charles_Augustus_Tulk,_12_February_1818
37. Mark 10:14.

## 2. BY CAME AN ANGEL

1. K672.
2. Swift, Jonathan, *The Prose Works of Jonathan Swift*, London: George Bell and Sons, 1898, retrieved from https://www.gutenberg.org/files/12746/12746-h/12746-h.htm

3. Ibid.
4. K157.
5. Gilchrist, Alexander, *Gilchrist on Blake, The Life of William Blake Pictor Ignotus*, Holmes, Richard (ed.), London: Harper Perennial, 2005, 365.
6. K729.
7. Gilchrist 2005, 9.
8. Ibid.
9. Ackroyd, Peter, *Blake*, London: Minerva, 1996, 23.
10. Gilchrist 2005, 10.
11. Tatham, Frederick, *Life of Blake*, London, 1832, retrieved from: https://en.wikisource.org/wiki/Page:The_letters_of_William_Blake_(1906).djvu/61
12. Bentley Jr, G.E., *The Stranger from Paradise: A Biography of William Blake*, London: Yale University Press, 2001, 105.
13. Ibid., 398.
14. Symons, Arthur, *William Blake*, New York: E.P. Dutton and Company, 1907, retrieved from: https://en.wikisource.org/wiki/Page:William_Blake_(Symons).djvu/433
15. Vickers, Salley, 'Why We Need Fairies,' retrieved from: https://www.salleyvickers.com/why-we-need-fairies/
16. K214.
17. Gilchrist 2005, 342.
18. Bentley Jr 2001, 166.
19. K539.
20. K538.
21. K622.
22. James, William, *The Varieties of Religious Experience*, London: Penguin Books, 1982, 14.
23. Storr, Anthony, 'The Sanity of True Genius,' in *Churchill's Black Dog, Kafka's Mice and Other Phenomena of the Human Mind*, New York: Grove Press, 1988, 249–68.
24. Coleridge, Samuel Taylor, *Biographia Literaria*, George Watson (ed.), London: J.M. Dent, 1975, 161ff.
25. Gilchrist 2005, 138.
26. Ibid.
27. Ibid., 344.
28. Barfield, Owen, *History in English Words*, Gt. Barrington, MA: Lindisfarne Books, 2007, 179.
29. Ibid., 176.
30. Ackroyd, 1996, 24.
31. K237.
32. Ibid.
33. Ibid.
34. Ibid.
35. Ibid.
36. K238.
37. Ibid.
38. K245.
39. Locke, John, *An Essay Concerning Human Understanding*, 1690, retrieved from:

https://enlightenment.supersaturated.com/johnlocke/BOOKIIChapterXXXIII.html
40. K550.
41. Symons 1907, retrieved from: https://en.wikisource.org/wiki/William_Blake_(Symons)/Extracts_from_the_Diary,_Letters,_and_Reminiscences_of_Henry_Crabb_Robinson
42. Gilchrist 2005, 343.

### 3. ALL THAT WE SEE IS VISION

1. K6.
2. K124.
3. K793.
4. K6.
5. K6.
6. K594–5.
7. Bentley Jr, G.E., *The Stranger from Paradise: A Biography of William Blake*, London: Yale University Press, 2001, 24.
8. K602.
9. Hill, Rosemary, *Time's Witness*, London: Penguin Books, 2023.
10. Ibid. 6.
11. K54.
12. Loxton, Alice, *Uproar! Satire, Scandal & Printmakers in Georgian London*, London: Icon Books, 2023.
13. K522.
14. K605.
15. Higgs, John, *William Blake Vs The World*, London: Weidenfeld & Nicolson, 2021, 338.
16. Shakespeare, William, *A Midsummer Night's Dream*, Act V, Scene 1, lines 8–9.
17. K97.
18. Murdoch, Iris, *Existentialists and Mystics: Writings on Philosophy and Literature*, Harmondsworth: Penguin Books, 1999, 374.
19. K520.
20. K521.
21. K181.
22. K431.
23. K124.
24. K191.
25. Conway Morris, Simon, *From Extraterrestrials and Animal Minds: Seven Myths of Evolution*, New Brunswick, NJ: Templeton Press, 2022, 161.
26. Francis Bacon, *Novum Organum*, 1620, Retrieved from: https://www.oxfordreference.com/display/10.1093/acref/9780191843730.001.0001/q-oro-ed5-00000644
27. Wolfe, Charles T., 'The Life of Matter: Early Modern Vital Matter Theories,' in *Notes and Records: The Royal Society Journal of the History of Science*, 21 June 2023, retrieved from: https://royalsocietypublishing.org/doi/10.1098/rsnr.2023.0049

28. Darwin, Charles, *The Expression of the Emotions in Man and Animals*, New York: D. Appleton and Company, 1899, retrieved from: https://www.gutenberg.org/cache/epub/1227/pg1227-images.html
29. Midgley, Mary, *The Solitary Self: Darwin and the Selfish Gene*, Durham: Acumen, 2010, 42.
30. Darwin, Charles, *The Variation of Animals and Plants Under Domestication*, London: John Murray, 1875, 8, retrieved from: https://darwin-online.org.uk/content/frameset?viewtype=text&itemID=F880.1&pageseq=1
31. Part of the reason for the delay is the novelty but also the politics of science communication, particularly in relation to Darwinian evolution, which is notably contentious. See my chapter, 'The Public Understanding of Biology: A Journalist's Perspective,' in Reiss, Michael J.; Watts, Fraser; Wiseman, Harris, *Rethinking Biology: Public Understandings*, Singapore: World Scientific Publishing, 2020, 323–31.
32. Ball, Philip, *How Life Works*, London: Pan Macmillan, 2024, in Prologue retrieved from Kindle. His italics.
33. K520–1.
34. K287.
35. Naydler, Jeremy, *How Caterpillars Acquire Wings*, Oxford: Abzu Press, 1995.
36. Plato, *Phaedrus*, 246.
37. K617.
38. K679.
39. K617.
40. Ibid.
41. Bentley Jr, G.E. 2001, 83ff.
42. K779.
43. K623.
44. K617.

## 4. CREATE A SYSTEM

1. K445.
2. K67.
3. K74.
4. Gilchrist, Alexander, *Gilchrist on Blake, The Life of William Blake Pictor Ignotus*, Richard Holmes (ed.), London: Harper Perennial, 2005, 327.
5. Bentley Jr, G.E., *The Stranger from Paradise: A Biography of William Blake*, London: Yale University Press, 2001, 77.
6. K386.
7. *Oxford Dictionary of Quotations*, Oxford: Oxford University Press, 2004, 339.
8. K211.
9. Paine, Thomas, *The Project Gutenberg's Complication of the Writings of Thomas Paine*, 2010, retrieved from https://www.gutenberg.org/files/31270/31270-h/31270-h.htm
10. Gilchrist 2005, 105.
11. See for example K741.
12. K171.
13. K682.

14. K433.
15. I stress the point because it is common amongst contemporary scholars of Blake to assume that, in spite of his clear rejection, he developed a naturalistic account of religion—or as it is also described, a non-realist theology of God: God as a useful hypothesis, as say an idealised figure projected into fictitious heavens. This theory of religion has become hugely influential, articulated soon after Blake died in *The Essence of Christianity* by Ludwig Feuerbach, who argued that theology is really just anthropology: when human beings seek God they are really just seeking themselves. And sometimes Blake can appear to advocate something similar, if sayings of his are taken in isolation. *God only Acts & Is in existing beings or Men*, he writes in *The Marriage of Heaven and Hell*, for example (K155). But here, the insertion of the word 'only' is not supposed to suggest that God can be done away with, as if God refers only to an aspect of the human, but rather is Blake's way of keeping the distinction between God as the source energy and God in existing beings or Men as the manifestation of that source energy. In other words, the relationship between God and existing beings or Men is another contrary: distinct but not separate. There is the divine source energy and then there are the actions of that divine source energy in existing beings or Men. So, these declarations of divine immanence, which he regularly makes, are not expressions of an implicit atheism but of his mysticism; he hears the *Universal Father* (K744) and the *Divine Saviour* (K641) not as if from afar but in intimate visions—a crucial aspect of his spirituality that we will come to in Part III.

    Intuiting God's transcendence as an eternal presence within the alert individual, as well as other created beings and things, is standard amongst Christian writers before the modern period. Blake summarised it in this way: *Therefore God becomes as we are, that we may be as he is* (K98)—a theological formula that was repeated throughout the early and medieval Christian periods by figures from Clement of Alexandria to Leo the Great. Moreover, there is good evidence that Blake directly knew of these so-called Church Fathers. His mother was a Moravian, a church that located its authority in the Eastern Orthodox Church, which, unlike Western Protestant Churches, was continually informed by directly engaging with the writings of these venerable theologians. In addition to that contact, recent research by Susanne Sklar has revealed that throughout Blake's adult life in London, he lived within a few minutes' walk of an Orthodox chapel that was led by Father Yakov Smirnov, a priest who is known to have welcomed writers and thinkers. (See Susanne Sklar's essay, 'Transfiguring Crucifixion,' in the forthcoming *Blake Sees Jesus*, edited by Helen Bruder and Tristanne Connelly.) Blake witnessed Orthodox mystical theology as a living practice, as is clear in some of his art, too: the image entitled 'The Virgin and Child' is clearly inspired by icon painting. In short, for Blake, theology is not anthropology, but quite the reverse: an awakened anthropology is theology.
16. Paine 2010, retrieved https://www.gutenberg.org/files/31270/31270-h/31270-h.htm
17. Porter, Roy, *Enlightenment: Britain and the Creation of the Modern World*, London: Allen Lane, 2000, 32.

18. K629.
19. K481.
20. K44.
21. Ibid.
22. K157.
23. Uglow, Jenny, *The Lunar Men: The Friends Who Made the Future, 1730–1810*, London: Faber & Faber, 2003.
24. See Schmitter, Amy M., '17th and 18th Century Theories of Emotions,' The Stanford Encyclopedia of Philosophy (Summer 2021 Edition), Edward N. Zalta (ed.), retrieved from: https://plato.stanford.edu/archives/sum2021/entries/emotions-17th18th/
25. K200.
26. Roland Barthes, *A Lover's Discourse: Fragments*, London: Penguin Books, 1979, 35.
27. Symons, Arthur, *William Blake*, New York: E.P. Dutton and Company, 1907, retrieved from: https://en.wikisource.org/wiki/William_Blake_(Symons)/Extracts_from_the_Diary,_Letters,_and_Reminiscences_of_Henry_Crabb_Robinson
28. Ibid.
29. Ibid.
30. K35.
31. K9.
32. K516.
33. K379.
34. Hume was deploying a 'bait-and-switch' strategy, as the historian of ideas, Peter Harrison, points out (Harrison, Peter, *Some New World: Myths of Supernatural Belief in a Secular Age*, Cambridge: Cambridge University Press, 2024, 19): setting up the argument on a hidden theistic premise, then deploying the argument to erode the premise.
35. K532.
36. K477.
37. K481.
38. K717.
39. K621.
40. K445.
41. See Thompson, E.P., *Witness Against The Beast: William Blake and the Moral Law*, New York: The New Press, 1993 – though, in line with subsequent scholarship, I don't think Blake was a Muggletonian and, for myself, reckon that aligning Blake with antinomianism, as Thompson suggests, is not quite right either, as we shall see.
42. Gilchrist, 2005, 350.
43. Carlyle, Thomas, *A Carlyle Reader: Selections from the Writings of Thomas Carlyle*, G.B. Tennyson (ed.), Cambridge: Cambridge University Press, 2001, retrieved from: https://learninglink.oup.com/access/content/schaller-3e-dashboard-resources/document-thomas-carlyle-excerpts-from-signs-of-the-times-1829
44. Machin, Anna, *Why We Love*, London: Weidenfeld and Nicolson, 2022, Chapter One, retrieved from Kindle edition.
45. K738.
46. K673.

47. Heisenberg, Werner, *Physics and Philosophy*, London: Penguin Books, 1990, 188ff.
48. Gunton, Richard M.; Stafleu, Marinus D.; Reiss, Michael J., 'A General Theory of Objectivity: Contributions from the Reformational Philosophy Tradition,' *Foundations of Science* 27, 2022, 941–55, retrieved from: https://discovery.ucl.ac.uk/id/eprint/10153750/3/Reiss_A%20General%20Theory%20of%20Objectivity_AAM.pdf
49. Isaacson, Walter, *Einstein: His Life and Universe*, London: Pocket Pockets, 2008, 94.
50. K237.
51. K363.
52. K689.
53. I am indebted to Merlin Sheldrake for expressions like 'entangled' and 'involution' that capture nature's imagination, in his book, *Entangled Life*, London: The Bodley Head, 2020.
54. K158.
55. K152.
56. K451.
57. K379.
58. Bentley Jr 2001, 83.
59. K287.
60. Ibid.
61. K533.


5. MONEY IS USELESS

1. Tatham, Frederick, *Life of Blake*, London, 1832, retrieved from: https://en.wikisource.org/wiki/The_Letters_of_William_Blake/Life_of_Blake
2. Ibid.
3. Ibid., 42.
4. Letter from Hayley to Lady Hesketh, 15 July 1802, in Bentley, G.E. (ed), *William Blake: The Critical Heritage*, London: Routledge, 1975, 101.
5. Gilchrist, Alexander, *Gilchrist on Blake, The Life of William Blake Pictor Ignotus*, Richard Holmes (ed.), London: Harper Perennial, 2005, 317.
6. Ibid., 65.
7. Corfield, Penelope J., *The Georgians: The Deeds and Misdeeds of 18th Century Britain*, London: Yale University Press, 2023, 63, 81.
8. Smith, Adam, *The Theory of Moral Sentiments*, Oxford: Clarendon Press, 1979, 180.
9. Ibid., 181.
10. K647.
11. K790.
12. K798.
13. K793.
14. K777.
15. K515.
16. K198.
17. K238.
18. K481.

19. The word 'misenchants' comes from McCarraher, Eugene, *The Enchantments of Mammon: How Capitalism Became the Religion of Modernity*, London: Belknap Press, 2019, 70.
20. K673.
21. Bentley Jr, G.E., *The Stranger from Paradise: A Biography of William Blake*, London: Yale University Press, 2001, 73.
22. K558.
23. K559.
24. K776.
25. K661.
26. K150.
27. K149.
28. K148.
29. K149.
30. Ibid.
31. Ibid.
32. Ibid.
33. K385.
34. K774.
35. Kant, Immanuel, 'Idea for a Universal History with a Cosmopolitan Purpose,' quoted in *Oxford Dictionary of Quotations*, Oxford: Oxford University Press, 2004, 441.
36. K152.
37. K647.
38. K613.
39. K156.
40. K81.
41. K306.
42. K79.
43. K149.
44. K150.
45. K151–2.
46. K151.
47. Ibid.
48. Luke 9:62.
49. K152.
50. K216.
51. 'Infant mortality by social status in Georgian London,' The Cambridge Group for the History of Population and Social Structure, University of Cambridge, retrieved from: https://www.campop.geog.cam.ac.uk/research/projects/georgianinfantmortality/
52. K481.
53. K215.
54. K218.
55. K97.
56. Ibid.

# NOTES

## 6. LOVE! LOVE! LOVE!

1. Gilchrist, Alexander, *Gilchrist on Blake, The Life of William Blake Pictor Ignotus*, Richard Holmes (ed.), London: Harper Perennial, 2005, 337.
2. The story is fully explored by Marsha Keith Schuchard in *Why Mrs Blake Cried: William Blake and the Erotic Imagination* (London: Pimlico, 2007). However, it is worth reading the review by the Blake scholar, G.E. Bentley, in the journal, *Blake: An Illustrated Quarterly*, Volume 40, Issue 4, Spring 2007, retrieved from: https://bq.blakearchive.org/40.4.bentley. In it, Bentley, who is the editor of *Blake Records*, the respected archive of all matters to do with Blake's life and work, appreciates the picture painted by Schuchard of the milieu in which the Blakes lived, but concludes: 'The primary problem of the book is that the biographical evidence for Catherine Blake's tears is extraordinarily slight.' It seems unlikely that William's Abrahamic request occurred.
3. Schuchard 2007, 38–9.
4. K149.
5. K151.
6. Corfield, Penelope J., *The Georgians: The Deeds and Misdeeds of 18th Century Britain*, London: Yale University Press, 2023, 111.
7. Letter to Godwin, cited in Wollstonecraft, Mary, Oxford Dictionary of National Biography, retrieved from: https://www.oxforddnb.com/display/10.1093/ref:odnb/9780198614128.001.0001/odnb-9780198614128-e-10893?rskey=xJUWZg&result=9
8. Darwin, Charles, *The Descent of Man*, London: John Murray, 1871.
9. K672.
10. K431.
11. Teresa of Ávila, *The Life of Saint Teresa of Ávila by Herself*, London: Penguin, 1957, 210.
12. Gilchrist 2005, 323.
13. Teresa of Ávila 1957, 210.
14. K219.
15. Wollstonecraft, Mary, *A Vindication of the Rights of Woman with Strictures on Political and Moral Subjects*, London: J. Johnson, 1792, retrieved from https://www.earlymoderntexts.com/assets/pdfs/wollstonecraft1792_4.pdf
16. K189.
17. I am indebted to Michael Ferber's interpretation in his book, *Romanticism: A Very Short Introduction*, Oxford: Oxford University Press, 2010, 82ff.
18. K191.
19. Plato, *Symposium*, 191D, translated by Alexander Nehamas and Paul Woodruff in the edition published by Indianapolis: Hackett Publishing Company, 1989, 27.
20. K189.
21. The psychopathology of Luther, and its impact upon the Reformation, is brilliantly analysed in Lyndal Roper, *Martin Luther: Renegade and Prophet*, London: Bodley Head, 2016, from which I've taken the quote from Luther's autobiography, too.
22. K770.
23. K481.

24. K189.
25. Ibid.
26. K817.
27. Ibid.
28. K189.
29. Ibid.
30. Ibid.
31. Ibid.
32. K190.
33. K191.
34. Ibid.
35. K190.
36. Ibid.
37. K195.
38. K192.
39. K191.
40. Ibid.
41. Murdoch, Iris, *The Sovereignty of the Good*, London: Routledge Classics, 2001, 100.
42. K194.
43. Genesis 4:1, King James Version.
44. K192.
45. K194.
46. K195.
47. The quote is inscribed on a bench in Ruskin Park, which is about all that remains of what Blake knew of *the lovely hills of Camberwell*, though I have not been able to locate its original source.
48. K194.

## 7. WHY DOES THE RAVEN CRY?

1. K576.
2. Ackroyd, Peter, *Blake*, London: Minerva, 1996, 99.
3. K238.
4. Gilchrist, Alexander, *Gilchrist on Blake, The Life of William Blake Pictor Ignotus*, Richard Holmes (ed.), London: Harper Perennial, 2005, 65.
5. K799.
6. Gilchrist 2005, 76.
7. K797.
8. Ibid.
9. K276–7.
10. K152.
11. K287.
12. K111.
13. Barfield, Owen, 'Form in Poetry' in Barfield, Owen, *The Riddle of the Sphinx: Essays on the Evolution of Consciousness*, Rory O'Connor (ed.), Oxford: Barfield Press, 2023, 1–8.

14. Barfield, Owen, *Romanticism Comes of Age: Essays on the creative imagination*, Oxford: Barfield Press, 2012, 3.
15. Barfield, Owen, *Poetic Diction: A Study in Meaning*, Oxford: Barfield Press, 2010, 44.
16. Barfield 2012, 2–3.
17. K153.
18. K90.
19. K98.
20. Psalm 139:14, King James Version.
21. K153.
22. Isaiah 20:2, King James Version.
23. Ezekiel 4:4, 15, King James Version.
24. K154.
25. Smith, Adam, *An Inquiry into the Nature and Causes of the Wealth of Nations*, London: W. Strahan and T. Cadell, 1776, retrieved from https://www.gutenberg.org/cache/epub/3300/pg3300-images.html
26. K337.
27. K207.
28. K154.
29. K207.
30. K729.
31. Gilchrist 2005, 124.
32. K668.

## 8. A MIGHTY & AWFUL CHANGE

1. Gilchrist, Alexander, *Gilchrist on Blake, The Life of William Blake Pictor Ignotus*, Richard Holmes (ed.), London: Harper Perennial, 2005, 103.
2. K799.
3. K481.
4. Price, Richard, *Observations on the Nature of Civil Liberty, the Principles of Government, and the Justice and Policy of the War with America*, London: Edward and Charles Dilly and Thomas Cadell, 1776, retrieved https://oll.libertyfund.org/titles/price-observations-on-the-nature-of-civil-liberty
5. K160.
6. K487.
7. K151.
8. K361.
9. K534.
10. K195–6.
11. K195, K159.
12. K195.
13. K196.
14. Ibid.
15. Ibid.
16. Ibid.

17. K197.
18. Ibid.
19. Ibid.
20. Ibid.
21. K198.
22. Ibid.
23. Ibid.
24. K199.
25. K214.
26. K200.
27. K498.
28. K509.
29. K647.
30. K203.
31. K202.
32. K396.
33. K200.
34. K389.
35. Plato, *Apology*, 31c-d; Mark 12:17.
36. K684.
37. K342.
38. K202.
39. Ibid.
40. Ibid.
41. K621.
42. K203.
43. K241.
44. Ibid.
45. K243.
46. K241.
47. K243.
48. K241.
49. K157.
50. K518.
51. K242.
52. Ibid.
53. K215.
54. K241.
55. K238.
56. K239.
57. K240.
58. Ibid.
59. K244.
60. K245.
61. K655.

## 9. SYMPATHY CAME FORTH

1. As quoted by Tom Chatfield in *Wise Animals: How Technology Has Made Us What We Are*, London: Picador, 2024, 146.
2. K265, K362.
3. K98.
4. K273.
5. K379.
6. Le Guin, Ursula K., *Cheek by Jowl*, Seattle: Aqueduct Press, 2009, quote retrieved from: https://www.ursulakleguin.com/cheek-by-jowl-review
7. K222.
8. Ibid.
9. Ibid.
10. Ibid.
11. Ibid.
12. K224.
13. Ibid.
14. K225.
15. Ibid.
16. K227.
17. K510.
18. Seth, Anil, *Being You*, London: Faber & Faber, 2022.
19. K228–9.
20. Ibid.
21. K230.
22. Ibid.
23. K649.
24. Taylor, Charles, *A Secular Age*, London: The Belknap Press of Harvard University Press, 2007.
25. K649.
26. Quoted in Eron, Sarah, "Bound… by their narrowing perceptions': Sympathetic Bondage and Perverse Pity in Blake's The Book of Urizen,' *Blake: An Illustrated Quarterly*, Volume 46, Issue 3, Winter 2012–13, retrieved from https://bq.blakearchive.org/pdfs/46.3.eron.pdf
27. Seth 2022.
28. K43.
29. K230.
30. K231.
31. K117.
32. K221. I am grateful for Rowan Williams's discussion of Blake's notion of pity in "The human form divine': Radicalism and Orthodoxy in William Blake,' in Bennett, Zoë & Gowler, David B. (eds), *Radical Christian Voices and Practice: Essays in Honour of Christopher Rowland*, Oxford: Oxford University Press, 2012, 151–164.
33. K217.
34. K231.
35. Ibid.

36. K233.
37. K235.
38. Ibid.
39. K215.
40. K236.
41. K237.
42. K249.
43. K790.
44. K250.
45. K240.
46. K254.
47. K236.
48. These references to Orc come from The Song of Los, another post-revolutionary poem that is a thought-experiment for Blake.
49. McGilchrist, Iain, *The Matter With Things: The Ways to Truth, Volume 1*, London: Perspectiva Press, 2021, 6.

## 10. NATURE, MOTHER OF ALL

1. K481.
2. Bentley Jr, G.E., *The Stranger from Paradise: A Biography of William Blake*, London: Yale University Press, 2001, 210.
3. K800.
4. K803.
5. K818.
6. K799.
7. K513.
8. Blake is close here to Aristotle, whom he read. The ancient Greek philosopher argued that a full description of anything that happens must incorporate four coincident causes: the material or quantitative, the efficient or mechanical, the formal or purposeful, and the final which is the value of what takes place.
9. K804.
10. K124.
11. K716.
12. K717.
13. K536.
14. Raine, Kathleen, in a lecture given at the first Temenos Conference in 1986, entitled, 'Nature, House of the Soul,' retrieved from: https://www.temenosacademy.org/the-first-temenos-conference-1986/
15. K213.
16. K211.
17. K213.
18. K150.
19. See K150.
20. K511–2, though I have changed the order of the paragraphs.
21. Raine 1986.

22. K536.
23. I have in mind Annie Dillard, *Teaching a Stone to Talk*, New York, NY: Harpercollins, 1982.
24. K315.
25. K290.
26. Whitley, Andrew, personal blog, retrieved from: https://www.breadmatters.com/hands-on-my-bread/
27. Midgley, Mary, *Wisdom, Information, and Wonder: What is Knowledge For?*, London: Routledge, 1989, 41.
28. Locke, John, *Second Treatise of Government*, Chapter V, Of Property, Section 32, 1764, retrieved from https://www.gutenberg.org/files/7370/7370-h/7370-h.htm
29. Ibid., Sections 42 & 36.
30. These thoughts are found in Shaftesbury, Anthony Ashley-Cooper, Earl of, *Characteristicks of Men, Manners, Opinions, Times*, Cambridge: Cambridge University Press, 1999.
31. Gill, Michael B., *A Philosophy of Beauty: Shaftesbury on Nature, Virtue, and Art*, Princeton: Princeton University Press, 2022, 1.
32. K693.
33. K583.
34. K660.
35. See Sheldrake, Rupert, *The Rebirth of Nature: The Greening of Science and God*, Rochester, VT: Inner Traditions, 1994.
36. Huxley, T.H., 'The Struggle for Existence in Human Society (1888), in *Collected Essays*, Volume IX, London: Macmillan & Co, 1893-95, retrieved from: https://mathcs.clarku.edu/huxley/CE9/Str.html
37. Darwin, Charles, *The Variation of Animals and Plants Under Domestication*, London: John Murray, 1875, retrieved from: https://darwin-online.org.uk/content/frameset?pageseq=1&itemID=F877.1&viewtype=text
38. K285.
39. K646.
40. K643.
41. Ibid.
42. K522, K611.
43. K611.
44. K738.
45. K633.
46. K717.
47. K151.
48. K179.
49. K622.
50. K484.
51. K828–9.
52. Ackroyd, Peter, *Blake*, London: Minerva, 1996, 244.

## 11. NO OTHER CHRISTIANITY

1. K831.
2. K844.
3. K851.
4. K563.
5. K548.
6. K849.
7. K432.
8. Bentley Jr, G.E., *The Stranger from Paradise: A Biography of William Blake*, London: Yale University Press, 2001, 336.
9. K622.
10. K757.
11. K153.
12. K98.
13. K516.
14. Ibid.
15. K18.
16. K526.
17. K97.
18. Evans, Pippa, *Improv Your Life: An Improvisor's Guide To Embracing Whatever Life Throws At You*, London: Hodder Studio, 2021, 51–2.
19. K115, K214.
20. K624.
21. K214.
22. Ibid.
23. K604.
24. K794.
25. John 8:7.
26. Heppner, Christopher, 'The Woman Taken in Adultery: An Essay on Blake's 'Style of Designing',' in *Blake: An Illustrated Quarterly*, Volume 17, Issue 2, Fall 198, 44–59, retrieved https://bq.blakearchive.org/17.2.heppner
27. Ibid. 49.
28. John 8:11.
29. K755.
30. K117.
31. K755.
32. K757.
33. K495.
34. Ibid.
35. K675.
36. K533.
37. K620.
38. K533.
39. K738, K744, K481.
40. K743.

41. K117.
42. K743.
43. K522.
44. K150.
45. *Bhagavad Vita*, III.19, translated by W.J. Johnson, Oxford: Oxford World Classics, 1994.
46. K623.
47. *Bhagavad Vita*, IV.22.
48. K716.
49. K621.
50. K623.
51. Bentley 2001 412.
52. K98.
53. K752.
54. K647.
55. Bentley 2001, 393.
56. K716.

## 12. FOUNTAINS OF LIVING WATERS

1. Bentley Jr, G.E., *The Stranger from Paradise: A Biography of William Blake*, London: Yale University Press, 2001, 381.
2. Ibid., 381.
3. Ibid., 364.
4. Ibid., 394.
5. Ibid., 361.
6. Ibid., 392.
7. The story is related in ibid., 408
8. Caption to the artwork at Tate Britain.
9. K635.
10. K288.
11. This is my suggestion, not Blake's, who had mixed feelings about Dante. At heart, he put Dante in the same league as Shakespeare and Milton, which is in the highest category of divine poetic genius. But at the same time, he disagreed with Dante on specific points, objecting, for instance, to Dante's advocacy of monarchy and veneration of pre-Christian poets, particularly those with martial tendencies like Homer; these classical authors had been co-opted by the warmongers of his day. He also concluded that Dante thought God exacted vengeance for sin, rather than offering forgiveness, though I present the case for Blake and Dante agreeing on the latter in my book on *The Divine Comedy* (see bibliography). I think that both Dante and Blake concluded that God brings salvation to all, without compromising on the seriousness of evil.
12. *Inferno* 1:1.
13. K818.
14. K666.
15. K632.

16. Sklar, Susanne, 'William Blake's Mythic System,' *Temenos Academy Online Papers*, Summer Term 2020, retrieved https://www.temenosacademy.org/wp-content/uploads/Blakes-Mythic-System-Dr-Susanne-Sklar-May-2020.pdf and K648.
17. Weinberg, Steven, *The First Three Minutes: A modern view of the origin of the universe*, London: Fontana Paperbacks, 1983, 149.
18. K97.
19. K609.
20. K238, K97, K647.
21. K661.
22. K623.
23. K200, K481.
24. K578.
25. K195.
26. K730.
27. K277.
28. K518.
29. K266.
30. K372, K271.
31. K516.
32. K613.
33. K513.
34. K632.
35. K222.
36. K481, K745.
37. K745.
38. K635.
39. Ibid.
40. Hoeveler, Diane, 'Blake's Erotic Apocalypse: The Androgynous Ideal in 'Jerusalem',' e-Publications @ Marquette, 1-1-1979, retrieved from: https://epublications.marquette.edu/english_fac/76/
41. Mark 12:25.
42. K656.
43. See, for example, K755.
44. K721.
45. K623.
46. Coleridge, Samuel Taylor, *The Table Talk and Omniana of Samuel Taylor Coleridge*, 1 September 1832, London: Oxford University Press, 1917, 201.
47. Woolf, Virginia, *A Room of One's Own*, London: The Hogarth Press, 1991.
48. Ibid., 92.
49. K665.
50. K664ff.
51. K522.
52. Bentley 2001, 432.
53. K868–9.
54. K744.
55. K871, K875.

56. K876.
57. K878.
58. Bentley 2001, 437.
59. K154.
60. K513.
61. K677.
62. K747.

# SELECT BIBLIOGRAPHY

Ackroyd, Peter, *Blake*, London: Minerva, 1996
Ball, Philip, 'Science as a Culture and the Science of Meaning,' in *Marginalia Review of Books*, 23 June 2023
———, *How Life Works*, London: Pan Macmillan, 2024
Barfield, Owen, *History, Guilt, and Habit*. Middletown, CT: Wesleyan University Press, 1979
———, *History in English Words*, Gt. Barrington, MA: Lindisfarne Books, 2007
———, *Poetic Diction: A Study in Meaning*, Oxford: Barfield Press, 2010
———, *Romanticism Comes of Age: Essays on the creative imagination*, Oxford: Barfield Press, 2012
———, *The Riddle of the Sphinx: Essays on the Evolution of Consciousness*, Rory O'Connor (ed.), Oxford: Barfield Press, 2023
Bentley Hart, David, *You Are Gods*, Notre Dame, Indiana: University of Notre Dame Press, 2022
Bentley Jr, G.E. (ed), *William Blake: The Critical Heritage*, London: Routledge, 1975
———, *The Stranger from Paradise: A Biography of William Blake*, London: Yale University Press, 2001
———, Review of Marsha Keith Schuchard, 'Why Mrs Blake Cried: William Blake and the Sexual Basis of Spiritual Vision,' in *Blake: An Illustrated Quarterly*, Volume 40, Issue 4, Spring 2007
Berlin, Isaiah, *The Roots of Romanticism*, London: Pimlico, 2000
Bindman, David (introduction), *William Blake: The Complete Illuminated Books*, London: Thames & Hudson, 2001
Bindman, David and Chadwick, Esther (eds), *William Blake's Universe*, Cambridge: Fitzwilliam Museum, 2024
Blackstone, Bernard, *English Blake*, Cambridge: Cambridge University Press, 1949
Carlyle, Thomas, *A Carlyle Reader: Selections from the Writings of Thomas Carlyle*, G.B. Tennyson (ed.), Cambridge: Cambridge University Press, 2001
Chatfield, Tom, *Wise Animals: How Technology Has Made Us What We Are*, London: Picador, 2024
Churchill, Winston, *A History of the English-Speaking Peoples, Vol III, The Age of Revolution*, New York: Bantam Books, 1963
Churton, Tobias, *Jerusalem: The Real Life of William Blake*, London: Watkins, 2015
Coleridge, Samuel Taylor, *Biographia Literaria*, George Watson (ed.), London: J.M. Dent, 1975

# SELECT BIBLIOGRAPHY

———, *The Table Talk and Omniana of Samuel Taylor Coleridge*, London: Oxford University Press, 1917

Conway Morris, Simon, *From Extraterrestrials to Animal Minds: Seven Myths of Evolution*, New Brunswick, NJ: Templeton Press

Corfield, Penelope J., *The Georgians: The Deeds and Misdeeds of 18th Century Britain*, London: Yale University Press, 2023

Damrosch, Leo, *Eternity's Sunrise: The Imaginative World of William Blake*, New Haven: Yale University Press, 2015

Darwin, Charles, *The Descent of Man*, London: John Murray, 1871

———, *The Variation of Animals and Plants Under Domestication*, London: John Murray, 1875

———, *The Expression of the Emotions in Man and Animals*, New York: D. Appleton and Company, 1899

Eliot, T.S., 'Blake' in *The Sacred Wood*, London: Methuen, 1920

Erdman, David V. (ed.), *The Complete Poetry & Prose of William Blake*, Newly Revised Edition with Commentary by Harold Bloom, New York: Anchor Books, 1988

Eron, Sarah, '"Bound… by their narrowing perceptions": Sympathetic Bondage and Perverse Pity in Blake's *The Book of Urizen*,' in *Blake: An Illustrated Quarterly*, Volume 46, Issue 3, Winter 2012–13

Evans, Pippa, *Improv Your Life: An Improvisor's Guide To Embracing Whatever Life Throws At You*, London: Hodder Studio, 2021

Ferber, Michael, *Romanticism: A Very Short Introduction*, Oxford: Oxford University Press, 2010

Feuerbach, Ludwig, *The Essence of Christianity*, trans. George Eliot, New York: Harper Torchbooks, 1957

Foster Damon, S., *A Blake Dictionary: The Ideas and Symbols of William Blake*, Revised Edition, Hanover, NH: University Press of New England, 1988

Frye, Northrop, *Fearful Symmetry: A Study of William Blake*, Princeton: Princeton University Press, 1969

Gilchrist, Alexander, *Gilchrist on Blake, The Life of William Blake Pictor Ignotus*, Richard Holmes (ed.), London: Harper Perennial, 2005

Gill, Michael B., *A Philosophy of Beauty: Shaftesbury on Nature, Virtue, and Art*, Princeton: Princeton University Press, 2022

Gunton, Richard M.; Stafleu, Marinus D.; Reiss, Michael J.; 'A General Theory of Objectivity: Contributions from the Reformational Philosophy Tradition,' in *Foundations of Science*, 27, 2022, 941–955

Harrison, Peter, *Some New World: Myths of Supernatural Belief in a Secular Age*, Cambridge: Cambridge University Press, 2024

Heisenberg, Werner, *Physics and Philosophy*, London: Penguin Books, 1990

Heppner, Christopher, 'The Woman Taken in Adultery: An Essay on Blake's "Style of Designing",' in *Blake: An Illustrated Quarterly*, Volume 17, Issue 2, Fall 1983, 44–59

Higgs, John, *William Blake Vs The World*, London: Weidenfeld & Nicolson, 2021

Hill, Rosemary, *Time's Witness*, London: Penguin Books, 2023

Hobbs, Angela, 'The Erotic Magus: Ficino's De Amore as a Guide to Plato's Symposium,' in John F. Finamore and Tomáš Nejeschleba (eds), *Platonism and its Legacy: Selected*

# SELECT BIBLIOGRAPHY

*Papers from the Fifteenth Annual Conference of the International Society for Neoplatonic Studies*, Lydney: The Prometheus Trust, 2019, 243–258

Hoeveler, Diane, 'Blake's Erotic Apocalypse: The Androgynous Ideal in "Jerusalem",' e-Publications @ Marquette, 1-1-1979

Holmes, Richard, *The Age of Wonder: How the Romantic Generation Discovered the Beauty and Terror of Science*, London: Harper Press, 2008

Hutchings, Kevin, *Imagining Nature: Blake's Environmental Poetics*, Montreal: McGill-Queen's University Press, 2002

Huxley, Aldous, *The Devils of Loudun*, London: Chatto & Windus, 1952

Huxley, T.H., 'The Struggle for Existence in Human Society (1888),' in *Collected Essays*, Volume IX, London: Macmillan & Co, 1893–95

Isaacson, Walter, *Einstein: His Life and Universe*, London: Pocket Pockets, 2008

James, William, *The Varieties of Religious Experience*, London: Penguin Books, 1982

———, *The Moral Equivalent of War*, Blackmask Online, 2001

Keynes, Geoffrey (ed.), *Blake: Complete Writings*, Oxford: Oxford University Press, 1966

Laing, R.D., *The Divided Self*, London: Pelican, 1973

Lewis, C.S., *The Great Divorce*, London: Geoffrey Bles, 1945

Locke, John, *An Essay Concerning Human Understanding*, Book II, Ideas, 1689

———, *Second Treatise Of Government*, Chapter V, Of Property, Section 32, 1690

Loukes, Andrew (ed.), *William Blake in Sussex: Visions of Albion*, London: Paul Holberton Publishing, 2018

Loxton, Alice, *Uproar! Satire, Scandal & Printmakers in Georgian London*, London: Icon Books, 2023

Le Guin, Ursula K., *Cheek by Jowl*, Seattle: Aqueduct Press, 2009

Machin, Anna, *Why We Love*, London: Weidenfeld and Nicolson, 2022

McCarraher, Eugene, *The Enchantments of Mammon: How Capitalism Became the Religion of Modernity*, London: Belknap Press, 2019

McGilchrist, Iain, *The Matter With Things*, London: Perspectiva Press, 2021

Midgley, Mary, *Wisdom, Information, and Wonder: What is Knowledge For?*, London: Routledge, 1989

———, *The Solitary Self: Darwin and the Selfish Gene*, Durham: Acumen, 2010

Milton, John, *A Treatise on Christian Doctrine, Compiled by the Holy Scripture Alone*, Charles Sumner (tr.) London: Cambridge University Press, 1825

Murdoch, Iris, *Existentialists and Mystics: Writings on Philosophy and Literature*, Harmondsworth: Penguin Books, 1999

———, *The Sovereignty of Good*, London: Routledge Classics, 2001

Myrone, Martin and Concannon, Amy, *William Blake*, London: Tate Publishing, 2019

Naydler, Jeremy, *How Caterpillars Acquire Wings*, Oxford: Abzu Press, 1995

Newfield-Cookson, Bernard, *William Blake: Prophet of Universal Brotherhood*, London: Crucible, 1987

Paine, Thomas, *The Project Gutenberg Works of Thomas Paine*, 2010

Paley, Morton D., *The Traveller in the Evening: The Last Works of William Blake*, Oxford: Oxford University Press, 2007

Peakman, Julie, *Libertine London: Sex in the Eighteenth-Century Metropolis*, London: Reaktion Books, 2024

Phillips, Michael, *William Blake: Apprentice & Master*, Oxford: Ashmolean, 2014

# SELECT BIBLIOGRAPHY

Porter, Roy, *Enlightenment: Britain and the Creation of the Modern World*, London: Allen Lane, 2000

Price, Richard, *Observations on the Nature of Civil Liberty, the Principles of Government, and the Justice and Policy of the War with America*, London: Edward and Charles Dilly and Thomas Cadell, 1776

Raine, Katheleen, *William Blake*, London: Thames & Hudson, 1970

———, *Blake and Antiquity*, London: Routledge Classics, 2002

———, *Golgonooza: City of Imagination, Last Studies in William Blake*, Angelico Press, Brooklyn, NY: 2021

Roland Barthes, *A Lover's Discourse: Fragments*, London: Penguin Books, 1979

Roper, Lyndal, *Martin Luther: Renegade and Prophet*, London: Bodley Head, 2016

Rowland, Christopher, *Blake and the Bible*, London: Yale University Press, 2010

Schuchard, Marsha Keith, *Why Mrs Blake Cried: William Blake and the Erotic Imagination*, London: Pimlico, 2007

Scruton, Roger, *An Intelligent Person's Guide to Philosophy*, London: Penguin Books, 1996

Seth, Anil, *Being You*, London: Faber & Faber, 2022

Shaftesbury, Anthony Ashley-Cooper, Earl of, *Characteristicks of Men, Manners, Opinions, Times*, Cambridge: Cambridge University Press, 1999

Sheldrake, Merlin, *Entangled Life*, London: The Bodley Head, 2020

Sheldrake, Rupert, *The Rebirth of Nature: The Greening of Science and God*, Rochester, VT: Inner Traditions, 1994

Shukla, Shikha, 'The Influence of the Bhagwad Gita on the English Romantic Poets Particularly on William Blake,' in *IOSR Journal of Humanities and Social Science*, Volume 24, Issue 7, Ser. 3, July 2019, 73–77

Sklar, Susanne M., *Blake's Jerusalem as Visionary Theatre: Entering the Divine Body*, Oxford: Oxford University Press, 2011

———, 'William Blake's Mythic System,' *Temenos Academy Online Papers*, Summer Term 2020

Smith, Adam, *An Inquiry into the Nature and Causes of the Wealth of Nations*, London: W. Strahan and T. Cadell, 1776

———, *The Theory of Moral Sentiments*, Oxford: Clarendon Press, 1979

Solomon, Andrew, *Blake's Job: A Message for our Time*, London: Palamabron Press, 1993

Storr, Anthony, 'The Sanity of True Genius,' in *Churchill's Black Dog, Kafka's Mice and Other Phenomena of the Human Mind*, New York: Grove Press, 1988

Swift, Jonathan, *The Prose Works of Jonathan Swift*, London: George Bell and Sons, 1898

Symons, Arthur, *William Blake*, New York: E.P. Dutton and Company, 1907

Szreter, Simon and Kevin, Siena, 'The pox in Boswell's London: an estimate of the extent of syphilis infection in the metropolis in the 1770s,' *The Economic History Review*, Volume 74, Issue 2, May 2021, 372–399

Tatham, Frederick, *Life of Blake*, London, 1832

Taylor, Charles, *A Secular Age*, London: The Belknap Press of Harvard University Press, 2007

Teresa of Ávila, *The Life of Saint Teresa of Ávila by Herself*, London: Penguin, 1957

Thompson, E.P., *Witness Against the Beast: William Blake and the Moral Law*, New York: The New Press, 1993

# SELECT BIBLIOGRAPHY

Vernon, Mark, *A Secret History of Christianity: Jesus, the Last Inkling and the Evolution of Consciousness*, Alresford: John Hunt Publishing, 2019

———, 'The Public Understanding of Biology: A Journalist's Perspective,' in Reiss, Michael J.; Watts, Fraser; Wiseman, Harris; *Rethinking Biology: Public Understandings*, Singapore: World Scientific Publishing, 2020, 323–31

———, 'The four-fold imagination,' Aeon, September 2020, retrieved from https://aeon.co/essays/what-we-can-learn-from-william-blakes-visionary-imagination

———, *Dante's Divine Comedy: A Guide for the Spiritual Journey*, New York: Angelico Press, 2021

———, '"Wars of Love": William Blake, Christian Idealism, and the way from Despair to Life,' *VALA: The Journal of the Blake Society*, Issue 4, November 2023

———, '"Enemies of the Human Race": Blake against the Deists, then and now,' *VALA: The Journal of the Blake Society*, Issue 5, November 2024

Weil, Simone, *Waiting for God*, New York: Harper Perennial Modern Classics, 2009

Weinberg, Steven, *The First Three Minutes: A modern view of the origin of the universe*, London: Fontana Paperbacks, 1983

Weir, David, *Brahma in the West: William Blake and the Oriental Renaissance*, Albany, NY: State University of New York Press, 2003

White, Harry, 'Blake's Resolution to the War Between Science and Philosophy,' in *Blake: An Illustrated Quarterly*, Volume 39, Issue 3, Winter 2005/2006

Whitney, William Dwight, *The Century Dictionary and Cyclopedia: A Work of Universal Reference in All departments of Knowledge with a New Atlas of the World*, Volume VI, New York: The Century Co., 1904

Whittaker, Jason, *Divine Images: The Life and Work of William Blake*, London: Reaktion Books, 2021

Williams, Rowan, '"The human form divine": Radicalism and Orthodoxy in William Blake,' in Zoë Bennett and David B. Gowler (eds), *Radical Christian Voices and Practice: Essays in Honour of Christopher Rowland*, Oxford: Oxford University Press, 2012, 151–64

Wolfe, Charles T., 'The Life of Matter: Early Modern Vital Matter Theories,' in *Notes and Records: The Royal Society Journal of the History of Science*, 21 June 2023

Wollstonecraft, Mary, *A Vindication of the Rights of Woman with Strictures on Political and Moral Subjects*, London: J. Johnson, 1792

Woolf, Virginia, *A Room of One's Own*, London: The Hogarth Press, 1991

Wright, Jason, *Blake's Job: Adventures in Becoming*, London: Routledge, 2023

# LIST OF ILLUSTRATIONS

*Images in Plate Section*

A. Portrait of William Blake made by Luigi Schiavonetti after the picture by Thomas Phillips. (Source: Yale Center for British Art, Paul Mellon Collection, B1974.8.13.)

B. Frontispiece to *Jerusalem: The Emanation of the Giant Albion*, showing possibly Blake stepping over the threshold, carrying a light, through the door of perception. (Source: Yale Center for British Art, Paul Mellon Collection, B1992.8.1(1).)

C. *The Marriage of Heaven and Hell*, plate 3, in which Blake presents lines that were to guide him in life, 'Without contraries is no progression'. (Source: Library of Congress, Rare Book and Special Collections Division.)

D. *Jerusalem: The Emanation of the Giant Albion*, showing Los being seduced by his Spectre, which is what Blake called the sense of self that believes we are individuals and isolated. (Source: Yale Center for British Art, Paul Mellon Collection, B1992.8.1(6).)

E. *Milton*, plate 42, showing a couple having made love. Blake advocated not free love but cultivating a love of all things, which I've called "large love", symbolised here by the eagle who sees across boundaries. (Source: Library of Congress, Rare Book and Special Collections Division.)

F. *Jerusalem: The Emanation of the Giant Albion*, showing Albion having his sense of connection with the cosmos stripped out of him by the daughters of memory who, unlike the daughters of inspiration, don't know of that connection directly. (Source: Yale Center for British Art, Paul Mellon Collection, B1992.8.1(25).)

G. *There Is No Natural Religion*, final plate, which summarises Blake's understanding of Christianity. (Source: Yale Center for British Art, Paul Mellon Collection, B1992.8.15(9).)

H. "Virgin and Child" painted by Blake after 1810. The image is clearly indebted to icon painting, indicating that Blake was influenced by Eastern Christianity and the Greek Orthodox Church in London in

# LIST OF ILLUSTRATIONS

particular. (Source: Yale Center for British Art, Paul Mellon Collection, B1977.14.91.)

I. *Jerusalem: The Emanation of the Giant Albion*, showing a pivotal moment in Blake's epic poem when his superhero, Jerusalem, rediscovers her divine life. (Source: Yale Center for British Art, Paul Mellon Collection, B1992.8.1(92).)

## *Images Inset in Text*

1. *Songs of Innocence*, plate 14, "Infant Joy." (Source: Yale Center for British Art, Paul Mellon Collection, B1992.8.12(9).) — 11
2. *Songs of Innocence and Experience*, plate 45, "The Chimney Sweeper." (Source: Yale Center for British Art, Paul Mellon Collection, B1978.43.1576.) — 15
3. *The Book of Thel*, plate 2, title page. (Source: Yale Center for British Art, Paul Mellon Collection, B1978.43.1335.) — 17
4. *Songs of Innocence and Experience*, "Infant Sorrow." (Source: Library of Congress, Rare Book and Special Collections Division.) — 21
5. *Songs of Innocence and Experience*, plate 39, "London." (Source: Yale Center for British Art, Paul Mellon Collection, B1978.43.1570.) — 23
6. Print entitled "Fear & Hope Are—Vision," 1793. (Source: Yale Center for British Art, Paul Mellon Collection, B1978.43.1498.) — 39
7. *Newton*, c.1804. (Source: © Tate Britain.) — 53
8. "Fertilization of Egypt" from *The Botanic Garden* by Erasmus Darwin, one of the engravings Blake provided for the book, in which Blake can't help but highlight a distinctly animate and supernatural element to the workings of nature. (Source: The Elisha Whittelsey Collection, The Elisha Whittelsey Fund, 1968, The Metropolitan Museum of Art.) — 56
9. *Jerusalem: The Emanation of the Giant Albion*, plate 14, detail showing Albion asleep, chrysalis-like, and Jerusalem, Albion's spiritual form, rising as a moth beneath the promise of a rainbow. (Source: Yale Center for British Art, Paul Mellon Collection, B1992.8.1(14).) — 59
10. "I want! I want!" from *For the Sexes: The Gates of Paradise*, 1793. (Source: Yale Center for British Art, Paul Mellon Collection, B1978.43.1494.) — 68
11. "Job Rebuked by his Friends," from *Illustrations of the Book of Job*. Blake's portrayal of Job being accused by his friends might be partly inspired by the story of Socrates being accused by his fellow

## LIST OF ILLUSTRATIONS

|     |                                                                                                                                                                                                                                                                                                                                                                                              |     |
| --- | -------------------------------------------------------------------------------------------------------------------------------------------------------------------------------------------------------------------------------------------------------------------------------------------------------------------------------------------------------------------------------------------- | --- |
|     | Athenians. (Source: Yale Center for British Art, Paul Mellon Collection, B1978.43.1512.)                                                                                                                                                                                                                                                                                                     | 69  |
| 12. | St Mary's Battersea from the north side of the River Thames. (Source: Author photo.)                                                                                                                                                                                                                                                                                                         | 80  |
| 13. | *The Marriage of Heaven and Hell*, plate 21, detail showing a man looking up to heaven. (Source: Library of Congress, Rare Book and Special Collections Division.)                                                                                                                                                                                                                           | 90  |
| 14. | "I found him beneath a tree," from *For the Sexes: The Gates of Paradise*, plate 3. In this image, Blake depicts a woman pulling a child out of the ground, which looks odd, until you wonder if the scene reflects a tryst under the tree that had longer-term consequences for the women than the absent man. (Source: Yale Center for British Art, Paul Mellon Collection, B1992.8.6(3).) | 97  |
| 15. | Image of the Transverberation or Ecstasy of Teresa, by an unknown seventeenth-century artist. (Source: SMK Open.)                                                                                                                                                                                                                                                                            | 100 |
| 16. | *Visions of the Daughters of Albion*, title page. (Source: Library of Congress, Rare Book and Special Collections Division.)                                                                                                                                                                                                                                                                 | 102 |
| 17. | *Visions of the Daughters of Albion*, frontispiece. (Source: Yale Center for British Art, Paul Mellon Collection, B1978.43.1580.)                                                                                                                                                                                                                                                            | 104 |
| 18. | *Visions of the Daughters of Albion*, "The Argument." (Source: Library of Congress, Rare Book and Special Collections Division.)                                                                                                                                                                                                                                                             | 106 |
| 19. | *Visions of the Daughters of Albion*, plate 3, detail showing the eagle and woman. (Source: Library of Congress, Rare Book and Special Collections Division.)                                                                                                                                                                                                                                | 109 |
| 20. | *Visions of the Daughters of Albion*, plate 7, detail showing a woman in a wave above a man. (Source: Library of Congress, Rare Book and Special Collections Division.)                                                                                                                                                                                                                      | 110 |
| 21. | *Songs of Innocence*, frontispiece. (Source: Yale Center for British Art, Paul Mellon Collection, B1978.43.1546.)                                                                                                                                                                                                                                                                            | 121 |
| 22. | *The Song of Los*, frontispiece. (Source: Library of Congress, Rare Book and Special Collections Division.)                                                                                                                                                                                                                                                                                  | 130 |
| 23. | *America a Prophecy*, title page. (Source: Yale Center for British Art, Paul Mellon Collection, B1992.8.2(2).)                                                                                                                                                                                                                                                                               | 132 |
| 24. | *America a Prophecy*, frontispiece. (Source: Yale Center for British Art, Paul Mellon Collection, B1992.8.2(1).)                                                                                                                                                                                                                                                                             | 134 |
| 25. | *America a Prophecy*, plate 10, showing figure in flames. (Source: Yale Center for British Art, Paul Mellon Collection, B1992.8.2(12).)                                                                                                                                                                                                                                                      | 138 |

## LIST OF ILLUSTRATIONS

26. *Europe a Prophecy*, frontispiece, "The Ancient of Days." (Source: Yale Center for British Art, Paul Mellon Collection, B1992.8.1(106).)    144

27. *Europe a Prophecy*, plate 13, showing the suffering of people in times of war, in this case depicting someone who has died of plague. (Source: Yale Center for British Art, Paul Mellon Collection, B1992.8.4(13).)    145

28. *The First Book of Urizen*, title page. (Source: Yale Center for British Art, Paul Mellon Collection, B1978.43.1419.)    154

29. *The First Book of Urizen*, preludium. (Source: Yale Center for British Art, Paul Mellon Collection, B1992.8.5(2).)    155

30. *The First Book of Urizen*, plate 11. (Source: Yale Center for British Art, Paul Mellon Collection, B1992.8.5(7).)    156

31. *The First Book of Urizen*, plate 6. (Source: Yale Center for British Art, Paul Mellon Collection, B1992.8.5(10).)    158

32. *The First Book of Urizen*, plate 14, showing figure tormented in flames. (Source: Library of Congress, Rare Book and Special Collections Division.)    159

33. *The First Book of Urizen*, plate 26. (Source: Yale Center for British Art, Paul Mellon Collection, B1978.43.1444.)    162

34. *The First Book of Urizen*, plate 19. (Source: Yale Center for British Art, Paul Mellon Collection, B1992.8.5(18).)    163

35. The Blakes's cottage in Felpham. (Source: Author photo.)    168

36. *Milton*, plate 36, showing the Blake's cottage in Felpham. (Source: Library of Congress, Rare Book and Special Collections Division.)    169

37. *Songs of Innocence and Experience*, "The Sick Rose," detail showing the bloom and the worm and a human figure emerging. (Source: Library of Congress, Rare Book and Special Collections Division.)    174

38. *Jerusalem: The Emanation of the Giant Albion*, plate 32, Vala with her veil tempts Jerusalem, as her daughters of inspiration urge her to think again. (Source: Yale Center for British Art, Paul Mellon Collection, B1992.8.1(32).)    181

39. *Chaucer's Canterbury Pilgrims*, 1810, similar to a picture Blake showed at his 1809 exhibition. (Source: Yale Center for British Art, Paul Mellon Collection, B1977.14.11092.)    189

40. *Songs of Innocence and Experience*, plate showing "The Lamb." (Source: Yale Center for British Art, Paul Mellon Collection, B1978.43.1556.)    196

# LIST OF ILLUSTRATIONS

41. *Songs of Innocence and Experience*, plate showing "The Tyger." (Source: Yale Center for British Art, Paul Mellon Collection, B1978.43.1573.) — 197

42. *The Woman Taken in Adultery*, c. 1805. (Source: William Blake, English, 1757–1827 *The Woman Taken in Adultery* (John VIII, 8–9), about 1805. Pen and watercolor over graphite pencil on paper. Catalogue Raisonné: Butlin 486. Sheet: 35.6 × 36.8 cm (14 × 14 1/2 in.) Museum of Fine Arts, Boston. Museum purchase with funds donated by contribution. 90.110. Photograph © 2025 Museum of Fine Arts, Boston.) — 200

43. *Milton*, plate probably showing Blake before Los, or his divine self, stepping out of a flaming sun. (Source: Library of Congress, Rare Book and Special Collections Division) — 203

44. *Milton*, plate 45, in which Blake shows the superhero Ololon in the form of Christ and ears of wheat with human heads, indicating that plant intelligence and human intelligence are unified in Christ. (Source: Library of Congress, Rare Book and Special Collections Division.) — 206

45. *Illustrations of the Book of Job*, plate 17, in which Job and his wife see God because they have perceived their divine humanity, unlike Job's accusers who turn away in fear and shame. (Source: Yale Center for British Art, Gift of J. T. Johnston Coe in memory of Henry E. Coe, Yale BA 1878, Henry E. Coe Jr., Yale BA 1917, and Henry E. Coe III, Yale BA 1946, B2005.16.18.) — 208

46. *The Schismatics and Sowers of Discord: Mosca de' Lamberti and Bertran de Born, from the* illustrations to Dante's *Divine Comedy*, Inferno XXVIII. (Source: William BLAKE, The Schismatics and Sowers of Discord: Mosca de' Lamberti and Bertrand de Born (1824–1827). Illustration for *The Divine Comedy* by Dante Alighieri (Inferno XXVIII, 103–142). Pen and ink and watercolour over pencil, with sponging, 37.0 x 52.7 cm (sheet). National Gallery of Victoria, Melbourne. Felton Bequest, 1920. 1009-3.) — 215

47. *The souls of those who repented at the point of death*, Blake's illustration of the flying souls, from the illustrations to Dante's *Divine Comedy*, Purgatorio V. (Source: William BLAKE, *The Souls of Those who only repented at the Point of Death* (1824–1827). Illustration for The Divine Comedy by Dante Alighieri (Purgatorio V, 37-57 and VI, 28–48). Pen and ink and watercolour over pencil and black chalk, 37.2 x 52.7 cm (sheet). National Gallery of Victoria, Melbourne. Felton Bequest, 1920. 1015-3.) — 217

## LIST OF ILLUSTRATIONS

48. *Dante and Statius sleeping, Virgil watching*, from the illustrations to Dante's *Divine Comedy*, Purgatorio XXVII. (Source: © Ashmolean Museum.)     219

49. *St Peter, St James, Dante and Beatrice with St John*, from the illustrations to Dante's *Divine Comedy*, Paradiso XXV. (Source: © The Trustees of the British Museum. All rights reserved.)     220

50. "Christ descending into the Grave," illustration for Blair's *The Grave*, in which the male Christ takes on androgynous form by being feminised. (Source: Library of Congress, Rare Book and Special Collections Division.)     224

51. Blake's recently restored gravestone in Bunhill Fields. (Source: Author photo.)     226

# INDEX

Page numbers in *italics* indicate illustrations

Abraham, 95
Ackroyd, Peter, 41, 186
Act of Toleration (1688), 30
Adam and Eve, 12–13, 127, 153, 162, 163
*Age of Reason, The* (Paine), 64
Ahania, 164
Albion, 59, 204, 227
*America a Prophecy* (Blake), 131–41, *134, 138*
American colonies, 9
    War of Independence (1775–83), 129–41, 146
'Ancient of Days, The' (Blake), 143, *144*
Ancients, The, 211–12
androgyny, 223–4
angels, 10, 27, 31–6
    'Chimney Sweeper, The', 14–15
    *Europe a Prophecy*, 143, 145
    Gabriel, 36
    'Infant Joy', 12
    'Infant Sorrow', 20
    Peckham Rye vision, 32, 35
animism, 55
antinomianism, 89
aphantasia, 37
*Aphorisms on Man* (Lavater), 88
apocalypse, 31, 141, 142, 153, 221
'Approach of Doom, The' (Blake), 115, 125
Aristophanes, 104

Arizona State University, 183
Arjuna, 117–18, 205
Arunachala, 179
Asiatic Society, 179
atheism, 9
Atlantis, 138
*atopos*, 68
'Auguries of Innocence' (Blake), 1, 3
Austen, Jane, 10

Bacon, Francis, 55, 65, 76, 168
Ball, Philip, 57
baptism, 29
Baptists, 9
Barfield, Owen, 41, 121–2
Barthes, Roland, 68
Basire, James, 47–8, 63
Beulah, 218, 223
Bentley Jr, G.E., 64
*Bhagavad Gita, The*, 4, 117–18, 179, 205
Bible, 12, 29, 95, 199–202
    Genesis, 12–13, 106–7, 153
    Gospel of John, 200–202
Birmingham, West Midlands, 68
Blake, Catherine (b. 1723), 10, 116
Blake, Catherine (b. 1762), 32, 79–81, 83, 85–6, 95, 96, 115, 116, 151, 190
    death of William (1827), 226
    Felpham, move to (1800), 167
    Fountain Court, move to (1821), 208–9

# INDEX

Lambeth, move to (1790), 126
Linnell, relationship with, 226
Robert, relationship with, 81
Scofield incident (1803), 185
South Molton Street, move to (1803), 187
wedding (1782), 79–80
Blake, James, 9, 10, 47–8, 116
Blake, Robert, 81, 95, 115–17
Blake, William
    art, 24, 46–9, 63, 125, 151
    birth and baptism (1757), 9, 10, 29, 31
    charisma, 63
    death (1827), 225–7
    death, views on, 115–19
    deism, views on, 64–6, 71, 142, 207
    education, 43, 45–9, 60, 63
    exhibition (1809), 188
    flat earth and, 69–71
    grave, 1, 5, 226, *226*
    illuminated printing, 125–6, 129
    Jesus, views on, 190, 193–207
    money, views on, 81–93, 188
    physical appearance, 79
    Scofield incident (1803), 185–6
    sex, views on, 95–114
    singing, love of, 25
    visions, 27, 32–43
    wedding (1782), 79–80
Böhme, Jakob, 191
*Book of Thel, The* (Blake), 17–19, *17*, 132
Boswell, James, 98
*Botanic Garden, The* (Darwin), 55–6, *56*
British Empire, 4, 9, 179
    slave trade, 16
Brothers, Richard, 31
Buddhism, 26, 157
Bunhill Fields, London, 1, 5, 226, *226*
Bunyan, John, 1, 218
Burke, Edmund, 151
butterflies, 58–60, 170–71

Butts, Thomas, 127, 167, 185, 201

cannibalism, 145
Catholicism, 88
cavern, 2
Charlotte, Queen, 66
*Chaucer's Canterbury Pilgrims* (Blake), *189*
Cheapside, London, 39
child labour, 14
'Chimney Sweeper, The' (Blake), 13–16, *15*
Christianity, 4, 29–31, 64–6, 190–209
    Catholicism, 88
    Church of England, 19, 29
    deism, 64–6, 71, 142, 207
    eroticism and, 96, 99
    Fall, 12–13, 106–7, 153, 223
    Nonconformism, 1, 9, 30
    Protestantism, 106
    Puritanism, 175
    sin, 13, 164, 200–201
    temptation of Christ, 179
    woman taken in adultery, 200
chrysalises, 58–60, 170–71
Church of England, 19, 29
Churchill, Winston, 9
Cicero, 190
'Clod & The Pebble, The' (Blake), 173
Coleridge, Samuel Taylor, 26, 38, 224
comets, 115
*Common Sense* (Paine), 135
compassion fatigue, 161
*Complaint, The* (Young), 151
Constable, John, 212
consumption, 115
contraries, 4, 86–7, 89, 98, 105, 116, 119, 129, 193, 220
    in *America a Prophecy*, 132, 135
    in *Europe a Prophecy*, 143, 146, 147
    Jesus and, 201
    in *Milton*, 202
Conway Morris, Simon, 55
Corfield, Penelope J., 9

# INDEX

counterculture, 10
Crabb Robinson, Henry, 43, 69, 206

*Daily Self-examinant, The* (Warren), 30
Dante, 31–2, 70, 117, 211, 213–20
Darent River, 212
*dark Satanic Mills*, 2, 66, 216
Darwin, Charles, 55, 56–7, 98, 180
Darwin, Erasmus, 55–6, 66
Dawkins, Richard, 38, 71
death, 115–19
Declaration of Independence (1776), 129, 137
deism, 64–6, 71, 142, 207
demons, 27
Derby, Derbyshire, 68
Descartes, René, 54
Devil, 85–6, 174–5, 179, 192, 202, 207
*Devils of Loudun, The* (Huxley), 15–16
Dickinson, Bruce, 1
Diogenes the Cynic, 124
Dionysius, 108
*Divine Comedy, The* (Dante), 31–2, 70, 117, 211, 213–20, *215*, *217*, *219*, *220*
'Divine Image, The' (Blake), 160–61
Dunbar, Robin, 161
Dürer, Albrecht, 47
Dutch Republic, 115

East India Company, 179
Edwards, Richard, 151
Egypt, ancient, 59
Einstein, Albert, 74
*Elements* (Euclid), 75
Ellul, Jacques, 151
engraving, 47–8, 63, 79–81, 95, 125–6
Enitharmon, 146, 147, 160, 162–3, 213
Enlightenment (c. 1637–1815), 49
Epicureans, 157
epilepsy, 37
equality, 130

Eternals, The (Zoas), 132–4
*Europe a Prophecy* (Blake), 41–2, 131, 141–7, *145*
Evans, Pippa, 192
*Everlasting Gospel, The* (Blake), 201, 207
evolution, 55–60
*Expression of Emotions in Man and Animals, The* (Darwin), 56
Ezekiel, 32, 122–4

fact, 24
fairies, 33–4, 41–3, 74, 90
Fall, 12–13, 106–7, 223
'Fear & Hope Are – Vision' (Blake), 39
fearless critique, 4, 62, 76
Felpham, Sussex, 167–70, *168*, *169*, 185, 190
female will, 216
feminism, 10
*First Book of Urizen, The* (Blake), 153–66, *154*, *155*, *156*, *158*, *159*, *162*, *163*
flat earth, 69–71
Flaxman, Nancy, 167, 187
'Fly, The' (Blake), 173–4
*For the Sexes* (Blake), *68*, 97
Founding Fathers, 65, 129
Fountain Court, London, 208–9
France, 115
    Revolution (1789), 41, 42, 129, 131, 139, 141–7, 201
Franklin, Benjamin, 130, 146
Fuseli, Johann, 33, 187

Gabriel the Archangel, 36
Garden of Eden, 12–13, 127, 153, 162, 163
'Garden of Love, The' (Blake), 91
gender, 81, 216, 223
generation, 215–18
Genesis, 12–13, 106–7, 153
George II, King of Great Britain, 9, 66
George III, King of Great Britain, 132, 137, 146

263

# INDEX

'Ghost of a Flea, The' (Blake), 212
ghosts, 39
Gibbon, Edward, 30
Gilchrist, Alexander, 32, 35, 39, 40, 95, 116
Gill, Michael, 178
Gillray, James, 48–9
God, 16, 32, 34, 38, 194–5, 202
    deism, 64–6, 71, 142, 207
Godwin, William, 98, 130
Golgonooza, 139–41, 147, 165, 218
Gordon Riots (1780), 88
Gospel of John, 200–202
Grand Tour, 46
Greece, ancient, 36, 68, 108, 113, 123, 124, 133
Guite, Malcolm, 1
*Gulliver's Travels* (Swift), 29, 67
Gunton, Richard, 74

Hagar, 95
Hamilton, Emma, 63
Hayley, William, 80, 117, 167, 185, 187, 188
Hazlitt, William, 25
hedonic treadmill, 164
Heisenberg, Werner, 74
Hell, 117, 213–15
Heppner, Christopher, 201
Hercules Buildings, Lambeth, 126
Herschel, Caroline, 115
Higgs, John, 50
high modernist poetry, 10
Hill, Rosemary, 48
*His Dark Materials* (Pullman), 42
*History of Rasselas, The* (Johnson), 49
Hobbes, Thomas, 163
Hoeveler, Diane, 223
'Holy Thursday' (Blake), 64
Homer, 133
Hooke, Robert, 40
*How Life Works* (Ball), 57
Hume, David, 9, 67, 71, 160
Huxley, Aldous, 15–16

Huxley, Thomas Henry, 180
hyperphantasia, 37
hypocrisy, 1

'I Rose Up at the Dawn of Day' (Blake), 84
illuminated printing, 125–6, 129
*Illustrations of the Book of Job* (Blake), 69, 188, 207–8, *208*
imaginal disks, 58
imagination, 4, 5, 36, 38, 49–62
    nature and, 53–62
India, 4, 117–18, 123, 179, 205
Indigenous peoples, 183
'Infant Joy' (Blake), 10–11
'Infant Sorrow' (Blake), 20–21, *21*
innocence, 4, 12–13, 14, 16, 17, 19, 26, 45, 54
Isaiah, 122–4, 127
*Island in the Moon, An* (Blake), 66
Israelites, 179

James, William, 38
James the Apostle, 219, 220
Jerusalem (emanation of Albion), *59*, 181, *181*, 182, 223
*Jerusalem: The Emanation of the Giant Albion* (Blake), *59*, 180–83, *181*, 188, 204, 205, 211, 227
Jerusalem (city), 5, 139
Jesus Christ, 36, 84, 96, 118, 141, 193–207
    androgyny and, 223, *224*
    birth, 194
    contraries and, 201
    crucifixion, 164, 204
    forgiveness, 190
    Logos, 193, 201–2
    temptation of, 179
    woman taken in adultery, 200
Job, 69, 188, 207–8
John the Apostle, 219, 220
Johnson, Samuel, 48–50

# INDEX

Kant, Immanuel, 87
Keats, John, 24
Khadijah bint Khuwaylid, 36
King James Bible, 29
Krishna, 118

'Lamb, The' (Blake), 193–4, *196*
Lamb, Charles, 26
*Lambeth Prophecies* (Blake), 41
Lambeth, Surrey, 126
Langford, Abraham, 47
language, 34, 40, 213
Lavater, Johann Kaspar, 88
Le Guin, Ursula, 153
Lewis, C.S., 41
Linnell, John, 84, 115, 212, 225
'Little Black Boy, The' (Blake), 16, 26
'Little Girl Lost, A' (Blake), 101
Locke, John, 43, 65, 76, 101, 123, 168, 178
London, England, 9
    chimney sweeps, 14
    finance in, 82–3
    Gordon Riots (1780), 88
    prostitution in, 90–91
    St Paul's Cathedral, 144–5
'London' (Blake), 21–2, *23*
Los, 107, 133, 134, 147, 157–8, 160–63, 213, 217, 222
love, 93, 99, 101–2, 104–5, 108–14, 117, 162, 164
Loxton, Alice, 49
Luddite movement (1811–16), 72
*Lunar Men, The* (Uglow), 67
Lunar Society, 66–7, 83
Luther, Martin, 106
Luvah, 133, 221–2

Machin, Anna, 73
Mammon, 84–5
Marianne, 201
*Marriage of Heaven and Hell, The* (Blake), 3, 4, 74, 75, 86–9, *90*, 96, 204–5
    contraries, 86–7, 89, 119

    illuminated printing and, 126
    Memorable Fancies, 122–4
    Milton in, 174
    Proverbs of Hell, 89–90, 97
    'Song of Liberty, A', 130
    *There is No Natural Religion* and, 92
    Urthona in, 136
Mary, Mother of Jesus, 33
Mathew, Harriet, 25
*maya*, 123, 181
McGilchrist, Iain, 165
*Mechanic's Magazine, The*, 72–3
mercantilism, 9, 85, 86, 93, 129
Meredith, William George, 75
metamorphosis, 58–60
Michelangelo, 36, 46, 47, 64, 223
Midgley, Mary, 56, 178
*Milton* (Blake), 51, 83, 118, 120, *169*, 174–6, 188, 202–3, *203*, *206*
*Miss Garnet's Angel* (Vickers), 34
modern perspective, 2
Mohammed, Prophet of Islam, 36
money, 81–93, 188
    mercantilism, 9, 85, 86, 93, 129
Moon, 53–4, 61
Moravians, 9, 96, 99
Moses, 154
Mother Nature, 180–84
moths, 58, 170–71
Muggletonians, 9
Murdoch, Iris, 51, 111
music, 24
myth, 4, 133–4, 143, 147, 152–3, 163
    Fall, 12–13, 106–7, 153

Napoleon I, emperor of the French, 14
Napoleonic Wars (1803–15), 129, 142
narcissism, 19
nature, 2, 4, 45–8, 119, 168–86
    evolving meaning of, 180
    imagination and, 53–62
    Mother Nature, 180–84
    trust and, 57
    wildernesses, 178–9

# INDEX

negation, 143, 146
negative capability, 24
Nelson, Melissa, 183
nervous fear, 3, 116, 168
Newgate prison, London, 88
*Newton* (Blake), 52–3, 214
Newton, Isaac, 40, 41, 52–3, 65, 66, 71, 72, 76, 84, 112, 142, 168
noble savage, 124
Nonconformism, 1, 9, 30
nymphs, 34, 105, 107

objectivity, 40–41, 48
*Observations on the Nature of Civil Liberty* (Price), 130
Ololon, 206
'On Sleeping in Church' (Swift), 30
Oothoon, 101–14, 119, 136, 217
openness, 27, 39
Oracle of Delphi, 36
Orc, 136–41, 143, 146, 147, 163, 165
Oriental Renaissance, 4
*Original Stories from Real Life* (Wollstonecraft), 101

Paine, Thomas, 64, 65–6, 130, 132, 135, 146
painting, 24, 46–9
Palamabron, 133, 146
Palmer, Samuel, 212
Parker, Anne, 95
Parker, James, 81, 95
Pars, Henry, 46
Paul the Apostle, 39
Peckham Rye, Southwark, 32, 35
perceptual openness, 4, 27, 39
Peter the Apostle, 219, 220
Pharisees, 200
*Pilgrim's Progress, The* (Bunyan), 1, 218
Plato, 59, 75, 104–5, 133, 138, 156, 190
poetic genius, 123
*Poetical Sketches* (Blake), 70
'Poison Tree, A' (Blake), 91

Poland Street, London, 95
polyamory, 95–6
Pope, Alexander, 40
Porter, Roy, 66
Pre-Raphaelites, 10
Price, Richard, 130
Priestly, Joseph, 66, 67, 130
prophecy, 1, 129–47, 152
    *America a Prophecy*, 131–41, *134*, *138*
    *Europe a Prophecy*, 41–2, 131, 141–7, *145*
prophets, 122–4
prostitution, 90–91
Protestantism, 106
*Proverbs of Hell* (Blake), 89–90, 97
Pullman, Philip, 42
Puritanism, 175

quantum theory, 74
Quran, 36

Rahab, 133
Raine, Kathleen, 172, 176
Ramana Maharshi, 179
rape, 105, 108, 109, 110, 136
Raphael, 47
regeneration, 147, 170–71, 180, 217–18
relief etching, 125–6, 129
repression, 91–2
Reynolds, Joshua, 63
*Rights of Man, The* (Paine), 64
Rintrah, 133, 146
Robespierre, Maximilien, 151
Romantics, 3, 26, 126
Romney, George, 63
*Room of One's Own, A* (Woolf), 224
Royal Academy, 63, 70, 76, 79
Rudd, Pauline, 75
Ruskin, John, 113

Sarah, 95
Satan, 85–6, 174–5, 179, 192, 202, 207
'School Boy, The' (Blake), 45, 54

# INDEX

science, 2, 52–60, 64–76
  deism and, 65–6, 71, 142
  evolution, 55–60
  flat earth, 69–71
  'selfish gene' biology, 57, 74, 112
Scofield, John, 185–6
*Select Collection of English Songs, A*, 25
selfhood, 202–3
'selfish gene' biology, 57, 74, 112
Seth, Anil, 157, 160
Seven Years War (1756–63), 9
sex, 95–114, 162, 164, 223
sexes, 81, 216, 223
Shaftesbury, Anthony Ashley-Cooper, Earl of 178
Shakespeare, William, 50
Sheldrake, Rupert, 180
Shoreham, Kent, 212
*shoshin*, 26
'Sick Rose, The' (Blake), 22–3, 172, *174*
single vision, 52–3
Sklar, Susanne, 214
slavery, 16
Smith, Adam, 10, 82, 85, 124, 160
Smith, John, 25
social media, 161
Society of Antiquaries, 48
Socrates, 68–9, 141
solutionism, 23
'Song of Liberty, A' (Blake), 130
*Song of Los, The* (Blake), *130*
*Songs of Experience* (Blake), 20, 22, 24
  'Garden of Love, The', 91
  'Infant Sorrow', 20–21, *21*
  'London', 21–2, *23*
  'Poison Tree, A', 91
  'Sick Rose, The' (Blake), 22–3, 172, *174*
  'Tyger, The', 35, 138, 193, 194–8, *197*
*Songs of Innocence* (Blake), 10–11, 13–16, 24, 25–7
  'Chimney Sweeper, The', 13–16, *15*
  'Infant Joy', 10–11

Introduction, 120–21
'Lamb, The', 193–4, *196*
'Little Black Boy, The', 16, 26
'Little Girl Lost, A', 101
'School Boy, The', 45, 54
South Molton Street, London, 187, 208
Southcott, Joanna, 31
Spiritualism, 36
Spurzheim, Johann Gaspar, 37
St James's Piccadilly, 1, 29, 31, 79
St Mary's Battersea, 79–80, *80*
St Patrick's Cathedral, Dublin, 30
St Paul's Cathedral, London, 144–5
Stoke-on-Trent, Staffordshire, 68
Storr, Anthony, 38
subjectivity, 41, 48
Swammerdam, Jan, 58
Swedenborg, Emanuel, 156
Swift, Jonathan, 29–30, 67
sympathy, 10, 158–60
*Symposium* (Plato), 104–5

*tabula rasa*, 123
Tamil Nadu, India, 179
Tate Britain, 10, 144
Tatham, Frederick, 10
Taylor, Charles, 159
Taylor, Thomas, 61, 75–6, 104
technology, 2, 23, 41
Teresa of Ávila, 99–100, 117, 191
*Theory of Moral Sentiments, The* (Smith), 82
*There is No Natural Religion* (Blake), 65, 92
Tirzah, 133
Tolkien, J.R.R., 41
transcendentalism, 10
transnomianism, 89, 90, 92, 101
transsexuality, 106
Trinity, 119, 220
trust, 57
tuberculosis, 115
Turner, J.M.W., 188

267

# INDEX

'Tyger, The' (Blake), 35, 138, 193, 194–8, *197*

Uglow, Jenny, 67
Ulro, 168, 171, 214, 222
United States
    Declaration of Independence (1776), 129, 137
    Founding Fathers, 65, 129
    War of Independence (1775–83), 129–41, 146
Urizen, 133, 134, 143, 147, 153–66, 168, 222
    in *America a Prophecy*, 140
    in *Europe a Prophecy*, 143–4, 146, 147
    in *First Book of Urizen, The*, 153–66, *154*, *155*, *156*, *158*, *159*, *162*, *163*
    in *Jerusalem*, 182
    in *VALA*, 176
    in *Visions of the Daughters of Albion*, 103, 112
Urthona, 136

Vala, 180–83, 223
*VALA* (Blake), 152, 176, 180
*Varieties of Religious Experience, The* (James), 38

Varley, John, 212
Vickers, Salley, 34
Virgil, 211, 216, 219
Virgin Mary, 33
'Visionary Heads' (Blake), 212
visions, 1, 27, 32–43
    fairies, 33–4, 41–3, 74, 90

Gabriel, 36
ghost, 39
God, 32, 34
Paul the Apostle, 39
Peckham Rye angels, 32, 35
Virgin Mary, 33
*Visions of the Daughters of Albion* (Blake), 54, 101–14, *102*, *104*, *106*, *109*, 133
Voltaire, 9

Warren, Robert, 30–31
Washington, George, 132, 137
waste lands, 178
Watt, James, 66, 67
Watts, Isaac, 1
*Wealth of Nations, The* (Smith), 124
Wedgwood, Josiah, 66, 67
Wesley, Charles, 25
Westminster Abbey, 32
Whitley, Andrew, 177
wildernesses, 178–9
Wilkins, Charles, 179
'Windsor-Forest' (Pope), 40
wine presses, 221
Winkett, Lucy, 1
Wollstonecraft, Mary, 10, 98, 101–2, 110
*Woman Taken in Adultery, The* (Blake), 200
Woolf, Virginia, 224
Wordsworth, William, 26, 73
Wren, Christopher, 144

Young, Edward, 151

Zen Buddhism, 26